WILDERNESS
JOURNALS

Head of the Minam River, Eagle Cap Wilderness, 1995.

WILDERNESS JOURNALS

Wandering the High Lonesome

JACK WARD THOMAS

FOREWORD BY
John Maclean

A BOONE AND CROCKETT CLUB PUBLICATION

Missoula, Montana | 2015

Wilderness Journals
Wandering the High Lonesome
By Jack Ward Thomas

Library of Congress Catalog Card Number: 2015940098
Paperback ISBN: 978-1-940860-16-9
Hardcover ISBN: 978-1-940860-21-3
e-ISBN: 978-1-940860-17-6
Published July 2015

Published in the United States of America by the
Boone and Crockett Club
250 Station Drive, Missoula, Montana 59801
Phone (406) 542-1888
Fax (406) 542-0784
Toll-Free (888) 840-4868 (book orders only)
www.boone-crockett.org

Printed in the U.S.A.

I dedicate this book to the memory of

Will H. "Bill" Brown

*long-time Director of the Northwest Region of
the Oregon Department of Fish and Wildlife,
who taught me many things, mostly by example,
including appreciation for Wilderness and
public lands—especially National Forests—
and how to pack and handle horses and various
tricks of the trade in hunting elk, mule deer,
white-tailed deer, pronghorn, and grouse in
what he called the "high lonesome" Wilderness
in Northeast Oregon and Montana. He was,
indeed, my mentor in many ways.*

CONTENTS

FOREWORD

> . . . down deep I know there is, in reality,
> no beginning and no ending—only an eternal turning. Dust
> to dust, it is said. I think that emphasis is wrong: what lies in
> between is the essence of everything.
>
> Jack Ward Thomas, *Wilderness Journals*

Wilderness Journals is the personal account of a burly and intelligent wildlife scientist from the Texas outback, Jack Ward Thomas. He loves the outdoors—especially its wildest parts—hunts and fishes, and thinks hard about what he's doing. He also served as chief of the U.S. Forest Service during a turbulent period in the life of the agency, from 1993 to 1996. Before, during, and after his tenure as chief he made many horse-packing trips into Wilderness Areas, most often with a sidekick named Bill Brown, and sat alone at the end of the day updating his journal by the flickering light of a campfire.

Wilderness provided him solace and refreshment of spirit. These are the familiar gifts offered by time spent in the bosom of nature, away from the hustle-bustle of a crowded life. And with each mess of brook trout that Thomas catches, dips in salt and pepper and breadcrumbs, and fries in bacon grease, that journal records a philosophical rumination or historical summary or meditation on life and death. It's his reflections on mortality in particular, and the way the theme plays out in the many years covered by his journals, that give the book an elevated narrative curve. There's plenty of wildlife gazing, trail riding, horse sweat, and fly fishing, enough to create envy in the heart of any fellow lover of the outdoors. But quietly and persistently, Thomas evokes the march of time as it plays its inevitable role in the lives of men and women in the book, whom readers come to know and enjoy through his portrayals and then to mourn.

And in this telling of human mortality lies an inevitable parallel to the life of wilderness itself. Fortunately, Thomas doesn't hammer the parallel: Earth abides, he tells the reader. But wilderness can be ruined and lost in many ways, from the slob elk hunters who leave behind a foul campsite to "range maggots," the flocks of sheep that overgraze once-pristine slopes, to the greater threats of encroaching development and vastly increased recreational use of the backcountry.

Thomas is a lover of wilderness, and as chief of the Forest Service he also played a significant role in the management of Wilderness Areas. As the author of this book, he will continue to play a role as an inspiration to the next generation to recognize the gift that has been passed on to them and to guard and even expand it for future generations. For without that support, the Wilderness Areas, the lands "untrammeled by man," as defined in the Wilderness Act of 1964, face a future in which they may be drilled, grazed, cut up by roads, logged, subdivided, and lost. These are not new arguments or sentiments. The strength of Thomas's journals is that they make the case through force of character, his own and that of others, and lots and lots of hands-on experience.

I first met Jack Ward Thomas shortly after the South Canyon Fire of 1994 in Colorado, the fire that killed fourteen firefighters—a dozen of them Forest Service employees. I had asked to interview the chief and was surprised at how readily Thomas agreed to see me. I had quit a newspaper job to write a book about the fire, which had become embroiled in controversy: two of the Forest Service's own fire investigators, for example, had refused to sign the official report. It was the sort of mess that Washington bureaucrats know how to dance around.

I was familiar with the dance; I'd spent most of my journalistic career as a Washington correspondent for the *Chicago Tribune*. I had run into stand-up people in the ranks of the federal bureaucracy, especially in agencies such as the Forest Service or the military where lives are on the line. But most had a gift for invisibility in a crisis, and I assumed the chief would give me a quote or two and the "agency perspective" on the event, which meant a spin session. After all, the South Canyon Fire had been the responsibility of another agency, the Bureau of Land Management, not the Forest Service: if mistakes were made, let the blame fall on the BLM or on Mother Nature itself.

Thomas is a big, imposing man and looks like he could be very tough. But when we met in his Washington office, he talked to me as though we were just two guys who understood and respected each other, both of us wanting to do the right thing. He said he appreciated someone from the outside committing to tell the story of the fire. He knew my father's book, *Young Men and Fire*, about the Mann Gulch Fire of 1949, another Forest Service disaster, and said he was glad to have me following in those footsteps.

He told me how he was awakened by a late-night call telling him multiple lives had been lost on a fire on Storm King Mountain in Colorado, the South Canyon Fire. At daylight, he packed his fire boots, grabbed a plane, and joined survivors of the fire at a bar in Grand Junction, where they had been bused in the aftermath of the disaster. He bought the firefighters drinks and shared stories. I later heard from survivors that the presence of the chief had been much appreciated, down to the White's fire boots.

At the end of that first conversation Thomas offered me the full cooperation of the Forest Service in my investigation of the fire. Frankly, I didn't believe him.

I've talked with Thomas many times since then about the South Canyon Fire, and he can't go over the story with dry eyes. Those young men and women died "on his watch," and the fire grieves him to this day. After the fire, he instituted many changes that improved wildland fire safety and remain in place today.

During the writing of the book, though, the time came when Thomas's hand was called. The two investigators who had refused to sign the investigation report cooperated with me up to a point, but balked at providing the email record of their exchanges with the Forest Service's Washington office concerning their refusals, which were key to understanding how the agency handled their dissent. The two investigators, Dick Mangan and Ted Putnam, objected to parts of the report, but they were loyal employees and rightly concerned about their careers. They sent a message to Washington asking what they should do.

Thomas sent them back a personal message: "Give Maclean everything he wants."

When I visited with Thomas last fall in Montana, the twentieth anniversary year of the fire, it was apparent that the march of time had taken its toll on him, but his courage and willingness to face reality remained undiminished. He's a man with the spirit of the wilderness in his heart.

John N. Maclean
SEELEY LAKE, MONTANA

John N. Maclean is the author of *Fire on the Mountain: The True Story of the South Canyon Fire* and other books about wildland fire.

Jack with Bill Brown in Sturgill Camp, Eagle Cap Wilderness, 1996.
This horseback pack trip included Undersecretary of Agriculture Jim
Lyons, who took the photo, and his daughter Elizabeth.

PREFACE

While working for the U.S. Forest Service (USFS) at its Range and Wildlife Habitat Laboratory in La Grande, Oregon, from 1973 to 1993, I became a close friend and regular hunting companion of Will H. "Bill" Brown, regional director of the Oregon Department of Fish and Wildlife for northeast Oregon. For reasons known only to him, he considered me a potentially influential player in increasing the USFS's enhanced attention to fish and wildlife. As he put it, he considered me to have "potential" while showing signs of being "trainable." He cultivated my friendship by inviting my wife Margaret and me to accompany him and his wife Bernice on horseback trips into the nearby Eagle Cap Wilderness on the Wallowa-Whitman National Forest. Over time, we became hunting and fishing partners, close friends, and—most of all—wilderness traveling companions.

Wilderness was Bill's passion. He spent all the time he could in the wilderness, working or playing and often mixing the two. When he couldn't be in the high lonesome, he talked about it, thought about it, and planned his next trip. We came to own a collective string of seven or eight horses and spent a month to six weeks a year on horseback trips to the wilderness, along with our various guests. Many of those trips centered on fishing and hunting mule deer, elk, ruffed grouse, and chukars. Bill schooled me until I was reasonably adept at riding, handling, and packing horses. He made sure that I understood the fine points of using such backcountry trips for "political purposes." After all, who could resist a wilderness foray on fine horses, even though it made them a captive audience.

There are two definitions of "wilderness" in Webster's dictionary. The first says that wilderness is "a tract or region uncultivated and uninhabited by human beings" or "an area essentially undisturbed by human activity together with its naturally developed plant community"; the second says that it is "an empty or pathless region." A wilderness area is defined as a "large tract of public land maintained essentially in its natural state and protected against introduction of intrusive artifacts such as buildings or roads." The Wilderness Act of 1964 said, "A wilderness, in contrast with those areas where man and his works dominate the landscape, is hereby recognized as an area where the earth and its community of life are untrammeled by man, where man himself is a visitor and who does not remain." Such areas that were, by act of Congress, made part of the National Wilderness Preservation System became known in the USFS as Wilderness, with a capital W.

Off and on, between 1986 and 1999, I kept detailed journals that included descriptions of backcountry trips and hunting and fishing experiences—many in Wilderness Areas—in the United States and several foreign countries. The journal entries that had to do with my experiences as chief of the USFS during 1993–1996 were incorporated into a book, *Jack Ward Thomas: Journals of a Forest Service Chief* (University of Washington Press, 2004).

By age eighty, the accumulated impacts from a very active lifestyle—a twice-fused spine, artificial knee, shoulder repair, artificial lenses, and heart bypass surgery—had put an end to my backcountry adventures. I could no longer ride deep into the wilderness, and my desire to hunt waned as my partners in such adventures passed on to the "happy hunting grounds" or to retirement homes. I came to treasure my journals, as they brought back experiences much as I felt them at the time of writing.

When I was first encouraged to publish excerpts from my journals relative to my wilderness adventures, I resisted. But those who encouraged me overcame my hesitation by telling me that I had a talent for "telling it like it was, is, and might be." If so, I thought, maybe these stories could help readers relate to the wilderness experience.

The stories related here are true to the original journal entries with a few exceptions: I've organized the trips into chapters, adjusted verb tenses, corrected spelling errors, removed extraneous or repetitive information, and occasionally added explanatory details. Additional inserts of information necessary to put the journal entries in context appear in italicized format.

WILDERNESS JOURNALS

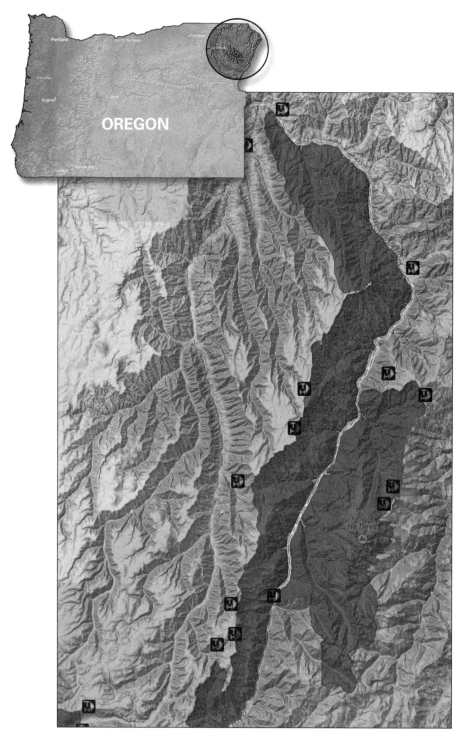

Hells Canyon Wilderness, Snake River Canyon.

CHAPTER 1

THE OLD FOREST SERVICE GUARD STATION AT MORMON—SNAKE RIVER CANYON

The Hells Canyon National Recreation Area and the Hells Canyon Wilderness were both established in 1975 through the Hells Canyon National Recreation Act— 130,095 acres in Oregon and 83,811 acres in Idaho for a total of 213,906 acres. Despite the grandiose title and the vastness, only a very few travel through the area, mostly via its crown jewel, the Snake River Canyon, and along the river itself. The Seven Devils Mountains across the river in Idaho were named She Devil, He Devil, Ogre, Goblin, Devil's Throne, Mount Belial, and Twin Imps, all topping 9,000 feet in elevation. There was a hint of danger and foreboding in those names that lay on the horizon reiterating the name Hells Canyon.

JUNE 19, 1986

For the past five days, my traveling companion, Bill Brown, and I had traveled via horseback the Snake River country, on the Oregon side of the river. We started from the Imnaha River, rode up Cow Creek, and made our first night's camp at the Wallowa-Whitman National Forest boundary. The next day we rode up the trail along Cow Creek and topped out at the location of the old USFS Guard Station at Mormon. The buildings were long gone, burned many years ago after being abandoned for many decades. All that remained was the sagging barbed-wire fence that had surrounded the house and the privy.

The next grass fire or the one after that will likely remove the posts and leave only the wire, or, given enough time, the posts will rot away. Sooner or later, a USFS crew will roll up the wire and haul it away. Then Mormon will just be another place-name on a map, and only a few will even know what or where Mormon was.

I wondered about the USFS men who had built the Mormon guard station. Who were they and how did they serve out their careers? For sure, they were tough and resourceful men! Mormon is difficult to reach today and must have seemed at the end of the earth when it was constructed. Everything used in its construction would have been packed in on horses and mules. The old guard station stood on a bald knoll overlooking the vastness of the Imnaha River drainage. Away to the west the Wallowa Mountains loom on the horizon. Almost surely the station was a fire lookout and a camping spot for the USFS man who was charged with overseeing the sheep grazing.

Down below in the trees along the stream bottom an old corral and a cabin are still standing. There is a spring nearby that had been developed to supply water to the old hollowed-out logs that served as watering troughs. The cabin, consisting of one room and a porch, was once the living quarters for the fire lookout. Then later on, it was used to shelter sheepherders and cowhands. We camped near the old cabin, which is no longer maintained and is slowly sinking into the ground as the timbers rot away from the ground up. Elk and deer hunters have used this same camp over the years, as revealed by the telltale meat poles tied between trees.

JUNE 20, 1986

We rode the high ground between the Imnaha and Snake River drainages and then dropped down into the Snake River Canyon via the Cougar Creek Tail. We made camp at the site of the old Kneeland homestead, which was abandoned in 1916 following the failure of the bank in Enterprise, Oregon, which cut off any access to cash money needed to support operations. In 1974, when I first passed this way, the old Kneeland house was still standing—two stories with a basement—along with a large barn. Both buildings are gone now, the house in a grass fire in 1983 and the barn in a fire in 1984. All that remains to testify to the Kneelands' struggles to make a go of their homestead in such tough country is a rock-walled basement and a rapidly decaying log springhouse.

We camped above the old homesite at the edge of a mature ponderosa pine stand. After we set up camp and gathered and cut adequate firewood to length, I stretched out on my back and studied the copse of trees that surrounded our camp. The area burned several years ago, probably in the same fires that destroyed the old homestead buildings. The big ponderosa pines, which had evolved to live with fire, had been severely scorched but survived. The thinner-barked firs that had begun to encroach on the area were killed by the fires.

Nearly all of the ponderosas have forked tops at about the same height above the ground. The locals call such trees "schoolmarms." They hosted a supposedly well-fed porcupine some thirty or forty years ago that gnawed away the tender, more easily chewed bark twenty feet above the ground. The girdled tops died, and the limbs emerging from the whorls immediately below turned upward and grew toward the light, forming the forks. The porcupines' mark will likely remain long after all signs of the Kneelands have decayed away.

The next day we traveled north following the bench trail along the canyon's side that lay halfway between the Snake River and the top of the canyon. We made camp at the old Somers Ranch. After camp was set up and the horses hobbled and loosed to graze, I looked over the old ranch house. I first saw this place some thirteen years ago when it was still being used by sheepherders. Inside there was a table and chairs and mattresses on two double beds. There was a back porch to provide shelter from the sun and a tool shed filled with rusting tools. The roof was still weather-tight.

But now time had taken its toll. The roof was gradually losing integrity, and water and time were working their deteriorating ways. The mattresses were gone—I wondered to where, and who would want them. All the furniture that remained was a stool made by cutting off the back and shortening the legs of an old kitchen chair. It sat in front of the wood stove. I imagined someone sitting there and warming his hands. The bed frames and springs were still here. There was a hook on the wall from which a pair of tattered jeans and two wool socks hung. Oddly, I remembered them hanging there thirteen years ago.

A woman had lived here once, her presence indicated by the flowered wallpaper in the main rooms and the delicate pastels of the paint on the kitchen cabinets. Where the wallpaper had peeled away, the newspapers and magazines that had been pasted to boards to seal the cracks were revealed. I spent several hours reading from those newspapers and magazines (especially the *Saturday Evening Post*). The dates on the newspapers identified 1924 as the time of the papering of the walls. I was especially taken by an advertisement for the latest automobile from the Dodge Brothers and the newest-model Radiola radio. The old, decaying building and the library provided by the newspapers pasted to its walls imparted a feeling of a moment frozen in time.

The old abandoned homesteads I have encountered in the course of my wanderings, whether in Texas, the Appalachians, New England, or the West, have always brought to the surface the same strange feelings. I felt that if I sat quietly and simply listened, I could hear—or maybe feel—the presence of the people who had lived there. I saw, among the rubble, the remains of a young girl's shoe. I imagined that I heard her laughter, or maybe was it her crying? What happened to her? Did she grow up straight and strong and marry, have children and grandchildren, and die old after an adventure-filled life? Or did she die young? Is she buried nearby in an unmarked grave? I wondered.

But 1924 was only sixty-two years ago—not so really long ago. Down below, where Somers Creek flows into the Snake River, archaeologists have dug up Indian artifacts said to be more than 5,000 years old. Will anyone know in a half century that the Somers family lived here in the Snake River Canyon for a brief time in the early twentieth century? Not likely.

The Snake River Canyon is conducive to such contemplation. It is so remote, so rugged, so lonesome, and so relatively nonproductive that it is relatively little changed in appearance since Europeans arrived on the scene. The changes made by the homesteaders are simply melting back into the landscape. It seems that the world's most barren dry places are the ones that were created to remind us of the once vast expanses of landscapes little influenced by mankind.

Jet boats come upstream against the torrent, the noise of the engines breaking the silence and reverberating between the canyon walls. The passengers sit back and sip their liquid refreshments while their captain yells out the names of the landmarks and recites the local history. The trip upstream affords the thrills provided by some real whitewater. Downstream come the rafters, looking for quiet and the thrills of running the rapids as "river rat" oarsmen alternately work against tremendous whitewater and lean on their oars and drift with the current. They pass one another, the jet boaters and the rafters— two kinds of beings, almost. They do not regard each other kindly. Both love and court the river, but they want different things from her. They live in uneasy compromise, each wanting and seeking a political advantage. After all, there are more and more suitors—of many kinds—and fewer and fewer such rivers to court as new dams are built. The ever-increasing need for clean energy and year-round sources of water for irrigation and cities does not, over the very long run, bode well for free-flowing rivers on public lands. "Preservation," I fear, is doomed in the very long term to be a "once upon a time" thing. But at least today's land allocation reserves a few choices for future generations. That, I think, will be increasingly valuable.

But each generation adjusts to present circumstances, while missing but little of what has gone before and it has not known. I tend, along with a few oddballs of my acquaintance, to retreat further and further into the "wilderness" in efforts to recapture the feelings and experiences of times past. As time passes, one place after another becomes too crowded, too used, too "now." I know those who come after me will enjoy their experiences in these same places. The so-called "person days" of recreational use per unit of land—the currency of the USFS's recreation managers—will mount gradually year by year, decade by decade. The USFS and other land management agencies have been, inevitably, co-opted by the "bean counters"—the purveyors of worship at the altar of cost/benefit ratios. We natural resource managers learned to play the game and, in so doing, produced a "monster of efficiency" that devours the cultural circumstance of human relationships to wild things and wild places that we set out to foster and preserve. It is a game that seems likely to end, given our societal proclivities, in increasing commercialization. No matter how we begin to measure values and costs, it eventually erodes into a metric of cost/benefit ratios measured in dollars and cents. Surely there are better—or at least different—ways to measure values.

JUNE 21, 1986

We rode along the bench trail from Kneeland place to the old Tryon Creek Ranch and then on to what we called Bear Camp. Just as we came to Tryon Creek, we encountered some fifty elk, mostly cows and calves along with two spike bulls in velvet. The calves were just old enough to follow the cows at a walk. Some cows, we suspected, had left calves in the thicket along the creek as they moved out across the hillside to graze.

Once we crossed the ridge above Tryon Creek and began our descent into Deep Creek, we were almost constantly in sight of elk. We flushed out one bunch of a hundred or more—all cows and calves. And we heard many other elk that we could not see. The racket of the alarm calls and the cows and calves "talking" to one another was, as Bill put it, a "pure wonderment!" We came up upon a cow, likely with a calf too young to move and secreted nearby, that stood her ground. She ground her teeth, laid back her ears, turned her head slightly, and rolled her widened eyes as the pack string passed within twenty yards. After the horses had passed, the cow offered to take on Bill's dog, who was trotting along last in line. Blitz wisely declined the challenge—or was it an invitation—by taking up a position in the trail between the last packhorses. The cow followed alongside, five to ten yards away, for at least a hundred yards.

When we arrived at our old campsite, we found a mess. The camp had been used earlier in the spring, judging from the "green" poles and tent stakes that had been cut to erect the camp. Poles had been left nailed between trees. Two sets of stovepipes were hanging in a tree. Numerous twenty-penny nails had been driven into living trees for some reason or another. We suspected the culprit to be a young man we knew in La Grande who had a guide's license and had packed some dudes into this area for the bear season. We spent several hours cleaning up the mess before we set up our camp.

Range conditions had improved dramatically over the past twelve years due to improved management of livestock, including the exclusion of grazing in some areas. Bluebunch wheatgrass and Idaho fescue had gained ground against the exotic cheatgrass. There was abundant elk sign everywhere. Every open ridge we crossed was marked by elk beds in the grass. From that location the resting animals had a 360-degree view for approaching threats and could catch scents in the breeze from any direction.

It is extremely difficult to make a viable operation out of seasonal grazing of livestock in the semiarid conditions in Hells Canyon. Why pretend otherwise? Is livestock grazing in the Snake River Canyon the area's "highest and best use"? This is one of the too few areas where the USFS manages both the summer and winter range of a major elk herd, which Bill and I both think has significant potential beyond its present numbers. After all, this special place is a National Recreation Area as well as a Wilderness. To be fair, the establishing legislation permitted grazing by domestic livestock to continue. Surely, the law is the law, but it doesn't say the USFS needs to go out of the way to encourage grazing or to tolerate abusive grazing. Grazing that causes deterioration of range conditions—or prevents or significantly delays recovery from grazing—should be judged intolerable.

JUNE 22, 1986

We stayed over for another day in Bear Camp. Why the name? When Bill and I camped here for the first time in the spring of 1983, a beautiful cinnamon-coated black bear, exhibiting no fear, strolled by just above camp. Fearful that the bear would raid our camp while we were away, Bill fired several shots from his Model 1911 Colt .45 pistol, aiming over the bear's head to speed it along to other environs. Bill could claim that it worked, as we didn't see the bear again.

We took a day ride down the Deep Creek trail to a prominence overlooking the Snake River. From there we saw down below us a small bunch of elk—ten cows and five calves. Upon our return to camp a little after midday, we decided to spend the rest of the day "resting from our labors." I finished reading *Out of Africa* by Isak Dinesen and, after a snooze, reread select parts of *A Sand County Al-*

manac by Aldo Leopold for what must have been the thirtieth time. Every time I read *A Sand County Almanac*, I remember with some pride that Leopold, a longtime USFS employee in the Southwest and then a professor at the University of Wisconsin, is the recognized father of my profession of wildlife management.

JUNE 23, 1986

We rode along the bench trail—mid-slope in the Snake River Canyon—to the Imnaha River, a major tributary of the Snake River. Just after we crossed Tryon Saddle and began our descent into Cow Creek, we encountered two cow elk and five calves lying on an open ridge—only the first of the many elk we would encounter this day. The cows, we thought, were likely "babysitting." For the next couple of miles we were never out of sight and hearing of elk. At one point, we counted at least 160 elk, including some 50 calves, moving out over the ridge to the north. Others remained behind in the side draws that we caught glimpses of as we rode past. Similar to earlier in the trip, one cow, likely with a calf too young to travel, charged Blitz several times and traveled alongside the pack string for a hundred yards or so, longing, I thought, for a chance to stomp on the dog. If a grinding of teeth indicates severe irritation, the cow was surely irritated.

In midafternoon we arrived at the mouth of Cow Creek, where our trucks were parked. Over the course of our eight-day trip we had not seen a single person. What a rare experience that was, in the Year of Our Lord 1986, to be able to cover so much country without encountering another human. The Snake River Canyon is a magical place produced and protected by sheer ruggedness, absence of roads, a brutally hot dry climate in summer, deep snows in the high passes in winter, and an absence of highly valuable resources, not counting the existing and potential dam sites on the Snake River itself.

As we relieved the horses of their packs and saddles at the trailhead, we discussed why we had seen less than a dozen mule deer and no fawns, only three blue grouse, two ruffed grouse, and no chukars. But there was certainly no scarcity of cow elk and calves. We wondered why we had seen so few bull elk. I pondered why, given all that we had seen, our conversation centered on those species. Our lifelong identification with hunting—and being longtime big game biologists—was a likely answer.

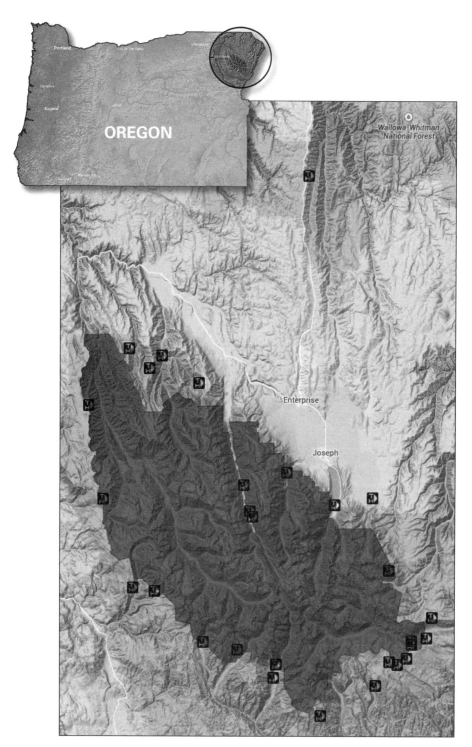

Eagle Cap Wilderness Area, in the Wallowa-Whitman National Forest.

CHAPTER 2

NO BEGINNING, NO ENDING, ONLY ETERNAL TURNING

The Eagle Cap Wilderness is located in the Wallowa-Whitman National Forest in northeast Oregon. In 1930 it was declared, by a USFS edict, that it would be managed as a Pristine Area, a designation that was changed, by law, to a Wilderness Area in 1940. In 1964 it was expanded by 73,000 acres (114 square miles), and the Wilderness Act of 1984 added 66,100 acres (103 square miles)—in total 361,446 acres (565 square miles). Eagle Cap Mountain, the area's namesake, is 9,572 feet above sea level. Four legally designated Wild and Scenic Rivers have their headwaters in the Eagle Cap Wilderness: Eagle Creek and the Lostine, Minam, and Imnaha Rivers.

AUGUST 26, 1986

We departed the trailhead—Bill and Bernice Brown, Margaret and I, seven horses, and one spotted dog (Blitz)—at Moss Springs at mid-morning and headed into the Eagle Cap Wilderness. I had never seen the trails so dusty. The fine particles of volcanic ash soil formed clouds of dust when stirred by the horse's hooves. We traveled most of the time with bandanas tied over our noses and mouths.

The horses traveled smoothly along well-maintained USFS trails. We needed only one stop to adjust packs and saddles in the course of our six-hour ride. The ride afforded me precious time and opportunity to appreciate my experience in this new habitat and cogitate. We arrived at a camp we called the Elk Camp, about a mile up the Minam River from its confluence with Elk Creek, with plenty of time to set up camp before dark.

As we lounged around the fire and darkness closed in around us, Bill gave his usual military-style briefing—which he delivered without notes—on what he figured we needed to know about the Eagle Cap Wilderness.

AUGUST 27, 1986

In the very early morning, I fished the Minam River for about a mile downstream from camp—unsuccessfully in terms of providing our lunch. I imagined that the fish would have a different view of my failure. I didn't really care all that much if I caught any fish. Just the doing—the being—was enough. The salmon were arriving in the Minam River at the end of their 600-mile journey up from the Pacific Ocean, via the Columbia, Snake, and Grande Ronde Rivers, to spawn and then—their mission complete—to die. We saw one or several, from time to time, in the crystal-clear water as they struggled mightily against the current, using up the last of their reserves to get to their special place in the river, near where they had been hatched, to reproduce their kind. There were no choices for the salmon, only the fulfillment of destiny.

My God, what a tremendous life force is focused in salmon! What a remarkable thing is life itself. Is the life on this little planet the only life in the universe? I watched the salmon hovering over their redds, knowing that they were only a few days—maybe just hours—away from the death in this place that was their destiny, foreordained by the evolution of their species. Now battered and nearly used up by the completion of their odyssey, they spawn and die. Then their decaying carcasses provide nutrients to streams essentially depauperate of such nutrients right at the moment they will be needed by their offspring.

Just before midday, we began our ride up the Cooper Creek Trail to near the summit. There we left the trail and set out cross-country to "Deer Camp," located just at timberline and several hundred feet below the mountaintop. There stands of subalpine fir give way to limber pines that can withstand the terrible winds and brutal cold of winter at 7,000-foot elevation. Such was a sterling example of adaptation—evolution in process. We set up camp in short order and were free to pursue our individual interests and urges.

A quarter-mile walk from camp, I came to a place among the bare granite rocks from where I could see the fingered drainages of the upper Minam River. Across the valley, I saw smoke from three separate still-smoldering wildfires of several hundred acres each. These fires, just at the edge of the tree line, were probably set off by lightning strikes during the "big bust" of lightening-set fires that had taken place over the previous three weeks. These fires had evidently been allowed to burn as part of the USFS's new policy for dealing with wildfires. Some USFS managers, however, seem a bit schizophrenic and maybe a little nervous about the new policy. Each morning and evening a small plane flew over for a look-see.

It is remarkable how range conditions have improved in these high mountain meadows since I first visited here thirteen years ago. Idaho fescue and bluebunch wheatgrass have reestablished themselves here and there on what was almost bare soil, dotted with occasional forbs, clumps of cheatgrass, and bunchgrasses. Likely these alpine meadows have not been grazed by domestic sheep since my last visit. It would have been difficult for me to justify—socially, economically, and ecologically—subjecting these high-elevation slopes, with their shallow soils and short growing seasons, to intensive grazing by sheep.

The reasoning that allowed such practices to continue for as long as they did seems to have rested in the political and social mores of the USFS to perpetuate a "traditional way of life"—plus the compulsion to actively utilize and manage resources and thereby prevent anything from "going to waste." Such "utilitarianism" too often fosters management decisions that, in retrospect, seem to make little economic or ecological sense. Obviously, politics, public opinion, and customs have their roles to play.

Yet with reduction in livestock grazing, especially sheep grazing, there has been a decrease in mule deer numbers. Is that coincidence? Coincident with that decrease in mule deer numbers had been an increase in elk numbers. Is that coincidence? Which came first—the chicken or the egg? There is still much we don't understand.

Perhaps we will never really know all the answers. It seems likely to me that reductions in livestock numbers, coupled with fire exclusion, have allowed development of range conditions to a state more and more dominated by perennial grasses, with a coincident decline in forbs and shrubs. Mule deer seem to have a much more restricted ability to utilize forage across the spectrum from succulent to fibrous, favoring the succulent end. Elk can handle the entire spectrum of vegetative conditions in addition to being bigger and tougher and more mobile. The vegetative conditions evolved away from those favored by deer and more toward those favored—or at least utilizable—by elk. When and where circumstances forced competition between deer and elk, elk seemed to have come out on top.

The USFS's new "let burn" policy may produce a bit better situation for deer as burned areas will go through the early succession of forbs and shrubs before tending back toward perennial grasses. It will be interesting to watch—in terms of wildlife response and the USFS's ability to hang tough with its policy. Just one or two "let burn" wildfires that spread over thousands of acres—or threaten homes and private property—will almost surely give rise to political backlash and perhaps revisions in policy. Climate change will come into play in decision making as wildfires become more prevalent and extensive. For certain, it will be an ongoing debate that will increase in intensity as temperatures rise, producing changes in rainfall amounts and distribution, and as wildfires become more of an ecological, economic, and social problem.

As I sat and watched the sun dip behind the ridge off to the west, I released my mind to daydream. When the sun disappeared from view, I felt a decided chill and smelled autumn in the air, which comes early up this high. Once upon a time, I looked forward to autumn and the various hunting seasons, but that passion is fading. Now, autumn more and more personifies an ending of an undefined something.

Of course, down deep I know there is, in reality, no beginning and no ending—only an eternal turning. Dust to dust, it is said. I think that emphasis is wrong: what lies in between is the essence of everything.

AUGUST 29, 1986

As daylight faded, dark boiling clouds began to gather, encouraging us to button up the camp, cover the woodpile, and prepare for rain. We were asleep early. Sometime in the early-morning hours, I heard thunder, seemingly far away. Then flashes of lightning occasionally lighted the top and walls of the nylon tent. When I saw the flash through the tent, I began to count slowly. At the count of five, I heard the resultant thunder. I was sleepy and could not remember the formula for computing the distance to the lightening. But it was too far away to worry about, at least not just now and likely not tonight.

The lightening flashes and the roar of the thunder—sometimes sharp like the crack of an artillery round and sometimes a prolonged rumble—continued for a half hour or so. We lay cuddled in the warm, dry cocoons of our sleeping bags, simultaneously dreading the storm and wishing its cleansing arrival. The storm passed away to the north, leaving us with only a sprinkle to remind of its existence. Then the horse bells, which had fallen silent when the horses moved under the trees as the storm approached, resumed their clanging.

Had there been danger? Maybe or maybe not. But surely there were spirits in the wind and mystery, all mixed together. I wondered if those things—the potential of danger and mystery—always come in a package. How dull it would be for those encamped in the high lonesome to be afraid to risk the first in order to experience the second.

Less than two hours after sunup, we were mounted and en route to "No Name Lake." We traveled cross-country to the Cooper Creek trail and then on up that trail to just beneath the lake. The lake was oddly perched near the ridgeline and was rarely visited by those of the human persuasion. As there was no clearly discernible trail to the lake, we called it "No Name Lake" to keep others from understanding exactly which lake we were discussing. Admittedly and quite selfishly, we tried to save the lake for ourselves—our guests would likely not know where they were and how they got there and were thus unlikely to return. We took the four saddle horses and one packhorse and traveled cross-country on up to the lake. In spite of a near adventure or two caused by the sliding of the horses' shoes on the smooth granite dome, we arrived at the lake with no real problems.

The eastern brook trout in the four- to five-acre lake had been stocked years ago by the State of Oregon's fisheries biologists. For reasons unknown to me, eastern brooks had been able to sustain themselves in this and other similar shallow cirque lakes where rainbow trout had a more difficult time. The fishing had varied somewhere between most excellent and phenomenal over the years. Three of us fished, and we each took the limit. The brookies rose to everything we laid in front of them: bucktail coachmen, black gnats, and grasshoppers. I took ten fish on the same bucktail coachman before it became too battered to be recognizable as a fishing lure. I accorded the beat-up fly a place of honor on my battered, somewhat greasy Stetson. Once we each had a limit of fish in hand, I retrieved a grill, frying pan, some bacon grease, and some salt and pepper from the packhorse and cooked up a bounteous fish lunch at lakeside utilizing an old fire ring.

We flushed four blue grouse on our ride up to the lake. They were safe—and seemed to know it. The hunting season for grouse opens tomorrow, and we had left our shotguns in camp. That was indeed fortunate for these feathered fellows, as we have our "collective lip" set for grouse stew. We flushed another four grouse—maybe the same birds, though I didn't think so—as we rode back to camp. If Lady Luck smiles, we thought we might encounter these same fellows tomorrow when we ride up this same way to our next camp, Sturgill Camp, located where Sturgill Creek joins the North Minam River.

Light is fading fast as I write this journal entry. The horses are grazing close at hand, their bells banging rhythmically. Fish are frying, and the women are laughing at some private joke. I feel warm and relaxed, inside and out. Maybe two generous drinks of good store-bought liquor have something to do with that. The world is as it should be. Things seem in order.

AUGUST 30, 1986

When day came, I was lying awake and listening to the early-morning sounds as my comrades began to stir, somewhat reluctantly. We intend to move camp today and need to make an early start. When I stepped out of the tent, it had become noticeably colder. I dug out a wool shirt from my saddlebag and put it on over my blue denim cotton shirt. It felt good. Our world was blanketed by a dense, cold fog that reduced visibility to fifty yards, maybe less.

We ate breakfast and broke camp with studied dispatch. We were mounted and on the trail some two hours after first light—I would have said "sunrise," but we could barely make out the sun rising through the heavy fog.

As we traveled through the fog, I tried to visualize the lay of the land—sometimes knowing precisely what was out there beyond the fog and sometimes not. I pondered if this was not the way we spend most of our lives, enmeshed in a fog produced by limited perceptions so that we can see only what is immediately around us, and maybe not even that. Most folks seem content with such limitations. The few that strain their minds against such fog piece together bits and pieces of what they can see or remember or reason mixed with a dash of the experience of others. Can that combination propel the mind beyond the tight circle of what can actually be "seen" to a broader vista of what might lie out there in and beyond the fog? Scientists call such a stretch of imagination a hypothesis—a potential new vision of reality that must be appropriately tested to be either accepted or rejected. I hoped we might ride this way again someday—"Lord willing and the creeks don't rise"—so that I might test my hypothesis of what lies out there shrouded by the fog. There will be no disappointment on my part if my hypothesis is rejected. To be able to formulate a vision and to wonder—and maybe test—seemed gift enough.

As we rode through the thick cold fog, Bill allowed Keno, his coal-black thoroughbred gelding, to pick his way. I thought of a friend, a scientist that I worked with in Pakistan several years ago. When we sat around our campfires in the mountains of the Hindu Cush and discussed the future, he inevitably ended his surmises with the statement "Allah willing" or "If it is the will of Allah." I concluded that I had different ways of saying the same things and expressing the same hopes. By the time we finished a month of working together in the mountains along the border with Afghanistan, he would say—in deference to the odd speech of his very strange American colleague—"Allah willing and the creeks don't rise." I could not help but laugh out loud every time he said it. He would smile with his black eyes flashing. I was pleased to leave behind some Texican culture in the Hindu Cush. Maybe my Muslim friend and I were not so different after all.

Thick mountain fog was a blessing as it closed off visual distractions and allowed me to focus my thoughts inward. As we rode along, I could see clearly only the rider and two packhorses in front of me and very little else. As we plodded on, hour after hour, my mind was freed up to pry into the nooks and crannies of long-neglected memory banks, and then to dash from the past into the future to dream without obligation or intent of action. I pondered many things. What were the horses thinking about? They did what they "hired out to do"—to take us and our equipment where we wanted to go. At the same time, they were conscious beings, and in doing their ordained jobs from time to time, they exercised behavioral interactions of laid-back ears, bared teeth, and kicks. Not so different from humans, I thought, in their ritual of demonstrating who the "top horse" was. Maybe for them, people were just part of their habitat—nothing more and nothing less.

We rode past Swamp Lake and then Steamboat Lake—at least, we believed that to be so, as we could not pick out the lakes down below in the clouds and the mist—and began our descent into the drainage of the North Minam River. Before we set out this morning, we discussed camping at one of the two lakes. Now we were cold and damp and just wanted to get down out of the chilling fog. The introspection induced by the dense cold fog was initially enjoyable. That feeling dissipated as I became more chilled. We descended some 2,500 feet to the Minam River. Shortly after we reached the Minam River Trail, Bill's mare, without guidance or hesitation, turned off the main trail and took us into one of our old camps about a mile above North Minam Meadows. She came to stop where the picket line was usually tied between two trees. I was once again amazed at the ability of some horses to remember such things and know exactly where they were. In this case, it was even more remarkable as the visibility all day had been less than a hundred yards.

Jack and Margaret with Kitty, Eagle Cap Wilderness, 1985.

We had initially planned to camp two and a half miles farther down the Minam River Trail. But by now we were cold, damp, tired, and hungry—and we could use a warming drink. So after a very short discussion, we rationalized that camping just a little early would be a good idea because the trails had been rough and steep and the horses were tired. Neither Bill nor I, in the *macho* tradition of the mountain men that we considered ourselves to be, mentioned that we were cold, damp, tired, and hungry and ready to make camp (though that was most decidedly so). The ladies, when asked, told it like it was—they were ready to camp right then and there. Why is it that in such circumstances "manly men" are reluctant to be the first to cry out "hold, enough!"?

So, blaming Bill's mare Manita for being tired (though she was just fine), as signaled by her turning off the trail, we made camp in midafternoon. There was no doubt that all members of the party, people and horses, were ready for that decision. The campsite was rechristened, as seemed appropriate, "First Chance Camp."

AUGUST 31, 1986

We intended to stay in First Chance Camp for two days to accommodate a planned ride up to our favorite high mountain lake, Green Lake, to try the fishing. We were dissuaded from a visit to the lake by the onset of lowering clouds, dropping temperatures, and the arrival of a persistent light cold rain. After some six hours of sitting under a tarp, drinking coffee, and watching the water drip off the tarp's edges, we decided to stay put in camp for today and then tomorrow move camp some four hours down to the Minam River. That would leave us with only a four-hour ride out to the trailhead the next day on our way home. Our next camp, on the Little Minam River, was a traditional camp for Bill for hunting, fishing, and family fun.

As we were finishing breakfast, a USFS Wilderness Guard rode in and gently chided us about our open fire. A fire closure order had been issued several days earlier in response to the very dry conditions at the time. Of course, we had no way to know about the order; besides, with persistent drizzling rain of 24 hours duration and temperatures just shy of fifty degrees, it had not occurred to us that we could possibly be in violation of a fire closure order. We promised to make sure the fire was extinguished when we pulled out. Hell's bells, we couldn't have kept the fire burning if we had tried. But we understood her plight. Orders are orders, and regulations are regulations until rescinded. We shared a laugh. After one more cup of cowboy coffee for the road, she mounted her horse, gathered up the rope to her pack mule, and rode on up the trail, having done her duty. We admired her horse and mule-handling skills. She did the USFS proud.

She had told us that she was one of only four full-time USFS Wilderness Guards patrolling the Eagle Cap Wilderness this year. She also told us there were no trail crews working this summer due to budget cuts. It is little wonder that "multiple use" sometimes seems something of a joke to the public. On the other hand, wilderness advocates and environmentalists are often their own worst enemies when it comes to cultivation of public opinion and political support. Some wilderness aficionados too much enjoy the sport of attacking or jousting with the USFS. Too often, even when they win their point—in court or otherwise—they refrain from becoming advocates for the USFS to execute aspects of land management that they claim to value, and many in their ranks have lost sight of their ultimate objectives. The smartest and most productive thing now would be for them to morph into a constituency for the USFS, at least so far as the management of Wilderness Areas is concerned. They could, and should, be a force for obtaining funds and personnel to do the job that they profess to want done. It is well past time for them to cease wandering about the old political battlefields bayoneting the wounded lest they loose a political backlash in the process.

We departed First Chance Camp in late morning and arrived at our next and last camp for this trip—at the junction of the Minam and North Minam Rivers—in late afternoon. We made camp just across the Minam River from the site of the "old dude" camp. The campsite clearly showed the impact of many years of heavy use—significant overuse in my judgment. I made a note to share my observations with the appropriate district ranger.

Bill and Bernice tried the fishing. The fish were the winners and lived another day to be tempted by the flies of some other fishermen on some future occasion. Neither fisher seemed especially disappointed.

I walked upstream and out of sight of the camp to take a significantly overdue cleansing dip in the very cold river. Afterward, while waiting for my goose bumps to subside, it came to me that dirty and smelly might have been the better state of being. It took me nearly an hour—plus a couple of snorts of apple brandy and two cups of steaming cowboy coffee—to quit shivering. Given my example, Meg eschewed a cold bath, insisting that lady riders, even after five days, did not give off the same vile aromas as those of the manly persuasion. Maybe it was the "sweet smellum" they used, even in the wilderness, that made the difference. When I proposed that hypothesis, the ladies rejected it out of hand, holding firm to their belief that the difference in aromas was genetic.

Just before the fire crumbled into ashes and we headed for our tents, the low-hanging clouds that had covered the skies for the past three days blew away. The effect was much like the lifting of the curtain at a stage show. The departure of the clouds revealed a moonless, crystal-clear sky and countless stars shining in all their brilliance. Such a display has become a rare experience for folks who spend their nights in the towns down below. Even if they cared to look up, the stars would be obscured by the glow of lights and the vapor particles condensed on the molecules of carbon monoxide spewed forth by a never-ceasing pulse of internal combustion engines and the burning of fossil fuels to meet ever-growing demands for electricity.

Many do not look even up at the night sky; in many urban environs, this can be quite rationally viewed as potentially dangerous. So the eyes of city dwellers are kept to the ground or on the next alleyway or toward approaching strangers. Many scurry from one lighted and enclosed space to another, for therein resides safety and warmth—but limited fodder for the spirit. If our lifestyles cost us the stars, it might be well to examine the benefit/cost ratios. Like many other treasures, the stars are fixtures—above and beyond the lights and the smog—for determined seekers. "Seek and ye shall find."

SEPTEMBER 1, 1986

In the late morning, after the horses were saddled, the packhorses packed, and the campsite cleared, we mounted up and headed downstream via the Minam River Trail. Our intent was to camp tonight at the junction with the Little Minam River. After a discussion around the campfire last night, which ended up being about grouse hunting, we had our "collective lip" set for a supper featuring ruffed grouse as the main course. Therefore, when we set out down the trail, Blitz was allowed to range widely on both sides of the trail. The shorthaired pointer eagerly shifted gears from traveling to hunting mode. It wasn't long before Blitz succeeded in pointing a black bear cub and put it up a tree, having managed to get herself all fuzzed up and present her most fearsome persona to the small cub. The farce lasted about a New York minute and ended when mama bear arrived on the scene, likewise all fuzzed up but much more impressively so than the dog. After a period of consideration, I figured somewhere between five and ten seconds, Blitz decided that she had hired out to hunt grouse and not bears. She ran in under Bill's horse and stayed right there until we were a half mile down the trail and she felt she could safely return to being a bird dog. With Blitz's help, by midafternoon, I had managed to bag four ruffed grouse, three juveniles and one adult.

We were only some two miles down the Minam River Trail below Red's Horse Ranch when the sky darkened and it began to sprinkle. That led to a quick decision to make camp, and just as we rode into our campsite, Blitz went point. Bill pulled up the string. Riding last in line, I dismounted, pulled my 20-gauge Citori over-and-under shotgun from its scabbard, walked up behind the dog, and with two shots added another two grouse to our pending banquet. Frankly, I was on a roll.

The lady chefs announced that tonight's supper was to be grouse corn chowder with dumplings, along with "spotted pup" (rice and raisins) for desert. Tang and rum served as pre-dinner, dinner, and post-dinner drinks. It beat the finest of wines. After finishing off three grouse and three drinks, Bill commented, "My God, this is a tough life—but, damn, somebody's got to do it!" I agreed wholeheartedly. The vote turned out to be unanimous.

SEPTEMBER 2, 1986

We were up with the first light of day. After a quick cold breakfast of spotted pup with canned condensed milk, we saddled the horses, packed up, and were on our way down the Minam River Trail to its juncture with the Little Minam River. From there, we took the trail up and over the ridge to Moss Springs.

Ruffed grouse were plentiful along the trail—tame and tempting. As the horses were lined out and traveling fast and easy, my shotgun remained in its scabbard. Bill philosophized that "there was a time under the sun for all things" and kept riding. Maybe next time.

When the trucks came into view through the trees, this trip into the wilderness was at its end—except in memory. Driving my truck and horse trailer down the dusty mountain roads, I pondered why the trip into the trailhead always seems so long and the trip back to civilization seems so short. There is real joy to an escape to the wilderness and real joy to return home, and therein lies the beauty of the thing.

CHAPTER 3

HELLS CANYON—JACK'S CABIN
AND THE OLD GRIMES PLACE

A bandoned homesteads are a fascinating attraction in the vastness of the Snake River Canyon. These old sites are unusual and rare, and their graffiti left on the landscape must have been created at a significant cost in human effort. They were highlights of this trip to the Hells Canyon National Recreation Area on the Wallowa-Whitman National Forest in extreme northeast Oregon.

JUNE 3, 1987

With two saddle mares, two gelded packhorses, and one spotted bird dog, Bill and I departed from the head of Freezeout Creek for our eight-day jaunt. Our whole outfit was soft—men, horses, and dog alike—after a long winter/spring layoff. The 2,000-foot, two-mile climb from the trailhead to Freezeout Saddle was a tough way for the horses to start the packing season. Keeping that in mind, Bill stopped frequently to let the horses blow and cool down so as to prevent their overheating and lathering up. After a couple of hours on the trail we reached Freezeout Saddle at midafternoon. We descended down the switchbacks from Freezeout into Saddle Creek, a major tributary of the Snake River. We dropped down another 2,000 feet following the Saddle Creek Trail, which had been inherited from the sheepherders and maybe the Native Americans before them and was clearly not laid out to USFS specifications.

I walked most of the steep downhill trail remembering the adage attributed by Bill to an old Nez Perce chief (it was an old Comanche chief who got the credit for the same saying from my grandfather when I was a boy in Texas): "It's a sorry horse that can't carry a man steep uphill, and it's a sorry man who won't lead a horse steep downhill." The trail led through the Saddle Creek Burn, which in 1975 killed nearly all the trees in its path, including several centuries-old ponderosa pines that had survived many previous fires. That this fire had been a genuine inferno could be discerned from the charred bark on the still-standing skeletons, or "snags," of ponderosa pines and Douglas firs. The dead pines were much larger than the dead firs, probably an indication that the firs began to grow many years after the pines. The encroachment of the firs on what was clearly a ponderosa pine growing site had been facilitated by the exclusion of fire by two factors—intentional fire control by the USFS and the removal of the bunchgrass each year, before the late-summer fire season, by heavy sheep grazing.

After the stands matured—now an admixture of pine and fir—the continued heavy grazing by sheep led to the development of a dense shrub understory of ocean spray, spirea, mountain maple, and various other woody shrub species in the creek bottoms. This shrub layer was what, when desiccated by the late-summer heat of the Snake River Canyon, had carried the long-delayed inferno up Saddle Creek Canyon. The year after the burn, the USFS used aircraft to seed the burned-over area with bunchgrasses. The seeding "took" and fourteen years later, combined with the shrubs sprouting back from their root collars, had produced outstanding forage conditions for elk. Elk tracks and fecal droppings were plentiful in the trail. The snags of the larger dead pines stood like gray ghosts over the resurgence of life, reminders of what was and what might be again a century or more in the future.

We made camp a mile or so down Saddle Creek from where the bench trail crossed in the first grove of live pines and firs that we encountered. The campsite had been heavily used. When we first camped here twelve years ago, the spot showed no signs of being used as a campsite. Now the evidence was abundant: a large area of bare ground devoid of vegetation, a large fire ring, bark chopped away from the massive pines at waist height to allow twenty-penny spikes to be driven into solid wood from which to tie horses, and a well-worn footpath to the creek to facilitate fetching water for the camp.

We made a note to avoid camping here again so that we would not add to the deterioration nor hinder the recovery process. We would find a new campsite. But in doing so, we knew down deep that the new campsite that we had "pioneered" would, sooner or later, attract others and might well become as overused as the one we were abandoning. Even in an area as remote and rugged as the Canyon of the Snake, humans leave their marks—not always lovely ones.

After supper, I sat on a downed tree trunk and methodically scanned the old burn through my binoculars. I assumed that the hundreds of standing snags would support the nesting and feeding of myriad woodpeckers and secondary cavity-nesting birds. But not in this case. Seemingly, the only bird that had made the old burn home in any numbers was Lewis's woodpecker. I could see some ten or twelve pairs moving about within their territories. This species has a poorly developed ability to excavate cavities for nesting and occupies cavities high up in the ponderosa pine snags where a limb has fallen away and decay has made excavation easier. This species—the only species of woodpecker in North America to do so—hawks flying insects and flies back and forth between perches in its feeding passes. Several elk and mule deer were venturing into view from over the ridgeline and down into the burn. It was getting late, and the fading light made it difficult for me to write in my journal. I left the area to them and joined Bill at our camp for a "sundowner" as a prelude to cooking up a supper of sausage, sweet onions, and cabbage.

JUNE 4, 1987

We traveled the bench trail north and arrived about noon at what we called the "Sheep Camp," located just before the trail crossed Rough Creek. Along the way, the dog pointed or flushed three grouse, two ruffed and one blue. The grouse flopped through the grass, feigning injury, and the dog believed the charade every time and dived off down the steep slope in pursuit of the distressed bird, only to be baffled when the flopping bird suddenly took to running and then flight.

Bill called the dog to heel each time before she blundered into the brood of young birds that was the hen's reason for the theatrics.

The environs of the Sheep Camp had also been heavily used and abused since my last visit here some five years ago. After we set up camp and finished our somewhat—by now—obligatory siesta, we set out on foot to locate a new campsite to be used when we come this way again. In the process I walked a half mile or so down a ridge toward the Snake River and sat for a while where the bench-country terrain broke off precipitously down to the river. I could see six cow elk in two bunches. They saw me but were too far away to be seriously disturbed. After a half hour, the elk decided that an enhanced degree of discretion was advisable and moved slowly into the nearby tree cover and were lost to my view.

Our campsite had been used for many years if not many decades by the sheepherders that drove their flocks through the bench country. There were several dozen worn horse and mule shoes hanging from nails driven into trunks of huge ponderosa pines. Were they hung there for good luck or, more likely, because they might be useful some day when a horseman found himself in serious need of a horse or mule shoe, even a used one? Or was it simply a sign that proclaimed, "I was here"?

In the course of searching for firewood, I encountered the hides and bones of a sheep and several mule deer that were likely butchered to provide meat for the sheepherders. It was a very long ride from here to a grocery store, and a deer eaten, whether legally acquired or not, spared a sheep that had market value. The chances of running afoul of the law this far removed from civilization were very small indeed.

As night closed in, Bill turned two horses loose to graze. The bells suspended by a strap around their necks signaled their location as they grazed. I pondered why the clanging of horse bells tend to keep "dudes" awake while the absence of the clanging will awaken old hands who fear that the horses might have departed for parts unknown. Context, after all, is everything.

JUNE 5, 1987

One of the consequences of traveling the backcountry without a lantern is that one quickly adapts to going to bed at full dark. That, in turn, dictates early rising—after all, sleeping eight or so hours on the ground atop a thin air mattress can make one long passionately for first light. Ordinarily, the horse wrangler is the first up. The clanging of the horse's bells inform him that the horses have eaten their fill and are getting restless. Restless horses sometimes take it into their heads to visit other areas, sometimes far from camp. And it is necessary to "change the guard" and let the horses that have been tied up all night have three or so hours to graze before they are saddled or packed for the day's travels.

There is something exquisitely satisfying about lying snuggled warm in a sleeping bag while the horse wrangler sets off to catch the grazing horses. Once those horses are tied, their bells are transferred to the horses that have been tied all night and are released to graze. Somehow, a code of the West developed that made it the duty of the horse wrangler to build the morning fire for the cook. As I was the designated cook in this lash-up, the idea seemed entirely logical.

An early rising meant that we were packed and on our way less than two hours after sunup. Such an early start would be more significant if we really had anyplace we needed to get to by any particular time. I doubted that either of us really had any definite idea of where we intended to end up when it was time to camp at the declared end of the day's travel, except that it would be somewhere along the bench trail.

A tad before noon we came upon the site of Jack's Cabin. We had camped here several times in the past, attracted by the dug-out flat place where the old cabin had once stood. Flat ground is scarce in this part of Hells Canyon, and sleeping on even a slight slope can be a bit of a challenge. We set up the tent on what would have been the floor of the old cabin. Water was close at hand in pools in the creek bed. There was a drawback to camping here. The very steep topography made horse wrangling difficult. When loosed to graze, the horses were disinclined to stay close to camp. The horse wrangler, when it was time to "change the guard," had to follow, over very steep ground, the sound of the bells to where the horses were grazing, catch and halter the lead horse, and lead them back to camp. Based on that experience, we decided to move on to Dead Failure, a place where a homesteader tried to make a go of it and did not succeed, hence the name.

We had traveled about a quarter mile along the bench trail when we came upon the recently remarked grave of the cabin's last occupant. He had been found near the cabin frozen to death with the carcass of a mule deer hanging from a tree nearby. It seemed to have been a case of "so near and yet so far." The grave, an oblong mound of stones, was graced with a marker that had been placed here since our last visit—a steel cross inscribed "Charles Gordon, 1901–1918." Had I noticed the mound of stones on previous visits, I would most likely have considered it to be a "sheepherder's monument," erected by a sheepherder as he passed the time away watching the sheep grazing on the adjacent slopes. It seemed to me to be a fine place to spend eternity. However, I felt certain that young Mr. Gordon would have preferred a different site—and much later in life.

When we arrived at Dead Failure, we encountered a sheepherder's camp. We could see sheep grazing and a sheepherder and two sheep dogs watching over their band of sheep a half mile downslope. The wind was blowing across the open green slopes in intermittent gusts. The sound of the wind was much like that of an approaching train as it encountered the stand of centuries-old yellow-bellied ponderosa pines. At first, the rush of wind and sound was a bit frightening. After a while, it morphed into an exhibition of the power of nature that seemed somehow magnified by the grandeur and ruggedness of the canyon.

Not wishing to bed down with the sheep or intrude on the privacy of the sheepherder, we decided to move on along the bench trail to where it crossed Temperance Creek. There an old homesteader's cabin was still standing, now known as the Old Wisnor place. We had never known the door to the cabin to be locked. Several years ago we had sought shelter here for several days from a steady rain and blowing wind.

There were fruit trees around the cabin, including an apple tree that bore the largest apples, green in color, that I have ever seen. One apple from that tree could make a small apple pie—no brag. Four or five years ago we carried some of the apples with us back home to La

Grande and presented them to two old fellows of our acquaintance who prided themselves as being experts on "pioneer apples." They testified that they had never seen apples like these. After several months of research, they called Bill and declared that the apple was a variety that had simply disappeared—or was a mutation.

At their request, the next year we brought out scion wood from the tree. The two fellows successfully grafted several trees in Union County, Oregon, with that scion wood—two of them in Bill's yard. The "Wisnor Place Apple" had been resurrected. They offered to name it the "Bill Brown Apple," but Bill passed on the honor.

Some thirteen years ago, Bill and I and a couple of companions rode into the Wisnor place from Hat Point, a prominence on the canyon's rim on the Oregon side, so named because an early USFS ranger's hat had been blown away into the canyon as he stood in this place. As we neared the cabin, we made out the back of a young lady with golden, shoulder-length hair sitting on a blanket in the grass in front of the cabin, face upturned to the sun—and totally nude. We were almost upon her when the "lady" heard us and turned to see what was coming down the trail. Then we saw the full red beard. That certainly broke the charm and anticipation of the moment!

Once he was dressed, we passed the time of day and rode on down Temperance Creek and made camp a half mile below the Wisnor cabin at a spot we dubbed "Greasy Grass Camp" in recognition of the rather loose droppings of what we assumed to be a large black bear in the tall bunchgrass. Later that evening, our new friend ambled into our camp and, as per our invitation, made himself at home. He had no way of knowing that our party was made up of wildlife biologists from the USFS and the Oregon Department of Fish and Wildlife—or maybe he just didn't care.

This young man with the flowing golden locks seemed lonely and needed to talk. He had returned eighteen months earlier from the war in Vietnam "a little confused," as he put it. He had retreated, on foot and leading a borrowed pack mule carrying all his gear, into the Snake River Canyon. He had lived in the canyon, more or less alone, for nearly a year and a half. Though he made occasional trips to civilization for supplies, he lived mostly off the land, with a little help from passing pilgrims who shared their food and other necessities with him.

When we encountered him, he was in the process making *charqui* (jerky) by drying thin slices of meat from mule deer in the sun. He offered us some dried apples and plums. There was a single-shot Remington bolt-action .22 caliber rim-fire rifle leaning against a tree.

As he didn't ask, we didn't tell him who we were. The therapy he had chosen for his wounded mind and soul seemed to be working. We figured that he had enough problems without any trouble with us. When we parted company, we left him a bag of rice, a bag of beans, six cans of chili, a chunk of cheddar cheese, two cans of Spam, flour, cooking oil, and some onions, carrots, and potatoes—and a skillet.

We arrived at our often-used camp on Temperance Creek in the late afternoon. After we dropped the packs from the horses, I headed immediately for the creek to drink my fill, cool my head, and soak my feet—it can be very hot, very dry, and very bright in the Snake River country in June. Frankly, I was a little queasy from the searing dry heat. Along the creek I made out tracks of mule deer and elk, a large black bear, and a cougar. Knowing that the cougar and bear might still be nearby, maybe even looking at me, sweetened the moment.

While soaking my feet in the cold waters of the creek, I became fascinated in watching a small white butterfly drying its wings in the sun, obviously having just emerged from the cocoon behind it on the branch. Suddenly the butterfly flew—directly into a spider web. I was inclined to free the insect and wish it well. But what then of the spider that had spun the web and now sat at its edge waiting for the butterfly to entrap itself further? After due consideration, I did not intervene.

JUNE 7, 1987

At daybreak we were jarred awake by the sharp crack of a big-bore rifle's report from just above our camp and over toward the sheepherder's camp at Dead Failure that we had passed yesterday. Some half hour later, as Bill tended the horses and I dealt with the beginnings of breakfast, the dog became alert and barked gently as the horses came to attention, erect and silent.

On the slope above camp we saw a sheepdog obviously trailing something. Just behind the dog was a sheepherder. Bill yelled to get his attention. But the sheepherder, carrying a lever-action rifle, doubled his pace and disappeared over the rise, headed in the direction of the old Grimes place, another abandoned homestead.

We wondered if the big bear or maybe the cougar that had left their sign where we drew water from Temperance Creek yesterday had given in to the temptation of an easy meal from the flock of sheep grazing above us at Dead Failure. If so, the diligent herder had probably wounded the unfortunate predator and was tracking the animal to ground. We heard no further shots, nor did we see anything else of the herder.

As we were eating breakfast, we became aware that three ruffed grouse were drumming nearby. As always, the odd drumming sound was somehow more felt than heard. It reminded me of the sound that my grandfather's old "one-lunger" John Deere tractor made from a cold start. Sights and sounds can stir up strange memories from the distant past.

The dog was a bit footsore after yesterday's twenty-mile or so trip from Saddle Creek. The trip was more like thirty miles for the dog, as she had explored all the interesting areas along the trail in search of the delectable aroma of grouse or chukars. We, of course, prided ourselves on how good we felt after our first twenty-mile ride of the season. Therefore, we blamed our decision to stay another night in this camp on the dog's sore feet, as if we really needed a reason. An excellent rationalization, I thought: the dog's feet get a rest and we feel proud of our compassion. And, in the bargain, we rested critical parts of our anatomy.

We spent the morning in pleasant conversation and reading, with a bit of journal tending on my part. Mostly we told each other the same old stories of youth and adventure and formative experiences. By now, we were old companions and had too much respect for each other to do anything but listen to the old stories again—and with more than feigned interest. Perhaps, as much as anything else, such respect was the coin of our real friendship.

After noon, we walked down to the old Wisnor place. The cabin was still being used, off and on, by sheepherders and maybe USFS folks from time to time, and it was therefore kept in some semblance of repair—at least to the extent of a rather recently installed tin roof. But it seemed inevitable that, sooner or later, the old cabin would be caught in a wildfire, or a big gust of Snake River wind would take off the roof and the old place would simply fall apart and, over time, melt into the ground.

The floor and the tables were littered with the dropping of packrats, and rodent nests (species unknown) adorned the tops of the old cabinets and the corners of the rooms. Yet the cabin was still in sporadic use, as evidenced by the wood supply for the stove and the appearance, since our last visit some three years ago, of a stove made from a fifty-five gallon oil drum.

The cabin's users had tried to chink the cracks between the twelve-inch planks of the walls, obviously a losing battle. The news-papers that served as wallpaper—and a buffer against cold winter winds—were from 1966, two and a half decades ago. I shuddered involuntarily—the old cabin must be a cold and lonely place to spend the winter. The names of sheepherders who had occupied the cabin over the decades were carefully inscribed on the walls along with the dates of their occupancy. The earlier-written names were followed with the listing of hometowns in Spain or the "Free Basque Nation." Those inscribed in the last few years listed hometowns in Peru. Evidently the origins of imported sheepherders changed along with the times.

It seemed to depend on sheepherders who were willing to accept the circumstances of living alone with the sheep in the Snake River Canyon for months on end and for the wages offered. That largely meant foreign nationals escaping from very desperate circumstances. Once here in Hells Canyon, they had little choice but to fulfill their bargain, as both pay and a ticket home came at the fulfillment of the contract.

There were several large black cottonwoods at the Wisnor place. Their resinous sap as well as the trees themselves were called "Balm of Gilead." As I looked over the vast panorama of Hells Canyon, the words of an old Methodist hymn came to me, "There's a balm in Gilead that makes the wounded whole." This country with its vast remoteness and grandeur was indeed a Balm of Gilead for me—and likely for Bill as well.

JUNE 8, 1987

Breakfast conversation centered on plans for the day. Relieved of any sense of urgency by this point in the trip, we concluded, after only the briefest consideration of alternatives, to go nowhere at all. We would remain here, a favorite camp, for yet another day. We would ride a loop along the bench trail and then follow the sheepherders' trails around the head of the tributary canyons to Temperance Creek and back down to camp. Along the way, we would visit an old homestead we knew of that did not show on our map.

The cabin site was not visible from the trail, as it was surrounded by trees and a thicket of ocean spray and hawthorn. I had discovered the old homestead several years ago while retrieving a blue grouse that I had shot and that had fallen behind the screen of shrubs. All that remained of the homestead was an old rock chimney and several scrubby apple trees. Nothing much remained that would be of interest to a hunter in early September except a grouse covert and a luxurious growth of blackberries planted by the homesteaders. The last time we stopped here was in the month of September—our wives, Meg and Bernice, were along. Our express purpose was to feast on the blackberries and perhaps gather enough for a cobbler.

While gathering berries, my attention focused on a tall green plant standing out dramatically against the desiccated vegetation that surrounded it. My eyes wandered about and I saw another such plant—and then another and another. Each plant was growing from a depression in which the soil was obviously wetted down. Finally, it dawned on me that we were standing smack-dab in the middle of a cultivated marijuana patch. And to make things even more interesting, the freshly watered soil indicated that the cultivator was close at hand—likely looking right at us. Bill retrieved his Colt pistol from his saddlebag and held it over his head so that it could be seen by anyone

who might be watching. He racked a round into the chamber, put on
the safety, and stuffed it under his belt. Following Bill's lead, I did
the same with the pistol in my saddlebag, a single-action .22 caliber
Ruger revolver. I figured that whoever might be watching wouldn't
know the pistol's bullet size.

We mounted up and rode out—without our blackberries for
supper. We were uneasy until we were far up the hillside. We saw
well over fifty marijuana plants on our way out of the thicket, and
there could have been many more. Such luxurious plants were said to
be worth maybe $25 or $50 each. And quite likely this was not the
only planting. The original homesteader had obviously been in the
wrong business.

It was seven days before we could report the location of the
patch and several weeks more before the law enforcement officers did
anything about looking for it. When they did look, the marijuana
had been harvested and all signs of its cultivation eradicated. There
were some pointed comments made by our friends in law enforcement
about our ability to recognize marijuana. We looked at each other and
shrugged. Next time, we decided, we would mind our own business
and let the growers mind theirs.

It seemed sad somehow that even in the remoteness of the
Snake River Canyon, the producers of illegal drugs operated more
or less freely. Of course, remoteness has always provided the haunts
of "moonshiners." In effect, marijuana was nothing more or less than
the new "moonshine." All the law enforcement efforts directed at
the problem didn't seem to do much beyond upping the price of the
final product.

After several hours' ride, we arrived at the site of the old Grimes
place. We had not seen a bear during the ride—a disappointment. In
riding this route a half-dozen times in the past, we had never failed
to see at least one bear. On one such trip we heard a scrabbling sound
in the rocks and saw a black bear cub climbing a leaning ponderosa
pine. The cub perched there looking down on us with curiosity, and
we returned the favor when mama bear came over the hill looking for
her errant offspring. She quickly decided that we meant the youngster
no good and came bouncing and huffing down the hill in a bluff

charge that worked beautifully. The horses did not like what they saw coming and were not difficult to urge into a rapid, somewhat undignified retreat.

The old Grimes place was marked by the flat place dug out for the cabin—there are few flat places in the "walls" of the Snake River Canyon except those dug out by man. There was some old farm machinery scattered about and a few apple trees. Of course, closer to or in town, such old cabins are classed as eyesores and removed with dispatch.

The same is true for the scenes of human deaths in the remote backcountry. All who are intimately acquainted with the Snake River country know of the sites of murders, deadly accidents, deaths from disease, and other forms of human demise. When such spots are encountered, the incidents are commonly recounted by those in the know for the edification of new pilgrims. But in populated places, who remembers the sites of the murders, the deaths from exposure of the street people to the cold and wet of winter, and the accidents— even those that took place last month or last week? Such incidents are relatively rare in the Snake River Canyon because humans were, are, and will likely remain rare. We were always aware that we were but visitors in the canyon and were not meant to stay.

JUNE 9, 1987

We followed the trail from the bench country, down Temperance Creek, to the Snake River. For most of the way the trail ran along the creek's bank and crossed the creek some twenty-seven times, but who was counting? Bill remarked that this was surely a great place for the horses to practice crossing creeks!

When we entered the creek bottom from the hot dry slopes that surrounded us, we abruptly entered "a whole 'nother world!" A canopy of alders closed over our heads, and the temperature dropped thirty degrees while the humidity increased dramatically. The shrubs took on gigantic proportions. Ferns and mosses were everywhere. Poison oak grew as high as our shoulders in places—and we were mounted on horses! The vegetation was sometimes so thick that visibility was limited to only a few yards. For long stretches the horses could not see the ground, which resulted in frequent stumbles over rocks in the stream bed.

A big black bear had taken this same trail, judging by how high it had left claw marks on the alders along the trail. Was the bear marking its territory, leaving a note to others of its kind? Or maybe it telling us: "Big Bear was here and may be nearby! Best you watch out for your happy ass!"

There was a stretch of the trail where the canyon's sides pressed in so closely that the trail had to go up the canyon wall and around such narrow spots. These narrow "passing places" had been blasted out of the rock face, and the footing for the horses was slick bare rock. With their feet clad in steel horseshoes, they slipped and skidded as they clamored over those spots. It was enough to tighten one's pucker strings.

A spot on this trail was called Brockman's Point after the first proprietor of the Temperance Creek Ranch. We were told that Mr. Brockman was leading a pack string past this point when there was a problem with one or more of the mules he was leading. He evidently dismounted and went back to deal with the problem. His saddle horse arrived at the ranch without him. Later he and several mules were found dead at the base of the precipice. I wished Bill had waited to tell me about Mr. Brockman's demise until we had passed this nerve-jangling spot. Once we came to the flats along the Snake River and turned our horses upstream, the countryside changed yet again, and the only trees were scattered hackberries and a few large ponderosa pines.

The open slopes above were covered primarily by cheatgrass and so-called poverty grass, both of which are largely unpalatable to livestock except when green and tender in the early spring. This section of the Snake River has a long history of overgrazing by sheep during the winter months. We felt a shock from the heat as the humidity neared zero and the temperature soared well over the century mark. When I commented on the oppressive heat, Bill's reply was, "Well, pilgrim, it ain't called Hells Canyon for nothing."

As we rode along the well-groomed trail that paralleled the Snake River, we saw jet boats occasionally pass by on the river below carrying tourists out for a quick look at the deepest canyon in

North America. The throbbing of the powerful engines reverberated against the canyon walls, and we were reminded of why we preferred the quiet of bench country. Twice we saw parties of rafters drifting downstream with the current. Some noted our presence and waved. We waved back. The use of the canyon and river by recreationists is partitioned by circumstance.

The rafters have the river pretty much to themselves in the upper stretches between Hells Canyon Dam and Granite Creek Rapids, a stretch of river judged a little too dangerous for jet boat captains with paying customers. Once the drifters—rafts and drift boats—are below Granite Creek Rapids, they encounter more and more jet boat traffic as they drift downstream toward the takeout points near Lewiston, Idaho. As the river has widened by that point, the potential for conflict is minimized. Then we encountered hikers for the first time who were walking the trail along the river on the Idaho side. The mid-canyon country, the bench country, seemed to be largely the province of horsemen and sheepherders slowly moving their bands of sheep. (I remember encountering only one hiker in some thirteen years of visits to these areas in May and June.) During mule deer and elk season in the fall, the canyon above the river receives more visitors than at any other time of the year, though many fewer than areas adjacent to the canyon.

There are comparatively few places in the Snake River Canyon to camp that have the requisite combination of adequate grazing for horses, water in close proximity, a wood supply, and relatively gentle slopes upon which to pitch a tent. Most of the places with that combination of attributes have been battered by overuse.

When we reached our campsite at the mouth of Sluice Creek, there was a thunderstorm building off to the west. This time, we won the race with the thunderstorm and had the tent and kitchen fly up when the rain set in. The grazing for the horses was poor. Clearly, we would have to move back up to the bench country tomorrow where the grazing would be better. We had flushed some thirty or so chukars while riding along the river, and some flew across the Snake River into Idaho. We joked about sending our friends in the Idaho Fish and Game Department a bill for services rendered.

I have never seen the Snake River running so low. The Idaho Power Company, in consideration of the very dry year so far, has closed the flow down to 5,000 cubic feet per second in order to fill the reservoirs above the Hells Canyon Wilderness Area and assure that the company can meet the power demands of its customers in the fall and winter. Bill told me that when the dams were constructed, it was agreed that water flows would never drop below 10,000 cubic feet per second and there would be no fluctuations greater than eight feet in river depth in any twenty-four-hour period and no more than two feet in any one-hour period.

Surprise! These agreements were nullified during the first "crisis" caused by periods of "less than normal snowpack" and then were never reinstated. This seems to be the way with too many conservation measures: they are gradually eroded in the face of an unexpected crisis and, too often, never restored. Scientists understand that "normal" does not mean the same thing to laymen—and certainly not to politicians, who equate "normal" and "average." Though it is quite normal to have years of precipitation well above and below average, too many in the general public equate anything below average to a perverse and exceedingly rare "act of God." Cries are then heard throughout the land for government action to deal with a terrible, unexpected, and undeserved blow from nature. There are few victories for conservation, and absolutely none are final.

JUNE 10, 1987

We made an early start up the Sluice Creek Trail and headed back up to the bench country. The climb of some 2,500 feet was slow going. As temperatures and humidity increased, the sweat from the horses did not evaporate readily, and they lathered up, a sign that they are near overheating. Stops for the horses to rest became much more frequent the higher we climbed.

About halfway up to the bench trail, we stopped to let the horses blow. A half mile below, I saw a cougar racing down a spur ridge toward the jungle of vegetation along Rush Creek. This sighting of a cougar was a first for me. I had never before seen a cougar in the wild except up a tree with dogs baying below, or in a trap, or caught for a moment in the headlights of a car or truck. I had seen tracks on numerous occasions, but this eyeball contact was a new experience for me—a spectacular trophy to be stored away in memory.

We reached the bench trail, halfway to the top of the canyon, in the late morning. After giving the horses an hour's rest, we mounted up and followed the bench trail to its crossing of Rush Creek and our intended campsite. Along the way we encountered five blue grouse, fifteen chukars, one cougar, and ten elk. Not a bad day for a couple of old wildlife and wilderness aficionados.

JUNE 11, 1987

We rode out today, back to the "real world." For me, this past week—and others like it—produced a time warp of sorts. When in the wilderness, we were ensconced in a different time with only the sonic booms and contrails left by the jet aircraft that passed over several miles above the canyon to remind us that it was but an illusion. Or just maybe that sleek aluminum speck that was speeding across the sky was the illusion and only this place and the few others like it are the last semblances of an earlier reality.

We broke camp quickly, made up the packs, saddled and packed the horses, and were on our way home earlier than usual. This was the tag end of the elk calving season. When we passed over this same trail eight days ago, we saw a few elk cows but no calves. Since then, the still-green forage in the old burn above and along Saddle Creek had attracted pregnant cows.

Now elk calves seemed to be everywhere. We could hear their mewling and the cows' answers from what seemed to be all directions. By the time we reached Saddle Creek, we had seen well over 200 elk—all cows and calves. Reluctant to leave their calves, the cows allowed us to approach much more closely than they would have at other times of the year.

They seemed more apprehensive of the dog than they were of us. One cow chased the dog fifty or sixty yards until she was safe in the midst of the pack string. The elk cow broke off her attack on the dog not more five yards from me, seated on my mare Shadow. Shadow didn't appreciate the elk's attention and shied away and off the narrow trail, which provided me with a quick shot of adrenaline.

The shorthaired pointer was a poor imitation of a wolf, but the old racial memories likely still existed in the cow elk. The dog triggered the cow's instinct to protect her calf from *Canis*—she cared not whether *Canis lupus* or *Canis domesticus*. We continued our climb up to Freezeout Saddle. We did not need to rest our horses as much as when we first rode into the canyon. The horses had picked up in condition and, like the athletes they are, strained, seemingly willing, against the slope and hot sun. I was convinced that they knew exactly where they were, what they were doing, and that now they were going home. They seemed to like that idea.

Halfway down from the top of the canyon to the trailhead on a road that paralleled the Imnaha River and that ultimately emptied into the Snake, we met the only two people that we had seen in eight days, outside of those traveling on the river. The man and his wife were longtime users of the backcountry. I could tell that by carefully looking over their outfits as they visited with Bill. Their gear was well worn yet carefully maintained. The horses and mules were fit and carefully and correctly packed. The ease of the saddle horses and their riders attested to the confidence that comes from many years of packing over long, dusty trails. Their two pack mules stood calmly switching away flies with their long tails.

Somehow, I felt envy—they were going, for a time, to where we would have loved to stay longer. But no one can enjoy the time warp forever. The consolation is that the time machine—the horses and the wilderness and the river—will be there to be used again when the desire to escape from the ordinary morphs from longing to desire and, finally, comes to border on compulsion. We waved good-bye to our fellow pilgrims as they passed out of sight. In doing so, we bade farewell to our own respite. The horse trucks were soon visible through the trees.

The time warp was over. I dug out my watch from deep in my pocket, where it had resided since the first day of the trip, and strapped it on my wrist. It read "11 June 3:45 p.m." The trip was over. I felt a knot in my throat, but it didn't last long. After all, we were going home. And home is always good.

Some ten years or so later, Bill and I discovered that the young man we encountered that day at Greasy Grass Camp had left the refuge of the canyon, married, had children, became a ranch foreman, and settled back into society. Sometimes I thought, "What's right" is not necessarily "what's legal." I have not regretted the decision we made that day to look the other way and leave the young fellow with the wounded soul alone to his healing.

Family and friends enjoying a Fourth of July weekend trip in the Wenaha-Tucannon Wilderness, 1987. Left to right, front row: *Celeste Thomas with Shiner and Bernice Brown;* back row: *Britt Thomas, Margaret, and Bill Brown.*

CHAPTER 4

A THREE-DAY WILDERNESS GETAWAY?
IT CAN BE DONE

The Fourth of July holiday presented a special opportunity and a problem: how to squeeze in a getaway to the wilderness and be out again in only three days. Trips into the wilderness are not necessarily long-term affairs. The Wenaha-Tucannon Wilderness, which Bill and I referred to as his "standby wilderness," was close to La Grande and therefore ideal for a three-day schedule. The Wenaha-Tucannon Wilderness (177,423 acres consisting of 66,375 acres in Oregon and 111,048 in Washington) was created with the passage of the Endangered American Wilderness Act of 1978.

JULY 3, 1987

Our party was made up of Bill and Bernice Brown, Meg and me, and our oldest son, Britt, and his bride, Celeste, who brought along their big black Labrador retriever, named Shiner for his glossy coat and disposition. We had four saddle horses for the "old folks" and two packhorses. The relative youngsters, Britt and Celeste, walked but didn't need to carry packs.

It was a two-hour drive from La Grande north to Elk Flat Meadows, which bordered on breaks into the Wenaha River Canyon. The horses had been saddled before they were loaded into the truck and trailer. The panniers and manty packs had been done up the day before. So upon our arrival at the trailhead, it took less than thirty minutes to put the packs on the horses, mount up, and be on our way into the backcountry.

Ten minutes down the trail we came to a USFS sign announcing "ENTERING WENAHA-TUCANNON WILDERNESS— NO VEHICLE TRAVEL BEYOND THIS POINT." At that point, as if by magic, we entered into another world—almost a parallel universe, a place without roads, four-wheel-drive vehicles, campgrounds, toilets, fire pits, trail bikes, chainsaws, and but very few people.

As we descended into the canyon, we passed through majestic stands of old-growth grand firs with almost-closed canopies. The trees were festooned with hanging strands of lichens, aptly called "old man's beard." The temperature became noticeably cooler as the sun was blocked out and humidity increased. We encountered signs of elk—beds, wallows, tracks, and pellet groups. The pungent smell of elk hung in the air. Wildlife biologists call such tall dense stands "thermal cover" as elk seem to seek them out, particularly on hot summer days and on very cold, windy days in winter, to moderate the impact of extremes of temperature.

I broke the silence with the comment that this place "looked like a piece of elk heaven." Bill pulled up his gelding, Keno, and studied a huge fir that seemed to stretch a good ways toward heaven. He commented that it was because of these increasingly rare old-growth stands that are so heavily used by elk that the boundary of the Wenaha-Tucannon Wilderness was moved from the river's edge up to midslope above the Wenaha River.

Bill leaned out from his saddle and touched the old tree and gazed up into the crown. His voice cracked a little when he said, "I helped make this canyon a Wilderness Area. Getting that done and helping with the lower Minam River additions to the Eagle Cap Wilderness were the accomplishments in my career that I'm proudest of." There were tears in his eyes, and his voice choked a little. We all pretended not to notice.

He seemed to be talking more to himself than to the rest of the party. Then, seemingly embarrassed, he drew himself erect in his old McClellan saddle and said, "Of course, there were a lot of people involved before it was all over. But I know in my heart that if it had not

been for me and Jack Kuykendall of the Washington Game Department, the Wenaha-Tucannon Wilderness would never have come to
be. We kept the issue alive, even when there were only a few of us who
believed there was any chance in the world that we could succeed.
Then gradually others took up the cause." He butchered a famous
quote—"Victories have many fathers and defeats are orphans"—but
it was close enough and we got the point.

He went on. "In the early 1950s, we made a deal with Charley Richter, the forest supervisor of the Umatilla National Forest, for
a 300,000-acre roadless recreation area along the Wenaha River. At
that time, there was only one primitive road into the breaks of the
Wenaha River Canyon, and that was over on the Washington side.
Charley had decided that the Forest Service would build a limited
number of Cat roads off of that existing primitive road to facilitate
the rehabilitation of some rangeland that had been badly abused by
sheep grazing in the 1920s. Once that was done, all the temporary
roads would be closed."

Then, in what Bill considered a violation of that "gentleman's
agreement," when the time came for the road closure, Richter retreated from his promise, saying he knew of no regulation by which he
could close those roads. Bill continued, "By the late 1950s, Wright
Mallory had replaced Richter as forest supervisor. He had a plan prepared to road the area, leaving only two roadless patches divided by
a road, with a one-mile-wide managed forest buffer remaining out
of the original 300,000 acres promised. Those of us who had been
privy to what we considered a handshake deal decided to quit playing
games and make a try at getting the area formally designated as Wilderness by an act of Congress.

"That turned out to be a slow, tedious process. By the 1970s,
Herb Rudolph had taken over from Wright Mallory as forest supervisor. Herb, who was genuinely and openly convinced that the Wilderness designation was inappropriate for the area, was a formidable
advocate for increased timber harvests, timber management, and
building access and logging roads into the Wenaha Canyon.

"At the time, the primary interests of environmentalists in
northeastern Oregon were additions to the Eagle Cap Wilderness on

the Wallowa-Whitman National Forest, particularly the lower Minam River additions. They had organized themselves as the Save the Minam group. Still, we kept the Wenaha country in their minds.

"The Oregon Department of Fish and Wildlife's politically appointed commissioners were, at best, wishy-washy about Wilderness designations. They had traditionally been big-time supporters of building roads into virgin territory to facilitate access for hunters and fishermen. The agency's director at the time was philosophically opposed to Wilderness and assigned his number two man to head off efforts to designate anymore Wilderness Areas in Oregon. With our agency officially on the sidelines, I worked through others to get the job done. In the end, those people got the credit. But a number of people involved knew the whole story of what really happened. They knew. I knew. That's good enough for me."

With that, Bill turned his horse and rode on down the trail toward the Wenaha River. He seemed to sit a little taller in his saddle for the rest of the ride. He had wrestled his demons, made his choices, taken his gambles, and paid the price. I wondered what I might have done in his position. The way that things really happen is, frequently, very different from what is generally perceived—or ensconced in the history books. Often the most effective movers and shakers, especially in bureaucracies, are known and appreciated only by themselves and perhaps a few others.

There is always "the rest of the story" to be told. There are two primary kinds of power in bureaucracies—hierarchical power (afforded by position) and influential power (emanating from knowledge, personality, influence, skills, connections, and achievements). Those with influential power often have more to do with change than those with hierarchical power—they just don't get the credit. Bill understood that, in the final analysis, achieving results is much more important than who gets the credit. After all, the doers—whether praised or cursed—know what they did. If their accomplishments persist, what does it matter—in the long run—who got the credit? Bill advised me never to worry about who gets credit. In the end, only achievement counts. Then he would smile and say, "Rewards come in heaven." I hoped he was right about that.

JULY 4, 1987

After a half day's ride along the river, we made camp where the two branches of the Wenaha River joined. We spent the rest of the day simply loafing around camp. I took the opportunity to feel Bill out on his feelings toward the USFS and the timber industry people he had sparred with over the years relative to Wilderness designations. I was surprised that he held most of his adversaries in high esteem as professional conservationists. As he put it, they "just saw things in a different way and fought as hard for their point of view as I fought for mine. They prevailed most of the time, but"—he smiled shyly—"not always, not always."

That was an attitude I wish more environmentalists would adopt in dealing with federal land management issues. Too many environmentalists make the political hassles over Wilderness designations and forest management personal. Too often their hubris leads them to castigate, ridicule, and question the integrity and honor of those in the land management bureaucracies who simply hold a different view and are, in many cases, compelled to obey laws and follow budget directives in spite of their personal preferences and biases. Often integrity and honor lie in the eye of the beholder.

I sometimes suspect that "professional" environmentalists adopt such belligerent attitudes and tactics for the primary objective of attracting and retaining membership in their organizations. They are certainly sophisticated enough to know that USFS administrators are not free agents. They are part of the executive branch of the federal government and subject to laws, regulations, budgets, plans, and court decisions.

The forest supervisor who consistently fails to meet the various targets set out through planning and budgets—timber, grazing, fish and wildlife, watershed, and recreation—will not remain a supervisor for very long. The regional forester who opposes administration policy or fails to heed the instructions of Congress expressed through budgets will likewise have short tenure. Skookum environmentalists—especially the professionals—understand that. In most situations it is the legal and political direction given to the USFS with which they vehemently disagree.

But too often the attack is directed at the operatives who execute that direction. Why? Perhaps it is safer and more satisfying to attack bureaucrats than members of Congress, governors, and presidents. Bureaucrats are easy targets, compelled to take the heat (woe to the civil servant who places blame or responsibility on Congress or the president) and unable to fight back (woe to the bureaucrat who suggests publicly that an attacker has ulterior motives or speaks less than the truth). As a result, environmentalists are often viewed by some in the USFS as antagonists or even as outright enemies. Environmental groups have learned to attack, to have land designated as Wilderness, to create National Recreation Areas, to establish requirements for multiple use and so on. But, in spite of such successes and those significant achievements, they have consistently failed to establish themselves as effective constituencies for the land management agencies to appropriately manage such areas. Much too often, they follow up on their victories with attacks on the failure to achieve new goals in spite of a lack of resources. It can be hoped that these circumstances will change as the environmental movement matures. Otherwise their victories may well prove to be pyrrhic in nature.

Bureaucracies are much like living organisms. The first concern of any organism—individually and/or collectively—is survival. The second is to prosper and grow. Fortunately, it is possible for an organization, like an organism, to evolve as missions and resources change. The necessary resources are obtained through political processes and the support of citizens—individually and collectively—who serve in symbiotic roles and are recognized as effective varied constituencies. This does not mean that tensions will not prevail between a bureaucracy and its constituents. The timber industry castigates the USFS—severely and routinely—over both real and imagined wrongs. However, the industry then turns right around and lobbies for USFS appropriations when it suits their purposes.

The environmental movement has persisted, grown, and bullied its way, against the odds, into a position of increasing influence. I have much admired that. In the beginning, much of the movement was anti-establishment. Suddenly the "system" accepted the environmental movement into the mainstream, and the game changed. Outsiders became, however gradually, insiders. But to retain influence and power, sooner or later insiders must play by insider rules. I am not certain that environmentalists can bring themselves to do that, at least not yet. There is no quicker way for successful revolutionaries to lose new-found power and influence than in failing to recognize victory—and face up to consequences of victory. After all, with victory comes responsibility. I believe the USFS stands ready to evolve to accept new roles and welcome the new constituencies represented by the environmental movement. However, until the environmental movement and all its parts mature to effective constituency status, little is apt to change in the status quo.

When the sun sank "below the yardarm," Bill pulled a flask of "good sipping whiskey" from his saddlebags and proposed a toast to the 200th anniversary of the signing of the Constitution. He noted that our powerful nation was born out of strife and still existed, now stronger than ever, through our collective ability to adjust and evolve. He noted that he was fortunate to be professionally active at such a great time and place for the work and dream of the conservation of natural resources—both as a professional natural resources manager and an involved, knowledgeable citizen.

What more could those of us concerned with the future of the national forests ask from life, he said, but to be alive at this critical juncture in conservation history—and with a real chance to make a difference. He noted that if "We the People" couldn't make it work, probably no nation could. And if we couldn't do it now, it was unlikely to ever be done as populations grow and wild lands and wild things shrink. It sounded a bit corny, but he meant every word. I agreed with those words. It wasn't just the sipping whiskey talking.

With bolstered exuberance we sat down beneath the huge old yellow-bellied ponderosa pines to a supper of pan-fried rainbow trout fresh from the Wenaha River. We would have to come down off our "wilderness high" tomorrow and get back to our jobs. But at this especially fine moment, we were filled with renewed confidence and hope.

JULY 5, 1987

We were on the trail at midmorning and arrived back at the horse trucks a bit after high noon. That rendezvous with the trucks marked the end of a three-day trip to what we thought of as our personal "backyard wilderness." Living in the backwater of sparsely populated northeastern Oregon may have deprived us of all but occasional encounters with opera, symphonies, plays, professional sports, and other extravaganzas of various sorts. But our proximity to wild country without roads, fences, and signs that read "Private Property—No Trespassing" was more than compensation enough. I had never heard a symphony lovelier or more inspiring than the sound of winds in the pines and the roaring of the river in the Wenaha-Tucannon Wilderness. It pleased me to know that, for at least a little while in the late twentieth century, it was possible to preserve such a place and such a symphony of sights and sounds as the Wenaha-Tucannon Wilderness.

But, I wondered, what about tomorrow? I looked at my son and his wife as they loaded the horses into the trucks. What will they decide? I don't know. The Bill Browns and others like them have seen to it that, in at least a few places, choices still exist. Just having such choices is in itself a precious legacy.

CHAPTER 5

MINAM RIVER IN THE EAGLE CAP
WILDERNESS—RED'S HORSE RANCH

Red's Horse Ranch was once an eighty-acre private in-holding within the Wallowa-Whitman National Forest. Owned and operated by "Red" Higgins, the dude ranch was a rustic resort with outfitter services for big game hunters and an airstrip for small aircraft. It could also be reached via a trail from Moss Springs or one up the Minam River from Highway 82. The property was "grandfathered" when the surrounding area was included in the lower Minam River addition to the Eagle Cap Wilderness. It had always been an economically marginal operation and was acquired by the USFS shortly thereafter.

The last few weeks had been hectic ones. A series of sixty-hour-plus workweeks and the pressures of starting a new high-risk, high-cost research study had drained me and my colleagues almost dry, both intellectually and emotionally. Perhaps a week in the Eagle Cap Wilderness would be just what an astute medical doctor would prescribe for the restoration of hope, energy, and spirit—and, in the process, remind me of why our profession matters and why it's worth what we put into it.

JULY 15, 1987

Bill and Bernice, Meg and I, seven horses, and Blitz entered the western edge of the Eagle Cap Wilderness from the Moss Springs campground a bit after midmorning. We had originally intended to take a trail that goes over a 7,000-foot-high pass, but the district ranger's office advised us that the pass was still blocked with deep snowdrifts. Caution directed us to change our route and then confine our wanderings to lower elevations, specifically the drainages of the Minam River.

Our second decision was whether to make our entry into the Eagle Cap via Lackey Hole, which would require fording the Minam River, or by way of Red's Horse Ranch, which would allow us to cross the Minam River via a bridge. There was no access to Red's except via foot or horse trails. As it had rained on and off for the past several days, we feared that the Minam would be running strong and deep, making fording the river risky.

When we laid eyes on the river, we found that we had worried too much about high water; it was running low and crystal-clear. We had an easy, short first day's ride in mind, as the womenfolk had not ridden any long distances since last summer and we aimed to camp just above what remained of the old splash dam, built in the days of the log drives between about 1910 and 1920. Splash dams were used by loggers to get logs from roadless mountain areas down the rivers to the mills. A dam of earth, logs, and rocks was built across the river during the period of low flow, leaving a sluice to let the water through. Logs were deposited behind the dam. When enough logs were in place and the river was running high, the sluice was closed and a lake formed behind the dam that floated the logs. At an appropriate time, the dam was blown out with dynamite. The surge of water carried most of the logs downstream to a mill site where the Minam inter-sected the Grande Ronde River. These repeated surges of water and the logs carried on those torrents had scoured the stream bed below the dam. The same technique was used in most of the major drainages into the Grande Ronde River system. Those waterways were still in the process of recovery.

The lower Minam River drainage had thus been logged without the construction of haul roads for timber. A primitive road alongside the Minam led from the highway all the way to Red's Horse Ranch, and on the basis of this road the lower Minam drainage had been excluded from the original Eagle Cap Wilderness, as the road showed evidence of "trammeling" by the hand of man (i.e., the area did not meet the definition in the Wilderness Act of an area "untrammeled by man"). It might have been a bit "trammeled," but it was still simply gorgeous country.

During the debates over the lower Minam additions to the Eagle Cap Wilderness, proponents argued that fifty-year-old stumps and a primitive road along the river should not be disqualifying, as they would simply "melt into the ground through natural processes" given enough time. So when Congress approved the lower Minam additions, a national precedent was established. Originally Wildernesses could include only land "untrammeled by man." Now lands were considered eligible for Wilderness status that had been relatively lightly exploited or had been exploited so long ago that the associated "trammeling" was disappearing. In short, "Wilderness" was what Congress and the president declared it to be.

The area above the old dam was overlain with soil that had been deposited behind the dam. The river was gradually reclaiming this built-up area, and much change was obvious between one of our visits and the next. We forded the river and camped in a nearby stand of mature white firs. There was a natural meadow farther back from the river that provided abundant grazing for the horses. The site was obviously a popular one for recreationists, and the river was heavily fished here, as could be seen by the footpaths paralleling the stream's course. Bill and I preferred more pristine areas for our fishing. At least that was our excuse to our wives for lying on the riverbank basking in the sun and shooting the bull rather than rigging up our fly rods.

Bill described the area as he remembered it from his first visit some thirty years earlier. The area above the splash dam was "salmon and steelhead proof" (i.e., the spawners coming up the Columbia to the Snake to the Grande Ronde to the Minam River could not get over the remnants of the old splash dam). With no competition, the native trout thrived above the splash dam, creating an outstanding— and little exploited—trout fishery.

In the 1940s and 1950s, crews from the Oregon Department of Fish and Wildlife twice blew up remnants of the old dam and constructed fish ladders over what barrier remained to give salmon and steelhead access to the upper Minam River for spawning. The salmon and steelhead gradually took advantage of the passage and now spawned in the upper Minam. In turn, the competition from the anadromous fish dramatically diminished the trout fishery. The Lord giveth and the Lord taketh away. Or, as Bill put it, "There ain't no such thing as a free lunch."

Bill pointed to a rock jutting out from the riverbank just across from our camp. He described how he used to bring his first wife, Blanche, and their two small children to camp in this meadow. Blanche, now long deceased, rode one horse with a son in front and a daughter behind while Bill led a packhorse. He looked intently at the rock as he described, tears in his eyes, how she sat on the jutting rock and knitted while he fished. It seemed to me that he could still see her sitting there in the warm sun—knitting perhaps? It was obvious that, for Bill, this place was filled with ghosts—"good spirits," as he put it. So wilderness serves that role, too: a reservoir for memories of times and faces fast fading into the past. I was perhaps the only person that Bill, stolid old soldier that he was, would allow to see emotion of any kind, and I was honored.

JULY 16, 1987

By midmorning, we had broken camp, packed up, and were on our way up the Minam River trail to the river's confluence with the North Minam River. We turned up the North Minam Trail. Just past the mouth of Sturgill Creek, we pulled up in an opening that we called Three Buck Camp from the time that Bill, Bernice, and I camped here on a mule deer hunt and we each killed a young buck on the first day of the season. Camp was so quickly set up that there was enough daylight left for a bit of fishing. Due to the steep gradient of the stream, this stretch of the river was not considered by most passing pilgrims as good fishing water and was therefore fished but little. When I expressed reservations, Bill showed me that, correctly done, a fisherman using a short rolling cast of a bucktail coachman under the overhanging canopy of alders could elicit strike after strike by eastern brook trout.

These misplaced members of the char family don't reach much size (six to ten inches), but they make up for it in their numbers, their willingness to take a fly, and their vigor in fighting the hook and tugging on the line. We had never failed to catch a bountiful supper here. Today was no exception. In fact, there were not only adequate fish for supper but enough left over for tomorrow's fish sandwiches. Admittedly, my rolling cast wasn't nearly as good as Bill's, and I lost a fly in the overhanging alders for every couple of fish that I caught. But it seemed a fair bargain that I would settle for anytime.

Night comes quickly in the tightness of North Minam Canyon. We stretched out on manty tarps and watched as the stars emerged in the cloudless sky. As the darkness deepened, we rose, one by one and without speaking, and sought out the warmth of our feathered sleeping bags. It seemed a magic moment.

JULY 17, 1987

Without debate, we decided to stay another night in Three Buck Camp and try our luck at fishing in Green Lake, a cirque lake perched some 1,200 feet above our camp. In addition to the fishing, the excursion would provide some exercise and conditioning for the horses.

Horseflies were numerous along the trail, and their stinging, blood-sucking bites made the horses a bit more skittish and difficult to handle. There was no lounging in our old cavalry saddles this day. Keeping a tight seat and a tight reign was *de rigueur*. We arrived at Green Lake after a two-hour ride just in time for lunch.

Bill had his fly rod set up and was whipping the mirror-like water of Green Lake while Bernice and I were still fumbling with our fishing gear. Meg, not being a fisherman, wandered down to the lakeshore in search of a bathing and swimming spot. I wondered if she had any idea how brisk the water was apt to be. Being the "clean freak" that she was, she would get the job done regardless—but I suspected it wouldn't take long.

"Fish on!" Bill cried out as I fumbled with tying a blood knot in my tippet for the third or so time. "Fish on!" yelled Bill again as I cleaned the grease and sweat from my reading glasses perched on the end of my nose in preparation for my sixth or so try at tippet-tying. "Fish on!" sang out Bill as I finally started down the bank toward the lake.

The fish were rising all around the lake—big-time. Bill hollered "Fish on!" again. His increasingly irritating announcement coincided with my expertly hooking an alder branch some eight feet above the ground on my first cast. I was beginning to think to hell with it—fishing should not be a competitive sport. One of Bill's least endearing attributes was that, for him, everything was a competition. He would compete with himself if nobody or nothing else was handy. By the time we met at the head of the lake, he had four ten- to twelve-inch eastern brook trout "keepers" in his creel; he also noted, just in passing, that he had let three or four little ones go. Bernice had three fish in her poke. Jack had none. Oh, I thought, the shame of it all! Actually, I really didn't give a damn—at least that's what I told myself. I lied.

I counted and sized up the seven fish we had in our collective possession, figured we could eat two apiece, and concluded we were one fish shy. I commented that we needed one more fish for dinner and began to unlimber my rod. Bill hurried down to the bank, made a cast, and sang out, "Fish on!" I gritted my teeth and reminded myself that fishing was *not*—or at least *should not*—be a competitive enterprise. That was what I told myself. That was not what I was feeling. There were times when I thought it would be soul-satisfying to be able to best the old bastard at something. Whenever I discovered what that might be, it was not apt to involve fly-fishing.

The ride back to camp was a bit too fast and furious for Meg, Bernice, and me. Bill was riding a young Morgan/thoroughbred cross gelding that had been, up to now, relegated to the pack string where he was compelled to simply follow the horse in front. This ride was not in that category, and in spite of Bill's work on the reins, the youngster set a pace a tad too fast to maintain good order for the following horses and riders.

Just after we hit the trail along the North Minam River, the two women and I dismounted and led our mounts the rest of the way to camp. Once in camp, Bill took care of the horse wrangling while I made the fire and cleaned the fish. The ladies then prepared our delicious supper: fish and spuds fried in bacon grease and garnished with yellow sweet onions.

And as a bonus, there were enough fish fillets left over for tomorrow's sandwiches. At home, we would likely complain if we were asked to eat the same thing for four meals in a row. But things were different here in the magic of the wilderness. We relished every mouthful and looked forward to more of the same tomorrow. There was little talking after the dishes were done as we sat around the fire staring into the flames. Talk would just have detracted from our private thoughts. One by one, we stood, stretched, and without comment retreated to our tents.

JULY 18, 1987

At daylight I emerged from my tent to find that Bill had already built up the fire and put the coffee water on to boil. I joined him at the fire. Meg and Bernice had declared last night that they were sleeping in. The dog was barking, without much enthusiasm, at something she thought she saw or smelled that required her to bring matters to our attention. Bill and I were leaning back against a log sipping our first cup of coffee of the day when the horses, still tied to the picket line, came to attention and focused their attention on the trees. From not more than twenty yards into the timber a bull elk with antlers in velvet emerged. The bull was perfectly aligned with one of the mares and created a momentary illusion that the mare had sprouted antlers. Just behind the first elk and a bit to the right was another bull with a magnificent set of developing antlers.

The elk and horses mingled for a few minutes, seemingly paying little attention to one another. The two bulls grazed around the edge of the clearing for nearly a half hour, never more than fifty yards away from where we sat, before they moved into the trees and out of sight. Bill's eyes met mine. How about that! I stood up to replenish the coffee in our cups and was just sitting down when Bill whispered, "The show's not over."

The smaller of the two bulls walked back into the clearing, alert and cautious but seemingly not frightened. He came slowly and carefully toward us until he was eleven long steps away, as paced later by Bill. We didn't even blink for fear of spooking the bull. He stood there without a twitch for perhaps a full minute and then turned and retreated slowly into the trees. His larger partner was more circumspect and remained half hidden in the edge of the trees. When the smaller bull joined him, they slowly sauntered out of sight, never looking back.

Just then, Bernice, who was brushing her hair, walked up to join us at the fire. We told her about the elk show and how much we regretted that she had missed the whole thing. But as this day's luck would have it, there was to be a curtain call. The two bull elk—now being referred to by Bill as Alphonse and Gaston—appeared again at the edge of the clearing. They stood there studying the camp for a very brief moment before again fading away into the trees, this time for good. I didn't believe that any of us would have traded that show for seats at a first-run Broadway musical. It was a truly golden moment, exceedingly rare and therefore precious. But such experiences do come, however rarely, to those who seek out the high lonesome. Well, maybe there was a little luck thrown in.

We dawdled over breakfast and were not packed up and ready to leave camp until nearly noon. We rode downstream to the trail's juncture with the main Minam River and turned upstream toward our next camp. We called this camp the Elk Camp, as it had been used off and on over the years by Bill and his hunting partners during the hunting season for elk. The camp was Bill's favorite in the Eagle Cap Wilderness—perhaps in the entire world. It was an almost sacred place for him where ghosts of family, hunting companions, horses, and long-ago youthful vigor resided in the shadows. To my mind, there were other prettier, handier, easier campsites nearby that we had shared over the years. But this was Bill's favorite and therefore a place to be visited when at all possible. I understood. Some places are indeed special and grow ever more special as life's shadows lengthen.

The USFS trail crew had just finished maintaining this section of trail, which made travel easy and uneventful. Just before we arrived at the confluence of Elk Creek with the Minam River, we watched a mule deer doe crossing the river. The snow-capped mountain in the background and the corridor of green firs along the river provided a perfect frame for the picture.

Occasionally, someone asks me, "Why don't you take many pictures?" My reply is that I don't want to be distracted by the rigmarole of taking photographs. For me, taking photographs is a low priority, as I have thousands of pictures in my memory banks, their resolution and color not only undiminished but rather enhanced by the passage of time. Still, I had the nagging feeling that I might regret that decision as time passed; after all, photos would be handy to illustrate the books and articles that I intended to write in retirement, should I live that long.

We arrived at the Elk Camp in the late afternoon and quickly set up camp. We had the drill down pat by now—practice does indeed make perfect. I think this camp was, for Bill, home to myriad friendly ghosts of old companions with whom he had shared this place and who had now passed over or were too old and too "stoved up" to venture so deep into the wilderness.

I think Bill sensed that at seventy-two years of age—and being increasingly crippled by arthritis and old injuries that nag at night and in cold weather—there would not be many more visits for him to such old, dear familiar places. That unspoken recognition made this visit all the more meaningful.

After camp was set up and the horses fed, Meg and I wandered downstream scouting for a place for a swim and a bath. The water was running cold and crystal-clear over the granite gravel bottom. After the first shock the rushing water that was snow only yesterday felt good and bracing as it washed away the sweat and trail dust and the heat of the day.

Supper was a delightful Bernice Brown concoction that she christened "Cheeseburger Impossible Pie," cooked in the reflector oven. The Eagle Cap Wilderness was a magical place that turned the commonplace into the delectable.

What seemed simple and easy when performed in a modern kitchen with all its gadgets is much more difficult when prepared from ingredients carried five days in a pannier on a packhorse and cooked using a reflector oven next to an open fire, especially when gusts of wind are stirring up both fire and ashes. Bernice, a former home economics teacher, seemed to take more pride in her camp cooking skills than in her gourmet cooking at home—and justifiably so.

While we were seated around the open fire eating supper, we looked up to see that a "camp doe" had dared to join the party. The mule deer doe was obviously used to human visitors at this commonly used campsite that was part of her seasonal summer range. Likely she was attracted by a combination of curiosity and a yearning for salt. This lust for salt sometimes led deer to gnaw at saddles and saddle blankets—especially the cinches—for the salt left behind from the evaporation of horse sweat.

Bill often put out a small block of salt to distract camp deer from the saddles. He had done so this evening, and it wasn't long before the old doe was joined by two younger does and a female yearling. Two of the does were nursing fawns, as evident from their swollen udders. But, as we had noted over the years, they seldom brought their fawns with them when they came to visit. After all, humans can be deadly dangerous.

JULY 19, 1987

There was a loud clap of thunder just at daybreak, and the causative lightening bolt struck close enough up the mountain to bring us wide awake. We snuggled deeper into our down sleeping bags and waited. Sure enough, a few minutes later, a tapping of raindrops commenced on the taut roof of the nylon pop tent. Meg nudged me and told me to zip the door to the tent closed. Now that I was awake, it dawned on me that we had not covered the woodpile with a tarp before going to bed. As I really wanted a good fire on this quite cool morning, I slipped on my boots and stuck my head out of the tent. I shouldn't have been concerned. I saw a flash of Bill's white long johns as he crawled back into his tent after throwing tarps over the woodpile and the kitchen boxes. That sight of his white-clad rump was rendered even more comical by the four deer that were running back and forth through camp.

Our "guard dog"—I use the term advisably—was either asleep or, more likely, just flat didn't give a damn. By this time, the rain had stopped. The three horses that had been left loose to graze all night heard us stirring around and ran into camp with their bells clanging, looking for a handout.

Just then, the dog charged out of Bill's tent to check things out. The morning peace and quiet suddenly resembled a wilderness version of a Keystone Cops movie—two horses running back and forth with bells clanging, deer getting the hell out of Dodge, the tied horses whinnying, the dog running in circles and barking, and Bill yelling at the dog as he hopped around on one leg and then the other, trying to get his pants on.

I was laughing quietly to myself, while being grateful that there were no outside witnesses. I was certain the scene would have seriously damaged our cultivated "old mountain men" image and credentials.

Bill and I were, by now, both wide awake and out of our tents, clad in long johns and unlaced boots. He quickly caught and tied the horses, which were standing next to the picket line just waiting to be "caught." The four horses that were tied on the picket line were turned loose for a couple of hours of grazing. I built up the fire and put the coffee on to boil. The two camp does returned after a half hour or so. It appeared that they had been rendered no more cautious by their earlier experiences. They patrolled around the camp at a discreet distance.

As we intended to spend the day in camp and nearby environs, there was no hurry to entice the ladies to rise and shine. Fish were rising in the river, and that was a temptation. But it was comfortable near the fire, and the coffee was hot, strong, and plentiful. Besides, there were stories—some new, some old standbys—waiting to be told. We settled in.

Just before midmorning, the ladies emerged from their nylon and feather cocoons. In short order, they whipped up a late breakfast of whortleberries (huckleberries)—picked along the trail yesterday—and oatmeal with a generous portion of canned milk and a bit of brown sugar. It seemed a most wonderful breakfast. Bill, as was his wont when canned milk appeared on the menu, quoted a short poem he claimed to have composed in his youth: "No teats to pull. No hay to pitch. Just poke a hole in the son-of-a-bitch!"

The ladies spent the midday hours walking downstream for a mile or so nibbling on wild strawberries they picked along the way. A little before noon, Bill cast a fly in the river at a spot only fifteen yards from the campfire and hooked and landed a fourteen-inch Dolly Varden. The second cast produced a twelve-inch rainbow. That did it. It was suddenly fishing time! I retrieved my rod and fishing gear and headed downstream. Bill went upstream. My fly supply was down to the most atrocious grasshopper imitations I had ever seen. The fish evidently agreed with my assessment, as they showed absolutely no interest in what I had to offer. So I gave up after a half hour, ambled back to camp, and immersed myself in briefing materials on forest policy to prepare myself for a training session that I was scheduled to address the day after we got home. Trips into the wilderness provided me clarity of mind to think and ponder in depth and at length.

There are curses that come with increasing professional recognition. The first is the danger of taking oneself too seriously. Second, given increasing hubris, it is possible to think you know and understand more than you do. The third is the demand on one's time, which renders further professional growth difficult and makes the synthesis of knowledge and the clarifying philosophical thoughts expected from "long-in-the-tooth" professionals ever less likely.

JULY 20, 1987

I was awakened by a camp doe nibbling at my boots, which I had parked just outside the door of the tent. Obviously, my boots would have been safer inside the small nylon pop tent, but there was the very significant factor of "essence of boot" to be considered. That less than delicate aroma was not a trivial thing. It led to Meg's insistence that my boots had to be deposited outside the tent. Her boots, of course, were safe inside. She coyly opined that "a girl's boots don't stink." I didn't argue. I could only win by losing.

My emphatic command to the deer not to chew my leather bootlaces led to a panicky retreat by the deer. Wide awake now, I dressed and crawled out into the early dawn. Last evening's rain clouds had blown away and left much of the earth's warmth to bleed away into the clear night sky. When the sun did rise, it was a small cold sun.

Once I had the fire blazing, it felt good on my bottom as I backed up to the fire. The hot coffee in my tin cup warmed my cold hands.

I crouched close to the fire with the dog between my legs, wondering what the dog was thinking while she had stood by shivering as I built up the campfire. Was her expression one of admiration for my exercise of such God-like skills, or was it merely a supplication for warmth?

I heard the clanging of the horse bells as Bill came into view leading the two horses that had been loosed all night to graze. The horses still tied to the picket line greeted him with a series of whinnies. Watching, I believed firmly that they were encouraging Bill to hurry up with their release. After all, it was their turn for rolling in the sand, drinking cold water from the river, and grazing in the meadow in the warming sunlight. What could be better than that—if one were a horse?

By midmorning, we had packed up the camp and were ready to go. We took the Cooper Creek trail to our so-called Deer Camp, located some 2,500 feet higher up in elevation. As the eagle flies, it was a journey of less than two miles. However, trails in the mountains aren't laid out as the crow flies. We figured the trip would take two hours to cover some five miles of trails that were, as Bill put it, "pretty much straight up all the way." The last two miles to our "hidden camp" would take us cross-country to the campsite nestled in a clump of large white firs.

The stand of trees hid a spring that emerged from the ground and disappeared, within fifty yards, into a bog. Bill had discovered the place some thirty years ago while he was hunting mule deer along the timber line. We had used it since as a camp from which to hunt for big Minam River bucks.

Over the years, each time we came and went from this camp we took care to use a different route to prevent establishing a trail for others to follow. This place had become very special to us, and we made every effort—selfishly or not—to keep it to ourselves. It was evident—from artifacts such as horse and mule shoes nailed to the trees—that the camp had been used by sheepherders until the USFS, somewhat belatedly in Bill's estimation, cut off sheep grazing in the area some two decades ago.

Each of our visits revealed high mountain meadows that were, in Bill's opinion, "healing up nicely" from many decades of overgrazing by sheep—faster, he opined, than he had once thought possible. I concurred. The plant species typical of early succession were giving way to perennial grasses, and erosion rills were clearly healing.

When we arrived at the Deer Camp, to our great disappointment, it was obviously no longer being used only by us. A dozen poles leaned against a tree at the tent site, a certain sign that elk hunters had discovered the place and had camped here last elk season. The sturdy poles were of the length and diameter and number to have supported two ten-by-twelve-foot wall tents. The remnant woodpile was made up of chunks of wood cut to fit Sims stoves. We figured that the elk hunters were a hardy lot with enough appreciation for the camp's secluded location to have taken the trouble to get here with a pack string with winter closing in on the high country.

We were far enough along in our trip to be increasingly well-practiced in a routine of setting up camp and caring for the horses. Those chores complete, we discussed the various alternatives we had for our afternoon activities. The women chose to hike the old sheep trail that contoured around the mountainside at 7,000 feet or so in elevation. The flowers that we encountered were blooming a month ago on the slopes above the Grande Ronde Valley. So, in a sense, it was still spring at this elevation. One of the magical properties of living near mountains is that spring can be prolonged by simply traveling higher into the mountains as summer progresses. On the other hand, winter comes early and stays long in the high lonesome.

Bill decided to hike over the ridge above us to find a new way to "No Name Lake," where we intended to fish tomorrow. A glance at the map indicated that he had about an 800-foot climb to the ridge above the lake. I retreated to a granite outcrop a quarter mile from camp that afforded a sweeping, spectacular view of the Minam River drainage, stretching from China Cap Mountain to Frazier Pass.

From my perch I saw places that stirred up good memories—a deer hunt up Elk Creek; rides over Sand Pass and Burger Pass; a big bull elk too far away to shoot at Tombstone Lake; and many more. Those experiences were fading, but not as much as memories associated with other places now much changed and changing still. The relatively unchanging qualities of the Eagle Cap and other Wilderness

Areas provided me a point of reference from which to look back—far back. That reference was valuable to today's ecologists and, I suspected, even more for those to come.

And, surely, this place too would change. The dead trees I saw across the canyon showed where wildfires had burned last year, and the needle-bare tops of the white firs showed the effect of a spruce budworm outbreak, both of which were in tune with the natural course of things. Such changes were but an illusion of immediate impact made dramatically real by the short lifetime of a man. I wondered if an ecologist who could live 1,000—or 5,000—years would view the process not as change but as a melding into sameness through repetition. At least for the immediate future, such a place as this would change relatively little. It was in such places that we could see and touch and feel our roots and know, or at least sense, where we came from.

Yet we could stay here for only the briefest time. There are far too many of us—and the pickings are too slim—to make staying longer while living off the land possible. Yet I thought the reference point was here—and similar other places—and should remain intact for that reason alone. Will such places as this exist in a hundred years? In a thousand? Who knows?

That will be a choice for those who come after us. We as a society have made our choices for now. It seems to me that we have not set aside—maybe "temporally preserved" are better words—as much as we should. Bill and other farsighted conservationists like him helped set aside as much as they could manage from pending exploitation. But they are old now, and the trails stretching out in front of them are short—and getting shorter by the day. Now it is someone else's turn to either pick up the torch or just turn away. They are heirs to the most valuable of inheritances—the ability to chose. There is much to be said for choices.

As I sat there and relived old travels and old hunts in my mind— and planned new ones—I thought of the admonition of one of my favorite philosophers, the baseball player Satchel Paige: "Never look back, something may be gaining on you." I think old Satchel meant never look back on the bad times. Now, looking back on the good times is a different matter. The wilderness had become a "lockbox" for me in which many of my memories of truly good times were stored. It was getting dark; the chill common to high elevations as the sun sinks in the west was at hand. I could smell the smoke from the fire in our camp down below. My longtime sweetheart—of thirty-two years now and counting—and my very good friends were seated around that fire waiting for me. Just now, that seemed the most desirable place in the world to be.

As I stood up, stretched, and started down the bare open ridge toward camp, the world was suddenly transformed as the sun, which had been hanging low on the western horizon, dropped below the cloud cover. The very tips of the mountain peaks were caught in the direct sunlight and glowed like candles in the gloaming. The phenomenon lasted less than a minute, and then suddenly the sun dipped out of sight. Darkness was coming—fast.

My comrades down below in the spruce thicket, their attention on the fire, were sipping coffee and awaiting supper. They were oblivious to the brief show that was perhaps mine alone. Suddenly it was noticeably colder, and I moved as fast as safety allowed down the ridgeline while I could still see where to put my feet. The campfire and the voices—and especially the ladies' laughter—were my beacon.

JULY 21, 1987

The temperature dropped significantly during the night. There was a layer of ice on the water bucket when I crawled out of the tent at daybreak to build a fire. Bill had left tracks in the frosty grass as he followed the sound of horse bells from the steep slope above camp. When he returned with the horses that had been grazing all night, we sipped scalding coffee, warmed our hands on the tin cups, and discussed options for the day. As the cold gray sky promised rain, we concurred that the eastern brook trout waiting in No Name Lake should remain—for today—unmolested. Likely conditions somewhat warmer could be found in a camp along the Minam River, lying some 2,000 feet lower down the mountainside. The ladies, after being coaxed from the tents with steaming cups of coffee, prepared breakfast while Bill and I saddled the horses, broke down and packed up the camp, and lashed the packs on the packhorses.

By midmorning, we were lined out on the trail down toward warmer climes. The steep downhill trail caused several of the pack-saddles to begin to slip, which made it necessary for us to stop, drop the packs, and readjust the saddle blankets and saddles.

During one such incident, I looked up to see the dog run into the midst of the horses with her tail tucked between her legs. She was being pursued by a mule deer doe that was giving every intention of a desire to stomp said dog into a blood puddle. It suddenly dawned on the doe that she was in the midst of people and horses—decidedly not an ordinary aspect of her habitat. She broke off her sally and departed the scene in the characteristic pronging gait peculiar to mule deer.

When the packs and saddles were in proper order, we proceeded on down the trail until we came to a large ponderosa pine across the trail. That forced us to take a detour through a fir thicket where, once again, we encountered our old acquaintance—the "attack doe"—and the reason for her uncommon belligerence. There was her fawn stretched out with its nose to the ground. Its spotted coat melded into the dappled pattern inscribed on the forest floor by the sun filtering through the trees. The doe stood her ground, stomping her front feet and snorting as we passed by not more than twenty yards away. I had never seen that behavior before.

When we reached the Minam River, we took the trail downriver for a half mile and turned in at what was commonly referred to as Minam Camp One. The name came from its establishment and use by commercial packers and hunting guides from Red's Horse Ranch.

Some old-timers called the place Tin Box Camp after a large sheet-metal-covered box that had once graced the site and was used by sheepherders to store salt and other necessities of their trade. The stacks of poles that were used to construct horse corrals and tent frames during the elk season were carefully stored against a giant ponderosa pine.

It appeared that we were the first horse party to camp here this year. As a result, grazing for the horses was plentiful. There was an ample supply of wood, cut to stove length and stacked, courtesy of last year's elk hunters. We judged this too pleasant a place—and too fortuitous relative to the wood supply—to pass up and quickly decided to make camp. After camp was set up and the horses cared for, the afternoon passed uneventfully. Bill and Bernice tried the fishing and were unsuccessful, except for one beautiful fourteen-inch Dolly Varden. Meg read while I spent the afternoon dozing in the sun and catching up on my journal entries.

The fishers returned to camp just a tad disgruntled—and very cold. Bill insisted that it must be five o'clock somewhere in the world, making consumption of a Rum and Tang an acceptable and attractive diversion. There was nary a word of disagreement. Such a round of drinks, combined with a blazing stand-around fire, drove away the chill. Suddenly the world was a brighter place, soon made even brighter by the aroma of a whole canned chicken, onions, and dumplings bubbling on the fire.

After supper, just before full dark, we made out the forms of three mule deer at the edge of the circle of firelight. They watched us cautiously, shifting from one forefoot to another, torn between curiosity and caution. Were they attracted by a vision of salt or some horse feed spilled on the ground? Or were we merely strange intruders in their home range and therefore something that warranted investigation? I wish I could communicate with the deer and tell them the old story of how curiosity killed the cat. It would be good wisdom that well might prove useful.

We discussed the likely fate of such curious deer when bowhunters began their hunts in late August and the deer would go from being entertaining curious camp does to fair game. Only some self-adopted ethical constraint against the taking of such foolhardy animals would prevent the easy harvest of these trusting, naïve creatures.

Bill slipped his hand into his saddlebag and came out with the Colt 1911a pistol that he had carried through campaigns in the Aleutians and Italy during World War II. He fired a shot over the heads of the deer, which responded with appropriate alarm. Maybe, he said, that would keep them from wandering into a bowhunter's camp.

JULY 22, 1987

No matter how enticing a sleeping bag is at dark, many nights of sleeping on the ground on a thin inflatable pad that gets even thinner as the

Red's Horse Ranch, Eagle Cap Wilderness, 1975. Left to right: *Pat Gill, Margaret and Jack, and Bill and Bernice Brown. The photo was taken by Jack Gill, Jack's former boss at the Forestry Sciences Laboratory in Morgantown, West Virginia.*

night wears on can make the coming of dawn increasingly welcome. Aching back and hips and a bum knee—plus a full bladder—made it a pleasure to greet the dawn and the cold world outside the tent.

The first thing I saw upon sticking my head out of the tent was the camp doe we had dubbed Old Bite Side from the nicks in her coat—likely earned in a disagreement with another doe over who was number one in their little hierarchy. The doe was nosing around the ashes of the campfire and gave way only with what I interpreted as reluctance when she saw me. She hung around within a stone's throw as I stirred up the embers from last night's fire and got the morning fire blazing. She finally faded back into the trees when Bill crawled out of his tent, picked up the halters and lead ropes, and walked out to catch the horses grazing across the meadow.

During the course of Bill's horse-wrangling exercise and my answer to the call of nature, we found two aluminum arrow shafts in the grass. That evidence settled our debate of the night before. Some folks are not above taking a camp doe during archery season. We agreed that shooting semi-tame camp deer was, by our lights, something less than good hunting ethics. But then all ethics, hunting or otherwise, tend to be personal and individual in nature. And there was nothing illegal in such an action. My grandfather once described ethics as what one does when no one else is watching.

When Bill and I got back to camp with the horses in tow, our wives were awake and dressed. The fire was blazing, and boiled coffee, my favorite kind, was waiting. It had begun to drizzle. The cold rain led us to congratulate ourselves on yesterday's now-prescient decision to move our camp down to the river from the high country. Now it was time to make new plans. Should we move on down the Minam River Trail to make our next camp so as to be closer to where the horse trucks were waiting if the weather continued to sour? Or did we want to stay in this camp for another night, leaving ourselves a twenty-mile ride out to the trailhead? We decided to remain another night and spend the day making a ride up the Elk Creek Trail.

During our ride up Elk Creek, we stopped in a small opening that had likely been created several years earlier by a lightening strike and the small wildfire that ensued. The ground was covered with wild strawberry plants, the fruits of which are diminutive compared to the bloated domestic varieties.

Soon, under the direction of the women, Bill and I were crawling over the ground picking the wild strawberries as if our places in heaven depended on obtaining an adequate supply for strawberry shortcake. The tiny fruits were incredibly tasty, as were the whortleberries that we had found several days earlier. Every other one went into our mouths, which slowed things down considerably. But so what? We were in no real hurry. During this "one for me, one for the shortcake" routine, I ruminated on why the native fruits had a much more intense flavor than the bigger, prettier domestic varieties. Wild strawberries, huckleberries, and plums all seem to have a much more intense taste compared with their domestic offspring. I remembered that this was true of the relatively small oranges and apples I had eaten while working in India and Pakistan.

As was my wont as a scientist, I formulated a hypothesis: the intensity of taste of a fruit per unit of weight is inversely related to the size of the fruit. This was followed by a corollary hypothesis: the intensity of taste per unit of weight diminishes with each step toward domestication. I fully intended to think on this more carefully and subject my hypotheses to a test at every future opportunity. Why not? I have used lesser excuses for trips into the wilderness. And sometimes I come to the wilderness—and stay long—with absolutely no excuse at all.

JULY 23, 1987

We were "up and at 'em" early, as we had a twenty-two-mile ride ahead of us. Unlike the other mornings on this trip, today all members of our party arose early and went about their chores with an early departure in mind. Bright eyes and bushy tails were not, however, immediately conspicuous.

The tents were collapsed and precisely folded into neat packages, sleeping pads were rolled and fitted into nylon sacks, and feather-filled sleeping bags were stuffed tightly into small bags. Within a half hour, the camp items were rolled and tied into manty packs or arranged neatly in panniers, ready to be loaded onto the horses.

Bill and I had three of the horses packed by the time the cooks announced breakfast—oatmeal with huckleberries and condensed canned milk. Ordinarily I am not fond of oatmeal, but this seemed somewhere beyond good, possibly because of the condensed milk that I remembered fondly from my youth.

My parents and grandparents had run a confidence game on me during the late years of the Great Depression when we were reduced to using condensed milk late in the months when money was short. To "make the medicine go down" they convinced me that condensed milk was a very special treat. I believed them, and still considered canned milk a special treat.

The dishes were packed away unwashed. After all, a dishwashing machine was waiting at the end of the trip. There were some things to be appreciated and short cuts to be exercised in bringing a wilderness trip to an end.

An hour after full light, we were mounted and lined out down the Minam River Trail. We passed a meadow that flanked the river, crossing at what Bill and I called Buckaroo Flat. Several years earlier, we crossed the Minam here on our way home at the end of an elk hunt. A big outfit—with maybe ten mules and ten or so horses—had been camped here for the elk season and were in the process of packing up to head for the barn. About six mules were already packed, and three riders were mounting their saddle horses preparatory to moving out up the trail toward Lackey Hole.

Then something spooked an untied mule, and it charged, bucking, kicking, and braying into the midst of the packed mules. A veritable explosion of horses, mules, and people commenced. Mules were bucking, horses were bucking, and bucked-off packs and riders seemed to fill the air. I was reminded of riding across a rodeo arena—with a rodeo in full bloom! Our horses rolled their eyes and danced a little. Fortunately they were disinclined to join the rodeo. Bill and I pulled our hats down and took a deep seat just in case. From there on out, the trip was uneventful. The horses knew where they were going—"home," where their feed came twice a day in the form of alfalfa, they were not tied to a picket line, and there were no saddles to tolerate and no loads to carry.

As we made the final climb up to the ridge between the Minam and Little Minam Rivers, Bill commented about the steepness of the slope we were traversing, "This slope would be pretty damn steep if it weren't for the trees." What? I pondered his observation. He was right. A rider tended to feel more comfortable riding a trail on a tree-covered slope than on an open slope. Within a half hour, we left the timbered north-facing slope on a trail that led into the Minam River drainage. The trail crossed the ridge and started down the treeless south-facing slope to the Little Minam. All the riders stiffened a little, whether they would have admitted it or not. Steep slopes without trees are steeper—at least in the mind's eye. Maybe the feeling is related to the possibility of having a tumble down the hill shortened by coming up against a tree. Who knows?

Riding along without conversation provided time and opportunity for such esoteric considerations. As we rode closer and closer back to the "real world" that lay waiting for us, my mind slipped slowly into thinking about the business that was waiting. That was okay, as it lessened the culture shock that always came with reentry into civilization.

I was even ready to stop by the Forest Service research lab on the way home to check the messages on my computer. On the pale green screen I noted the origin of the messages—Portland, Oregon; Washington, D.C.; Fort Collins, Colorado; and Missoula, Montana. I was suddenly struck by the contrast between our yesterdays in the wilderness and my today in a modern research laboratory. I didn't know whether to laugh or cry. Maybe just little appreciation and gratitude for the wilderness and the escape and contrast it provided would be adequate.

Margaret and her Appaloosa mare, Kitty, Eagle Cap Wilderness, 1987.

CHAPTER 6

NEW PILGRIMS IN THE WILDERNESS— FAST LEARNERS PREFERRED

D r. James Applegate, a professor of wildlife biology at Rutgers University and a longtime colleague and friend, was spending a year's sabbatical leave with my USFS unit in La Grande. His eldest daughter, Katie, had shown up in the course of her travels following high school graduation, and it had been arranged, with Jim's permission, that part of this rite of passage should involve a short horseback trip into the Eagle Cap Wilderness. The party consisted of Bill Brown, Meg, Katie, and me—with seven horses and one spotted dog.

JULY 24, 1987

Bill decided that we would enter the Eagle Cap via East Eagle Meadows, as it was only a six-mile ride into some alpine lakes and would allow Katie to experience some "real mountains"—up close and personal. The only drawback was that the journey entailed a three-hour haul from La Grande to our jumping-off point at a private, now-closed mountain resort and outfitter's headquarters called Boulder Park. The good news relative to the long haul was that the road traversed backcountry forest lands still relatively free of roads and, mostly, still "unmanaged" (not yet logged and without roads). That relatively pristine condition was in the process of dramatic alteration.

The road along which we traveled was festooned with plastic ribbons of orange and blue and red tied to the wooden stakes used by USFS civil engineers to designate soon-to-be roads. Farther along the road, construction of the network of logging roads was well under way, with logging to follow hard on the heels of road construction. And in that process, *de facto* wilderness would shrink by another increment. Whether this was good or bad was not so clear, but there was no doubt that the change in this piece of the earth, likely the first of an ongoing series of such changes, was irrevocable. What had been for many centuries would very soon be no longer—and would never be again. Thereby, land managers were asserting their God-like ability to manipulate the forest while, at the same time, betting that their knowledge was adequate and their techniques fine-tuned enough to maintain that forest in a viable and productive state forever.

Most of the foresters and forest managers I know well enough and respect enough to ask seem fully confident that we have the knowledge, wisdom, and technology to accomplish that task. Others—I being among them—hear whispers in the night, warning that we know too little about forest ecosystem function over the very long term, that our experience with managing these forests is very brief and, therefore, limited in application, and that we would be wise to proceed very slowly learning each step.

To my mind, that situation cries out for caution and some dampening of hubris. We speak readily about fully regulated forests and second-, fifty-, or even tenth-stand rotations. Those things lie hundreds of years into the future. Clearly we are engaged in a great ongoing experiment and are learning in the process. It might be prudent if we dared admit that we are engaged in the testing of a hypothesis—nothing more and nothing less. But, on the other hand, what choice is there? We *Homo sapiens* ("wise ones") probably have no choice; like all species, we must exploit our environment in order to live and prosper.

We were seemingly condemned to this course of action when our species evolved from hunters and gatherers to agriculturists and learned to manufacture and buy and sell and consume more and more. "Wealth" was and is most commonly defined by more and more consumption. That removed, or at least dramatically eased, the controlling mechanisms on population growth of our species.

Now we are firmly committed to a race between technological development along with increased—hopefully sustainable—exploitation of our environment and increasingly likely disaster. At this point, the question is not whether to exploit natural resources but how and at what rate. The trick to the survival of *Homo sapiens* over millennia is to make sure that "renewable" natural resources are indeed maintained as "renewable"—century after century, literally forever.

As we saddled up and lashed the packs on the packhorses, we could hear logging machinery hard at work to get logs to the mill while simultaneously removing one more "buffer" between the legally designated Wilderness and the "managed forest." Even after riding several miles up the trail, we could still hear the loggers at work down below, busily engaged in the first steps to bring these pristine forests "under management." When we turned off from the last newly laid out logging road and passed the signs informing us that we had entered into the Eagle Cap Wilderness, both our habitat and our state of mind changed. We had entered a different world in terms of reality and perception.

Yet even here was the mark of human hands modifying the purity of the vision stated in the Wilderness Act of 1964, which described such places as "untrammeled by man." The groomed trails were beautifully engineered and maintained by USFS personnel. We rode the six miles to Echo Lake without ever having to stop to let the horses catch their breath or even cool down. We met two pack strings, and the lead horseman in the second group informed us that "the trails get better from here on up—not as tough as they are down here." I had just commented to Bill that the trail we were traveling was a beautifully engineered "freeway" for horses and hikers. Beauty is, after all, in the eye of the beholder.

Some two hours after departing the trailhead, we arrived at Echo Lake. We passed through several meadows choked with fleeceflower, a tough plant that thrives on the bare mineral soil conditions that were partially the result of abusive grazing by bands of sheep around the turn of the twentieth century. Given the status of the soils today, maybe we should thank God for the likes of fleeceflower. Without it, more and more of the crumbly granite soils would be clogging the streams down below. The original soil layers still exist here and there and support fescue and sedges that are increasing their share of the growing space.

Given enough respite from grazing, especially by domestic sheep, the meadows might to some degree be recaptured by more palatable species. If so, it will be a very slow process. Plant succession is slow above 6,000 feet, and the situation is delicate where ecosystems exist in an ongoing argument between bare rock, evolving soil, and a tenuous hold for plant life and the creatures that vegetation supports. Human exploitation of such environments through grazing, especially sheep grazing, proved to be risky business. Is it a risk worth continuing?

Even exploiting ("making productive use of") these sites for recreational purposes involves risk, which therefore demands careful, flexible management. As we approached Echo Lake, the impacts of recreational use—bare ground, fire rings, soil damage where horses had been tied, etc.—became increasingly obvious. We came upon a USFS sign proclaiming "NO CAMPING OR GRAZING WITHIN 200 FEET OF THE LAKE." A good rule, but one too long delayed and inadequately complied with or enforced.

Oddly, some dream of the wilderness as land "untrammeled by man," and yet in the process of their visits they "trammel" those same lands. We literally want to have our cake and eat it too. But what is new about that? Management of Wilderness Areas will be, by definition, a tricky business that will require varying degrees of management. Over the long run, there will be much more to wilderness management than drawing lines on maps and occasional visits by friendly rangers passing the time of day with visitors. Those who advocate and fight for Wilderness designations must, upon achieving success, become advocates for the necessary resources to manage those areas—including their use. With increasing recreational use of such high-elevation, relatively fragile environments, there is increasing probability of such impacts accumulating and interacting. Managers will not long be able to ignore those impacts and will be forced invariably—and much against the instincts of some—into more intensive "management" of human and livestock use.

The necessary managerial constraints are the antithesis of "wild." Implied in the concept of "wilderness" is the opportunity to escape the world of intensifying regulation and to experience the world as it was before man became the dominant animal force—i.e., before we entered what some have called the Anthropocene. There will be an increasing conflict between the desire—expressed in law— to maintain wilderness in a state "untrammeled by man" and the accommodation of increasing human use. Resolution will not be easy, and it won't be insignificant in terms of cost. Maintaining wilderness will increasingly require more careful management.

For people like Bill Brown, who have long experience in the use and management of wilderness, the trends toward more and managerial control is both perceptible and painful while being recognized as inescapable. Seemingly he has adjusted and takes things as they are. Yet I think he believes, as a matter of faith, that wilderness has been the savior of his mind and soul—maybe even the "salvation" of his "world" in the tradition of John Muir.

Bill seemed philosophical about the diminution of the "wild" in wilderness. He looked at Katie, our bright young companion from New Jersey, and whispered to me, "Watch her eyes. Try to see what she sees—and how she sees it. She doesn't know what it was like before. She only knows what she sees—right here, right now. And the wilderness she sees is huge and beautiful and *wild*. Our time, and what we have known, is coming to an end. Hers is just beginning. Focus on that, and it will likely change the way you see things." He was right.

We made camp a half mile above Echo Lake. The pasturage for the horses was good, and we were camped far enough away from the lake to assure that the hobbled horses would not drift down to overgrazed areas closer to the lake. Through our binoculars we could see circles in the water that came and went with increasing frequency— fish, potentially tomorrow's supper, were rising in the lake. We would have to see what we could do about exploiting that opportunity.

JULY 29, 1987

We awoke with the clear intent of moving camp over the ridge above camp and down into the Trout Creek drainage and then on down to the Minam River. On the other hand, we were in no hurry to begin that journey. As we sat around the fire and sipped our cowboy coffee, our breaths made small temporary clouds in the air of the high lonesome.

We waited impatiently for the sun to emerge over the ridge and take away the frost and the cold. We watched as the sunlight crept down the rock bluffs, talus slopes, and snow patches that towered above Echo Lake. It was a glorious show of light and shadow that changed rapidly with the angles of light produced by the rising sun. No words passed between us—such would have been superfluous and perhaps even considered rude, much as spoken words would be in a great music hall with a performance underway. The only sound was our breathing and the soft rattle associated with the occasional replenishing of the steaming coffee in our metal cups.

When Meg emerged from the tent, she asked, "What have you two been up to?" I answered, "Taking communion." She looked at me quizzically. Then she smiled her beautiful smile and issued instructions for me to get off my fanny and get the wood she needed for a cooking fire. As I stood and turned to get the wood, I caught Bill's eye. He was poking at the fire with a stick and smiling to himself. He understood exactly what I meant—and he was in complete agreement.

We quickly broke down the camp, caught and saddled the horses, packed things up, and lashed the packs onto the packhorses. We had the drill down pat. Well, almost. Strange as it seemed, every year of travels into the wilderness required a shakedown period as the old skills—all rusty from lack of use—came back, and confident routine replaced hesitation and uncertainty. That led us, after some cogitation, to agree that what we needed was more practice! Unfortunately, the demands of the real world interfered far too often.

When we reached the ridge between the East Eagle and Minam River drainages, we dismounted to loosen the horse's breast collars and tighten their britchens in preparation for the steep descent into Trail Creek. We stood, literally, on top of the world, at least this part of the world, and all the land we could see in every direction was part of our nation's Wilderness Preservation System. Bill and Katie snapped pictures to remind them of this time and place. I stored away my pictures in my mind. Our descent down the trail to Trail Creek seemed an interminable repetition of switchbacks across a very steep, open slope marked by granite rocks and rubble at the top and alder-covered snow-slide areas toward the bottom. The scenery was beautiful, but there was little time to contemplate it, as the pack string absorbed our full attention. Human pucker strings were tight. I couldn't say about the horses, though I had my suspicions.

We had a beautiful campsite in mind: just where the trail crossed Trail Creek. The spot was situated in a grove of very large, very old spruce trees and tucked in out of sight of the trail at the base of a large meadow. Just before we rode into the cathedral stand of spruce, we stopped and looked back up at the granite slopes of the mountain we had just descended. It was impossible not to be impressed with the workmanship and skills of those who had engineered and constructed that trail. Trail Creek carried, at the moment, a mere trickle of water. But it was also home to a series of crystal-clear pools. After we gave the horses a "little blow," Bill and I agreed that, with our fly rod lines sporting a Carey Special or black gnat at the end of our tippets, a suitable mess of trout might be attained for our supper—but just not today. We marked the spot for a more opportune time. Today we needed to move on down the trail to the Minam River and then several miles farther downriver before we made camp. We wanted to be in position to move tomorrow to our last camp of our too-brief trip, just below Tombstone Lake.

There seemed to me to be two kinds of wilderness trips: those with a definite plan and those of the more ad hoc variety. I had come to prefer the semi–ad hoc variety whereby we moved (or not) as the spirit moved us, camping when and where things were sufficiently seductive. And sometimes it just seemed like the right thing to do to take a new fork in the trail. While I preferred ad hoc, I would take a wilderness trip any way I could work one in.

On the descent down to Trail Creek, we came to a boggy spot in the trail not more than ten feet across. It was such a mess that the USFS trail crew had laid down a pad of eight- to ten-inch-diameter logs laid side by side, making twenty feet of corduroy road that had been in place long enough to lose integrity. The first three horses scrambled across with moderate difficulty, but in the process the logs began to shift, and several of the more rotted ones broke. My mare and the packhorse I had in tow finished the job of destruction as they lunged out of the hole in a bit of a panic.

In following me too close behind, Katie's mare plunged in up to her chest and went down on her side, with Katie's left leg pinned underneath. To her great credit, Katie kept her cool and stayed with the mare as she struggled to right herself and lunge out of the hole. The kid was a little pale but didn't say a word. Later that evening, we found that her knee was bruised to the point of it turning spectacular hues of red and black and blue. But Katie was one good kid—smart and "PDT" (plenty damn tough) to boot. I suspected that, in her place, I would have sniveled a least a little. She had said nothing.

Several miles farther down the trail we met another pack string. I recognized the lead rider as a colleague of mine in the USFS's research division in Portland, Richard "Dick" Woodfin. Dick had been a companion on several rides at the USFS's Starkey Experimental Forest and Range in the Blue Mountains when we were showing our bosses from the Washington office a good time and, in the process, hoping to develop some understanding and appreciation of our work. I had found that there were few gimmicks that beat "politicking on horseback." Dick and his wife, LaDonna, were real horse people and fellow lovers of wilderness, especially the Eagle Cap Wilderness.

It seemed strange to me how many friends and acquaintances I had encountered over the years in the course of my wilderness travels—and they didn't have to be close to home. Several years ago Bill and I and our wives were on a pack trip in the Bob Marshall Wilderness in Montana. We had been camped two days' ride down the Sun River from the jump-off point at the Bench Mark Campground. I was busy fishing when I heard a voice say, "Don't you speak to old friends?" I looked over my shoulder to see, judging by his appearance and gear, an old mountain man watering his horse in the stream. It was Jake Callentine, an old USFS colleague. Several years earlier, we had worked closely together on the Range Research and Development Program on the Malheur National Forest in northeast Oregon. We had last seen each other at his retirement party in John Day, Oregon, some five years earlier.

What were the chances of two old friends, both more than 300 miles from home, meeting in the middle of the Bob Marshall Wilderness in Montana? Jake was soon joined by a fellow rider, a USFS employee that Jake had hired over thirty years earlier when he was a brand-new district ranger for this part of "the Bob." The "young fellow" was retiring, and he and Jake were taking one last ride together to check out "their wilderness." After a prolonged coffee break at our camp, Jake and his friend mounted up and moved out down the Sun River. As they rode out of sight, I sensed the passing of an era in USFS history. Those men had passed on their responsibilities to a new generation of folks to treasure and care for the Bob. I only hoped they passed on their deep sense of responsibility and caring, too.

We rode on down Trail Creek to the juncture with the Minam River and then down the Minam River Trail to the old commercial elk camp once maintained by the now-defunct Boulder Park guide outfit. The campsite lay just across the river from the bottom of an alder snow slide—a long narrow opening in the timber that ran from the river to the tree line on the steep slope above. The clearing was the result of occasional avalanches of snow and ice in late winter or spring.

Our usual campsite had been washed out in last spring's high water except for the upper portions, but there was still room enough for our camp and ample grazing for the horses. The site's most appealing feature—for this particular trip—was the neat stack of cut-to-stove-length wood kindly bequeathed to us by last season's elk hunters. Cutting and splitting wood for the stove was far down on my list of favored chores. To make matters worse, we had managed to leave our "Swede saw" in the horse truck.

With water only fifty feet away, a precut wood supply, a flat place for our tent, and an alder snow slide for the horses to graze— what was left to be desired in a wilderness campsite? For me, one of the foremost beauties of the wilderness is the way it simplifies things.

Just before dark, seven elk crossed the snow-slide area just above our tent. Only moments later, a doe and a yearling mule deer began nosing around camp. I lay stretched out flat on my back on a manty tarp next to the fire—with Bill's dog cuddled tight to my side for warmth—and watched the bats flitting back and forth against the fading sky. Finally, at full dark, the aerial spectacle disappeared in the darkness, though I could still hear the bats mixed with the other night sounds. I was tempted to seek out my sleeping bag, but not just yet. I continued to gaze into the fire as it burned down to coals while dozing off and on in the process. When the glowing coals became ashes, I awoke cold and stiff and ready for bed. To get warm seemed a wonderful prospect. My down sleeping bag was calling and promised to do that job.

JULY 30, 1987

When I crawled out of the tent just at sunrise, frost covered the grass and the kitchen fly. Bill was wrangling horses. The dog sat staring at the ashes of last night's fire and wagged her tail when she saw me crawling out of the tent. I imagined what she was thinking: "Here comes the 'warmth maker' just when I need him most." I worked my magic and the fire blazed up. I sat down on a campstool and opened my hands to soak up the increasing warmth while waiting for the coffee water to boil. The dog settled in between my legs, and we stared into the fire. I wondered what she was thinking—or was she simply feeling?

I looked up to see Bill returning to camp with the horses, each leaving a trail through the frosted grass. The coffee seemed especially good—almost as good as the fire but not quite. We watched the tips of the mountains as they began to glow brighter with the rising sun. When the sunlight finally reached down into our camp, the frost quickly morphed into bright beads of water. No wonder that the sun seemed a worthy god over the centuries to so many.

We were packed up and riding out of camp at midmorning, a decent enough starting time to begin the day's journey—especially when escorting a young lady from the East on a wilderness adventure. Frankly, our instinct had been to stay over another day—to hell with the schedule. But schedules are schedules, and Jim would worry about Katie if we did not emerge from the wilderness at the promised time. In contrast, nobody would worry about Bill and me until we were two days overdue—and maybe not even then.

It was five miles down the Minam River to the first spot where we could safely ford the river and take the trail up Elk Creek to its head and then on up the switch-backed trail to Tombstone Lake. We pitched our camp in a beautiful five-acre meadow some two miles below Tombstone Lake. We had a personal rule-of-the-trail for our excursions in the Eagle Cap Wilderness: "Don't camp near a high mountain lake, as that is the privilege of backpackers." Back-packers seemed drawn to the high lakes "like good ole boys to beer and barbecue." They seldom camped between the trailheads and the lakes, not even in the good spots. And like most backcountry horsemen, Bill and I didn't ordinarily camp at the lakes. It seemed a fair way to divide up the world. The horse bells that are music to our ears could be a form of pure aggravation for backpackers. It was big country, and there was no need for unnecessary problems. Live and let live.

Meg and I set up camp while Bill and Katie rode on up the trail to Tombstone Lake to try the fishing. After we had put up the tents, gathered in a wood supply, and set up the kitchen, Meg and I took a much needed swim in the creek. The stream at the edge of the meadow ran along the edge of a boulder field that came down from the granite walls looming above.

The car-sized boulders next to the creek and the smaller boul-ders farther up were home to pika. Their sharp calls kept us aware of their presence. Through our binoculars we could see the pika, off and on, as they gathered "hay" and left it on the tops of the boulders to dry. It was late July, and the living for pikas was easy. But instinct—and thousands of years of experience—told the pikas to make hay while the sun shines. They stored the hay in "barns" under the rocks where they would spend their days when the snow buried this place six feet under.

Across the creek a small meadow had two large spruce trees growing in its center. Smaller trees were encroaching around the edg-es of the meadow, but there was still adequate grazing for the horses. The surrounding granite ridges formed a huge semicircle around the camp. Three trails led out of this semicircle in various directions back to the real world in a long one-day ride. But for this precious moment, the ridges formed what seemed to me to be a huge nest for us in the midst of the wilderness—a nest that we had all to ourselves.

Just at dark, two mule deer does emerged from the cover of the trees and grazed alongside the horses in the open meadow. Their visit added flavor to the bucolic scene that was all too soon obscured by darkness. There was no moon in the crystal-clear sky—it was a night meant for stargazing. Above 7,000 feet there was no pollution to interfere with our view of the heavens. The stars emerged from the cloak of diminishing light—one by one at first and then by the dozens and, suddenly it seemed, by the hundreds and maybe thousands. Finally, the cloudless sky was awash with tiny dots of light. As the hours passed, we made out some half-dozen satellites moving across the sky. The incongruity between our surroundings and these products of space-age technology streaking across the sky struck me. I found that if I refused to notice, the satellites weren't there. Then only the real stars shone, and it seemed easier to pretend at isolation and immersion in a more primitive world. The open, star-filled sky was a glorious sight but carried a penalty, as it seemed to suck away the heat from the earth, making things quickly uncomfortable for pilgrims hunkered down around a tiny campfire at 7,000 feet.

When the anticipation of down-filled sleeping bags overcame the wonderment of the star-filled sky, it was time to crawl into the taut domed nylon tents and sleep. Sleep did not come quickly, and the sights and sounds and smells of this glorious day played over and over in my mind. The world had become a more simplified place where I could shut out the confusing cacophony of the political battles raging over the future of the national forests and my role in those battles.

JULY 31, 1987

I rose in time to get dressed, build up the campfire, and wait for the sun's appearance on the surrounding mountain peaks. There were still a few stars lingering in the clear, cold sky. This was one of those mornings when coffee seemed more of a necessity than a pleasurable indulgence. When the coffee was ready, Bill and I crouched close to the fire and sipped the scalding liquid with a certain reverence, holding our tin cups in two gloved hands to absorb the warmth. We blew softly across the coffee's surface, making small brief clouds. A visitor from outer space would surely have thought that he had come upon some religious rite. In my case, such an assumption wouldn't be far off the mark.

The tip of a mountain peak was suddenly alight with the new day's sun, and then in quick succession, another and another. The dramatic effect softened as the sunlight crept down the face of the mountains. We watched silently until the sun enveloped our campsite. Then we stood and stretched and poured ourselves more coffee.

Our version of "Sunday services" in the wilderness was complete—except for the music emanating from the upslope breezes in the spruce trees, the water sounds from the stream, and the periodic whistles from the awakening pika in the boulder field. I enticed Meg from her sleeping bag with a cup of coffee delivered to her in the tent. Once dressed, she and Katie prepared breakfast while Bill and I saddled horses, broke down the camp, and packed up.

The trail back down to civilization took us up 2,000 feet in elevation past Tombstone Lake and over a 7,000-foot-high pass before descending into the Eagle Creek drainage. We encountered a family of six camped at Tombstone Lake. They had been delivered to the lake by Charlie Short, a commercial packer and a friend, who would return for them in a week. This was their first encounter with the wilderness. Given their wonderment and excitement, I suspected it would not be the last.

We reached the pass about noon and continued on down the trail to Eagle Creek. The trail was washed out in two places, requiring us to do some plain and fancy sliding with the pack string to get around the problem. After we cleared the second slide area, we began to worry about what might lie ahead, as retreat back up the trail was no longer a safe option. Luckily, we encountered no further problems.

The lower portion of the trail was beautifully laid out, having been rebuilt by the USFS trail crew just the previous summer. There were more switchbacks per mile along this section of trail than I had ever seen before—maybe more than thirty. Now, I thought, this was the place to come with a pack string that needed to practice negotiating switchbacks! We arrived at the trailhead at midafternoon, and in less than an hour we were loaded up and on the road to home. Within a mile we encountered a four-wheel-drive pickup with hugely outsized tires that was, more or less, under the control of a young man clutching a beer can. He took his half of the road out of the middle, forcing us into the borrow ditch, fortunately a shallow one. The horses displayed their displeasure at being thrown around by giving the trailer a few swift kicks. The driver that forced us off the road never looked back. I seldom employ the middle-finger salute, but in this case I made an exception—with both hands—and threw in some of my best obscenities to boot. Somehow it made me feel better, if only slightly, and not for long.

We had to unload the horses—no easy task—given the tilt of the truck with wheels on one side in the shallow borrow ditch. Then it was necessary to execute some fancy maneuvers with a chain and a Handy-Man jack to get the horse truck back up on the road. During that process, I formulated a hypothesis: the IQ of the driver of a four-wheel-truck in the backcountry is inversely and closely correlated with the size of the tires relative to the size of the vehicle. I thought, welcome back to "where the peoples is!" Our interlude in the high lonesome was at an end.

CHAPTER 7

DOES WILDERNESS HAVE THE POWER TO HEAL? MAYBE

This trip into the Elkhorn Wilderness was what Bill called "a weekender." The Elkhorns are an isolated mountain range lying southeast of the much larger Eagle Cap Wilderness. The trailhead was only a one-hour drive from our home in La Grande, just off a paved road that also provides access to the Anthony Lakes Ski Area.

SEPTEMBER 7, 1987

I had forgotten that today is my fifty-third birthday—maybe because I wanted to. Meg remembered, however, as she always did. I was the pleased recipient of a "big ole Happy Birthday kiss"—a birthday present impossible to beat.

Meg and I had been blessed just two weeks earlier with the arrival of a seventeen-year-old foster child who had been in and out of mental hospitals and purportedly had problems with alcohol, drugs, and inappropriate social behavior. Last year she had lived in a group home in Portland. "Jan" was excited about the trip and rattled on incessantly on the drive to the trailhead. She said she had ridden horses before and was obviously thrilled at the prospect of riding Wendy, a tall, beautiful, thoroughbred mare. She seemed fascinated with the packing operations. I had to warn her several times to stand clear of the horses, especially their kicking end. Bill and Bernice, Meg and I, and Jan made up our party of five, leaving us with only two packhorses. Accordingly, we were traveling light.

After two hours of easy driving on a just-groomed dirt road, we arrived at Dutch Flat, a large, wet meadow some three-quarters of a mile long by one-half mile wide. A narrow stream—four to six feet wide—was incised two or three feet deep in the floor of the meadow and meandered its way from one end of the meadow to the other. After camp was set up, there was enough daylight remaining for a try at fishing for small eastern brook trout.

As I headed for the stream, I spotted a black bear about a quarter mile away. I thought it likely that the bear was feeding on the guts and heads of fish discarded by fishermen. I called to Jan and motioned for her to come to me. She was certain that I was teasing and joined me reluctantly. The sight of the bear convinced her that she wasn't at the Portland zoo, and her excitement began to break down her studied reserve.

The fishing for brook trout was almost too easy; it seemed that my every second cast produced a fish for the frying pan. It took less than thirty minutes to catch enough fish of adequate size for our supper.

A chill wind arrived with twilight, holding the hint of approaching winter. I lay stretched out flat on my back on a manty tarp by the dying fire and watched the bats emerge and begin their patrol for insects through and over the treetops. Soon it was too dark for me to trace their erratic flights, but I knew they were there. Cold toes and fingers signaled that the fire had died down to ashes and it was time for bed.

Meg, long toasty warm in our double-size down sleeping bag, protested mildly at the entry of my cold body, but neither long nor persistently. Fluffy down sleeping bags and crisp nights are a prescription for the best cuddling. I lay awake and listened to the intermittent winds in the trees and the night sounds. I pondered the consequences of our agreement to take in a foster child with significant problems at this stage in our lives.

Sometimes, being married to a lovely lady who is a dedicated Christian has significant consequences. But that was what made the lady who and what she was, and I very much appreciated the result, heathen that I was. And she was beautiful to boot—a combination hard to beat.

SEPTEMBER 8, 1987

When I emerged from our tent at dawn, I was surprised that there was no campfire blazing. My first thought was that Bill had uncharacteristically slept in. Then I saw him crouched low at the edge of the trees. When he heard me, he gestured for me to join him by crawling and moving as quietly as possible. He was watching six elk—four cows and two calves—feeding, mixed in with the horses. The breathing of the animals made fog in the cold crisp air.

We watched until something startled the elk—maybe the bear we saw yesterday. The too-brief show came to an end as the elk retreated to the cover of the trees at the edge of the meadow, their heads up and noses to the wind. Bill left camp to wrangle the horses, leaving me with my usual duty of getting a fire started.

After a breakfast of fried fresh fish, we spent the day reading, hiking, bird watching, and fishing. Jan took me up on my offer of fly-fishing lessons. She quickly developed—and stayed with—the "overhead flop" method of casting. She played out eight to ten feet of line that was back-cast onto the grass. Then, with a two-handed, overhead motion, she flopped the line, fly attached, into the stream. In using her newly developed technique, it was important for Jan to approach the stream bank on hands and knees at a right angle in order to hide the would-be fisher from the fish.

Execution of the overhead flop not only looked funny but also had a propensity to lose flies that hung up in the grass on the back flop. However, nothing succeeds like success, and Jan caught some fish. It was hard to believe. Of course, she lost a number of flies, but I was able to retrieve most of them from the grass. Hey, whatever works. I nodded my appreciation to heaven.

Sometime during the night, Meg's twenty-year-old white Appaloosa mare, Kitty, had been on the short end of a horse argument and was barely able to walk. She was a gentle, sweet mare, not much inclined to participate in the ongoing horse disputes relative to establishing and maintaining the herd's pecking order. She was at the bottom of the pecking order and seemed content with that. Much of my day was spent keeping cold compresses on her hock. We were worried about whether we would be able to get her down the mountain to the horse truck.

Supper produced yet another overindulgence in eating crisp-fried eastern brook trout. Jan was certain that she could identify the fish she had caught, even after they had been beheaded and fried. She seemed certain they were superior fish in all regards, including taste. Nobody disputed her observations—certainly those were the best-tasting of all the fish in the pan.

After supper, we built up the fire, took seats around it, and spun fishing and hunting yarns until the participants, one by one, sought out their sleeping bags. I was the last liar left sitting near the dying fire. As I watched the embers crumble into gray ashes, I was conscious that it had been a very good day. I felt a tinge of regret at the passing of such a wonderful moment. Meg's voice called me to share our double sleeping bag and snuggle up to get warm. I could not imagine a better ending to a wonderful day. Likely old Kitty might feel a bit differently. I felt the wind coming up and felt compelled to drown out the fire before I crawled in my sleeping bag.

SEPTEMBER 9, 1987

Bill and I were up before the sun. It seemed a shame to deprive the ladies of their beauty rest, but we were apprehensive about getting old Kitty down to the horse trucks. She seemed even worse this morning and was barely able to hobble along. We knew that there were two really bad places on the trail that might give her serious problems. The first was a "rocky scramble" made up of loose rocks on a very steep fifty-yard-long incline. The second was a series of three bogs, each about thirty yards across.

We started out with Bill and me leading the packhorses and Meg "tailing" Bernice's mare—walking holding onto the mare's tail and being towed along, a technique especially useful when going up a steep trail. It was a neat trick to have in reserve, as sometimes a rider ends up on foot on a pack trip due to injuries to horses or the need to pack out a dead elk or deer on a saddle horse.

Kitty had no choice but to tough it out and stay up with the string of horses or be left behind; she managed, with difficulty, to keep up with the much slower pace. We stopped frequently to give her time to pick her route and to rest. We arrived at the trucks, loaded up, and were on our way without incident. Jan announced that she had had a wonderful time and almost immediately fell sound asleep. She seemed much more open and animated than at the beginning of the trip. Meg and I hoped that this was the start of something better for her.

CHAPTER 8

"THE PROMISED LAND ALWAYS LIES ON THE OTHER SIDE OF A WILDERNESS"

Bill had phoned me with an emphatic proclamation: it was Snake River time! His proclamation came just at a time when I needed to recharge my emotional batteries, which had been depleted by implementing a controversial, expensive, and very risky research study as well as the stress of dealing with a newly acquired, difficult foster child. It took some scrambling, but I cleared my work schedule. There are times when being the boss man is a good thing. There is nothing like an escape to the Snake River and the Hells Canyon Wilderness to bring things into perspective.

MAY 31, 1988

Bill and I would have this trip all to ourselves. When we finished loading the horses into the truck and trailer, I could feel my cares begin to peel away. All our other supplies were already loaded in the back of my old Ford truck. As was our custom for this particular venue, we stopped at Imnaha for our traditional lunch—fried chicken gizzards and coffee at the bargain price of $4.50 for two. There are some great bargains left in this world if you know where to look.

Contrary to the opinions of some, Imnaha is not the end of the world, though some of the locals insist that you can see it from there. It is the sort of place that TV commentator Charles Kuralt might pick for a segment of his *On the Road* show. There is a carefully cultivated and maintained atmosphere among Imnaha residents that they are the last to deny the arrival of the late twentieth century. Much of isolated rural America must have been like Imnaha once upon a time.

We traveled up the gravel road along the Imnaha River, and as we drove alongside the river, I couldn't help but imagine how I would guide a drift boat through the rough stretches. I knew I was a much better river-rat oarsman in my imagination than in reality, but my state of mind facilitated the fantasy. By the time the road turned away from the river, I had run my imaginary drift boat through twenty miles of pretty tough whitewater and never even clipped a rock—nary a one! Could this be the same oarsman who is touted by his friends as a prime example of persistent mediocrity in guiding a rubber raft?

We came to what had been, when we were here two years ago, the end of the road and the start of the horse trail. Now the road continued on for another half mile before it entered a new, larger, and much-improved parking area. Wonder of wonders, there was even a newly installed composting toilet. The road continued from the other side of the parking area on up Freezeout Creek; it had been constructed to afford access for loggers to the big yellow-bellied ponderosa pines we saw marked for cutting when we hunted elk here two years ago.

Bill told me that, when he was a regional supervisor for the Oregon Department of Fish and Wildlife, his agency had struck a bargain with John Rogers, then supervisor of the Wallowa-Whitman National Forest, to allow construction of a road to the jump-off point if the road would never be extended. That bargain, a gentlemen's agreement sealed with a handshake, had been honored only so long as Rogers was supervisor. By now there had been three different forest supervisors since John's retirement, and the old bargain had been forgotten—it mattered little whether inadvertently or knowingly. People change, times change, politics change, and so the world changes. A handshake is good only as long as the people who made the bargain hold power. Though disappointed, Bill seemed philosophical about the changes. He did comment, with some irony, that the camp we had used for several late-season cow elk hunts was now buried in the middle of the new parking lot. That was a painful realization.

A young couple walked up to us, and for some reason, the man asked if I worked for the Forest Service. When I said yes, he said he wanted me to know how much he and his companion appreciated the new improvements—i.e., the newly paved road and parking lot. He hoped that the Forest Service would be able to accomplish more of the same and as soon as possible. I tried to be philosophical. Was it a matter of "different strokes for different folks"?

When the couple moved on, Bill snorted, "To hell with standing around sniveling about parking lots and buried campsites. Let's hit the trail." Within a half hour, we were on the trail and climbing toward Freezeout Saddle, where we would cross over into the Snake River Canyon. We found Freezeout Saddle blanketed by snow—not much, but enough to remind us that this was harsh and unpredictable country. We might encounter temperatures of one hundred degrees before we returned this way, but today it was probably twenty-five degrees at Freezeout Saddle, and a trace of snow crunched under the horses' hooves. Temperatures warmed rapidly as we descended into the Snake River Canyon to the bench trail. Our intended camp lay ahead where the trail crossed Rough Creek.

When we reached the bench trail, which stretched the length of Hells Canyon some halfway between the top of the canyon and the Snake River, it seemed that we had retreated to another, very different time, one that operated under simpler rules of engagement. Violations of those rules could produce swift and sometimes disastrous consequences.

We came across a place where a packhorse had obviously rolled down the steep hillside, leaving a trail of broken pack boxes and some of their contents. The remains of the horse, or what the vultures and other scavengers had left—marked the end of the trail of debris. There had been quick, sure, and deadly consequences for some mistake not discernible from the remaining evidence. It was a disappointment that there had been no effort to clean up the debris. But maybe someone had been injured and needed medical attention. We stopped, picketed the horses, and gathered and stacked the debris next to the trail for a USFS trail crew to pick up.

When we came to Two Buck Creek, Bill told of coming upon a sheepherder's camp here several years ago while he was elk hunting. He had filed the location away in the back of his mind as a potential hunting camp. We noted that firewood was plentiful, and running water was close at hand. So, disregarding our earlier plans, we decided to make camp. Oh well, I thought, so much for careful planning—one day in the wilderness and we had already changed our previous well-thought-out plan.

Our campsite was surrounded by huge ponderosa pines that the locals call "yellow bellies." Their bark showed signs of being scorched, over and over again, by the many grass fires that have passed this way during the past century or two. The ability of this species to survive repeated fires was key to the ecological makeup of the site. In the span of several more decades of generalized timber harvest, only places like this will harbor the remnant stands of such "big ole yellow-belly pines." But knowing that these giants would stand a while longer—maybe a lot longer—gave me some comfort.

This campsite had been used for many years, likely many decades, by sheepherders, hunters, and just plain travelers—and probably Native Americans before that. I wondered how many people had camped here before us over the centuries and then how many more would camp here over decades or even centuries to come. We were in no hurry to eat, and the stew simmered down to a mush—the way Bill likes his stew.

When the sun descended behind the rim of the canyon, it was time to cease writing in my journal, enjoy a cup of rum, and then eat some simple food with my friend. As Bill watched the sun sink below the canyon's rim, he noted, "It just doesn't get any better than this!"

JUNE 1, 1988

I came awake sometime in the very early morning while it was still pitch dark. After brief resistance, I gave in to the need to answer nature's call. Bill and I had joked when we went to bed about who would give in and get up first. He heard me scrambling to get out of the sleeping bag and asked, "Where are you going?"

"To see the blue moon" was my answer. It had popped into my head that this was the night of a blue moon, which occurs once in four years when there are two full moons in one month. Entranced by the prospect of seeing a blue moon, Bill joined me.

As we emerged from the tent, it was obvious that we would see no blue moon this night. The fog was thick and wet and cold. Flashlight beams reflected back from swirling mist. We spent the minimum possible time answering nature's call before we dived back into the tent. My sleeping bag felt good. Just at dawn, we heard the beginning of a slow tattoo of raindrops on the taut nylon over our heads. The first thing I saw upon emerging from the tent was my wrong-side-out rain jacket draped over a nearby stump. Oh well, I thought, there is nothing like starting off the day cold and soggy.

I prepared breakfast in a drizzling rain. Our plan had been to continue on the bench trail to the site of the old Wisnor Ranch headquarters at Temperance Creek. Now we decided to take the Sluice Creek Trail down to the Snake River instead. While it might be raining down along the Snake, it would likely be much warmer there.

We broke camp with dispatch and were mounted and on our way not more than an hour after daylight. We rode in and out of swirling mists—clouds, really—and the canyon's wall across the Snake River in Idaho appeared now and again through low-lying fleecy clouds. The scene seemed primordial and gave me the impression of an ancient landscape—the same in near time but always in transition. A verse from Ecclesiastes kept running through my head: "One generation passeth away, and another generation cometh; but the earth abideth forever."

On the way down Sluice Creek Trail to the Snake River, we encountered nineteen adult elk on the opposite slope. They had seen us before we saw them but gave no indication of being unduly perturbed—after all, there was well over a quarter mile separating us. The cows were heavy with calves that would be born in a few days or weeks, and they were taking it easy. They watched us pass.

Temperatures warmed noticeably as we descended toward the river, but the intermittent rain and mist did not abate. We passed the remains of the rapidly deteriorating old homesteader's cabin at Sluice Creek. Half the cabin had fallen in, and the corrugated tin roofing over the other half had been half peeled back by the winds. The decision had been made by the USFS managers not to repair the damage, so the rate of decay will increase as the rains periodically wet the unprotected timbers. The generations, and their leavings, come and go, but the earth abides.

We made an early camp on a little bench just above where Sluice Creek joins the Snake River. It was good to get the fly up, get out of the mist and rain, get a fire started, and shed our raingear. Hot coffee quickly rekindled our cold-numbed spirits and loosened our stiffened joints. The world soon seemed a brighter, better place. A lull in the wind and rain gave us a chance to get the tent up. No sooner was the tent up and our gear stowed under manty tarps than the alternate bouts of drizzle and mist changed to a steady, cold, blowing rain. We retreated into the tent to read. The Coleman lantern not only provided light but warmed the tent until it seemed both secure and cozy. The additional warmth provided by my sleeping bag draped over my shoulders, the residual glow of the rum and coffee, and the drumming of rain on the tent quickly lulled me to join Bill, who was already snoring, in a nap.

When we awoke, after an hour or so, the rain had stopped and the sun angled into the tent from the western canyon rim. We could see blue sky through the clouds. Suddenly, life seemed much brighter. After supper, the dog and I walked down to the Snake River. The river's "bank" was a jumble of boulders polished over the centuries by the sand carried by high water. Some call this glaze on the boulders "Snake River patina." From the position of the driftwood, it was easy to discern the river's recent high-water mark—a full twenty feet higher than the present level of the river.

The Snake River seems a formidable and frightening thing even at this level—and awesome to think of what it was like before the upstream dams were built and the high water deposited the driftwood at my feet. But that was many years ago—before the Oxbow and Hells Canyon dams plugged the Snake River. Now the high flows are trapped behind these dams for later controlled release to turn turbines to generate relatively cheap hydropower. The dams, located far upstream, are out of sight and out of mind for sojourners in these parts. Likely few visitors to this spot even know about such things. A few more decades and the driftwood marking the high-water marks of the old floods will have finally rotted or burned away and will no longer inform visitors of what was "once upon a time." Only the Snake River patina on the boulders will remain as a reminder of what the mighty Snake River was once and, given enough centuries, might be again.

JUNE 2, 1988

The new day arrived all bright and shiny—and blessedly dry and warm. This campsite was a good one, with relatively flat ground, cheatgrass still green and thick, and plentiful dry firewood to be "harvested" from the hackberries and gnarled old apricot trees that have survived from the homesteader days. We judged this camp too pleasant and too comfortable to leave after only a single day.

We saddled up and set out at midmorning for a ride down to the Snake River and back. The slopes and benches were recovering from the decades of overgrazing, mostly by sheep, which Bill refers to derisively as "range maggots." I will say this for Bill: it's not difficult to tell what he's feeling. He had the knack of describing complex feelings succinctly and clearly.

When I first visited this place some thirteen years ago, the ground cover was composed mostly of poverty grass—some call it "Democrat grass" due to its spread in the canyon during the New Deal era of the 1930s. Poverty grass is essentially unpalatable to grazing animals due to its high content of silicates—i.e., it's gritty as hell. As Bill said, "Not nothing, nohow, no way, eats Democrat grass—not ever, never, and at no time." But that was good news of a sort. The grass took over the overgrazed sites and held the soils together until better controls on grazing gave more palatable grasses a chance to take hold.

Cheatgrass, an annual grass, has come to dominate the site. Cheatgrass, an accidental import from the Middle East, tends to occupy sites that have been overgrazed and is palatable to grazing animals in the spring when it is green and succulent. Here and there, a new clump of bluebunch wheatgrass—the ancestral possessor of the site—was regaining a foothold. With continued good grazing practices (or maybe no grazing at all by domestic livestock for a long period), the bluebunch wheatgrass may gradually reclaim the site. Closer examination of the flat showed that it had been farmed, or at least mowed, during the homesteader days. There were no rocks on the flat, as they had been gathered up and stacked in piles around the edges.

An irrigation ditch ran along one side of the old field. After the field was abandoned for agricultural purposes, it was graded with a horse pulling a Fresno for use as an airstrip for light aircraft. Bill told me that he had been airlifted out of this strip to attend his mother's funeral several decades ago.

There was an arrow formed with whitewashed stones that pointed upstream to warn pilots that this was a one-way airstrip. A large circle of stones, also whitewashed, outlined an appropriate landing spot for helicopters. It was identified by the number "3-70"—also formed by whitewashed stones. Maybe they are artifacts left by the dam builders as they studied the river. The area is now officially designated as Wilderness and a National Recreation Area by an act of Congress. The bare dirt runway was filling in with weeds, and the whitewash was fading from the painted rocks. These too have become artifacts of man's former uses of the canyon.

Just upstream of the river trail crossing on Sluice Creek, there is a small campsite snuggled between the creek and a wall of twenty-foot-tall boulders. The small plot of flat ground is surrounded by large hackberries on the uphill side and by cottonwoods and alders nearer the stream. The effect was that of a green cave formed by the tree canopies, somewhat secure from winds in winter and an air-conditioned paradise in the God-awful midsummer heat of the Snake River Canyon.

The running, tumbling waters of Sluice Creek and the tree canopy combined to provide something of a natural evaporative cooler. The site had been well used by campers, as evidenced by the absolutely bare ground and the absence of dead wood for several hundred yards in every direction. The rock wall was blackened by smoke from the many fires built against its face by passing pilgrims. I could visualize the people—both ancient and modern—standing around those fires in winter, basking in the warmth radiating out from the rock. And gathering here in midsummer to escape the blistering heat and the glaring sun.

I had no doubt that an archaeological dig of the floor of the ancient campsite would reveal evidence of prehistoric use by humans. And today's people still leave their similar marks. I saw, partly buried in the ashes of the campfires, wads of aluminum foil and a Coleman fuel can stuffed with more foil. In the bushes I saw several discarded aluminum beer cans, with "Oregon Refund 5 cents" stamped on the lids.

I flattened the cans and gathered the foil so that we could pack the trash out with us. Under the adjoining stand of alders I found three elk skeletons—two cows and a calf. The skeletons showed signs of having been sawed in half between the second and third ribs. This made the portions of the carcass weigh the same and made for a balanced load on a horse or mule; such careful attention to weight indicated that the hunters came and went via horses or mules rather than by boat. Judging from knife marks on the bones, the meat had been stripped from the carcasses along with the hides and heads (so that the Oregon Department of Fish and Wildlife officials might discern the sex). The jawbones were left behind. I felt compelled to carefully bury the jawbones against the stone wall, a likely place for hunters of antiquities to dig at some future time.

After all, such curious diggers should not be perpetually disappointed. I picked up that philosophy from an old colleague early in my research career. He was a premier maker of flint arrowheads. When VIPs visited our USFS Research Work Unit, we usually took them to the Starkey Experimental Forest and Range in the Blue Mountains. In the course of events, we just happened to visit "an old Indian campsite," and our guests were invited to scuff up the soil where my colleague had sequestered several of his best renditions of flint arrowheads. The guests were always delighted with their finds. We hoped that the experience inclined them to listen more carefully to our appeals for support. Better yet, it left the real thing for the real archaeologist.

And so the use of the logical campsites goes on—generation after generation and civilization after civilization—and "artifacts" accumulate. Upon reflection, it seemed strange that today's garbage becomes, given enough time and appropriate circumstances, precious artifacts for future generations providing clues from the past. Will archaeologists, 200 or 300 years hence, be as fascinated with aluminum foil, fuel canisters, empty cartridges, and beer cans as we are with flint projectile points?

We continued our ride down the Snake River, turned up the trail along Rush Creek, and climbed toward the bench country. The only water in Rush Creek was in pools. The cover along the creek was composed primarily of hackberries, poison oak, and cheatgrass. At the juncture of Rush Creek and Pony Creek we encountered a sheepherder's camp. We hoped the resident herder, likely a contract worker from Peru, was immune to poison oak. His tent was set up in the midst of a decidedly vigorous patch of the shiny, three-leaved plant. As we continued our climb toward the bench trail, we saw the sheep a mile or so away, grazing along the divide between Rush Creek and Sluice Creek. We could barely make out the individual animals as they moved along in a mass that reminded me of the amoebas I watched under a microscope in my high school biology class. A "pseudopod" of sheep reached out from the mass and then the body flowed into that area while another arm extended out from the herd in another direction.

The trail was very steep, so we made frequent stops to let the horses blow. The pioneers—or maybe the Native Americans—who established these trails seemed likely to have been more cognizant of time and distance of their travels than solicitous of the welfare of their horses and mules. About noon we topped out in the saddle between Rush Creek and Sand Creek. The view was spectacular down the Snake River Canyon to the north. The canyon rims were still covered with a blanket of snow that shone brilliant white in the bright sunlight.

We hobbled the horses and removed their bridles, allowing them to graze. We hobbled them not so much to keep them from running away, which was unlikely, but to keep them from lying down and rolling to give their backs a scratch. No matter how satisfying to the horse, this activity tends to be quite hard on saddles and the contents of saddlebags. We took advantage of the break for the horses to enjoy a lunch of canned meat, crackers, and raw sweet onions. The sweet onions were a special treat reserved for all-male trips far from the delicate olfactory sensibilities of our mates. We also treated ourselves to a short siesta—just to give the horses a little more of a break, of course.

Our plan from here was to take the Salt Creek Trail to the Snake River, as indicated by our official USFS map. We started out on a faint graded trail. But after we traveled a quarter mile, we concluded it had not been used, except by elk and maybe deer, for some years. It was time for a consultation. We both thought we remembered that the trail went off the saddle between Rush Creek and Sand Creek—a full mile away from where it was indicated to be on our map.

We were right, though it took us an hour of cautious exploring to make certain. I made a note to tell the manager of the Snake River National Recreation Area that there was a problem with the map—or was there? The trail from the saddle followed an old wagon road that had, decades earlier, provided a mowing machine and hay rake access to the gentle ridgetop. We wondered why that road was constructed. There was no homestead along the bench trail at the end of the ridge. The homestead at Dead Failure seemed too far around the bench trail, which was passable only to horses and foot traffic. I made a note to ask Al Defler, the USFS's district ranger in charge of the Snake River National Recreation Area, for clarification. As Bill put it, it was a genuine puzzlement. Yet these genuine puzzlements were part of the charm of Hells Canyon.

Hearing sheep bleating and looking north, we spotted sheep grazing on the open slopes above the head of Salt Creek. It was amazing how their bleating carried so clearly across the one and a half miles or so that separated us. It takes time to adjust to the absence of the cacophony of the sounds associated with the city and suburbs. We could distinctly hear the sheepherders calling directions to their dogs and the bell clanging on a grazing white horse—surely the sheepherder's mount—that we could barely see on the far slope.

The absence of sensory overload for the past few days had facilitated our innate ability to simply see, hear, and feel more easily. Somebody (was it Henry David Thoreau?) said, "In wildness is the preservation of the world." I don't know about that. But wilderness—"wildness"—had rejuvenated my tired mind and weary soul. Or, as Havelock Ellis put it, "The Promised Land always lies on the other side of a Wilderness."

Before we mounted and started our descent, we looked over the far slope with the aid of our binoculars and saw nine sleek red-tinged elk lying in the sun, ruminating and watching us as closely as we watched them. We walked down the very steep slope, leading the horses in order to spare them our weight digging into their shoulders. Keeping a close watch on our feet on such steep ground, we glanced up occasionally to see if the elk were still there. They continued to watch us without moving until, between one glance from us and the next, they were gone, seemingly melting away into the scrubby hackberries. The Snake River country, as wide open as it is, is not what most sportsmen would visualize as elk country. Yet elk are present in large and increasing numbers.

The absence of roads equaled rarity of human contact, and that likely made all the difference. We hypothesized that elk are much more adaptable to various and constantly evolving habitat conditions than is commonly recognized. What elk do not tolerate well is the presence of people with intermittent intentions of doing them in. Even elk managers who have been declared to be "certified wildlife biologists" by The Wildlife Society (the professional society for wildlife biologists) lose sight of the fact that a main cause of death for elk is now bullets—e.g., humans, in nearly all cases, are their number one predator.

The Snake River Canyon, when coupled with a paucity of people, provides highly suitable habitat for elk—except perhaps during hunting season, when numbers of *Homo sapiens* temporarily increase. There was an ongoing recovery of range conditions—including re-establishment of some of the primary species of vegetation preferred by elk—bluebunch wheatgrass and Idaho fescue. That, coupled with the rugged terrain and limited human access, made it likely that the elk population in the Snake River Canyon would continue to prosper with appropriate adjustments in hunting regulations. The Snake River country, unlike most habitats, contains an almost complete array of predators on elk and deer that existed prior to 1850—humans, black bears, cougars, and, probably soon, wolves and grizzly bears.

Where the Sand Creek Trail reached the canyon bottom, we came across a large "elk lick" where an outcropping of diatomaceous earth—a soft, chalky white earth derived from the remains of small sea creatures with calcareous shells—had been exposed by erosion. Diatomaceous earth attracts ungulates, including deer and elk. Over thousands of years, deer, elk, and wild sheep had eaten away tons of the exposed deposits to obtain minerals supposedly deficient in their diet. The marks of their incisors could be clearly seen on the face of the deposit. Droppings were plentiful.

We stopped briefly at the Oregon Department of Fish and Wildlife cabin at Sand Creek to eat lunch in the shade. We left a note for our colleagues for no other reason than to say "Howdy." Greetings left in such a place have a special meaning to those in the ranks of professional conservationists. To find such notes in remote cabins and campsites says, across time and space, "We share and love the same things! We too were here! Keep the faith!"

The trail from Sand Creek to Rush Creek ran through bluffs just above the Snake River. One spot on the trail, called the Eagle's Nest, was well over 100 feet above the river. It had been blasted out of the rock face and was just wide enough, with enough height and width, to accommodate a tall rider on a tall horse leading a packhorse. It resembled, in spots, half a tunnel hacked out of the side of the cliff face. It seemed a very dangerous spot, though not as dangerous to traverse as it appeared at first glance. Rafters floating by on the river below looked up and saw us. We could tell that their conversation was animated and obviously centered on the seemingly dangerous pastime in which we were engaged.

Likely they didn't know it, but in rafting down the Snake River through Granite Rapids and Wild Sheep Rapids, they had done an equally dangerous thing. Of course, my view may be biased by the fact that I once made a pretty damned good try at drowning myself in Granite Rapids. And on two other float trips down the Snake, one of our party had been tossed out of a raft in Wild Sheep Rapids. In those trips we had an adventure that stimulated our adrenal glands to maximum production while providing a little taste of just what physical courage might entail. Better yet, we survived to feel better about ourselves and our abilities to deal with challenges. For a brief time, nothing seemed to exist but the moment, the boiling water, and the task at hand. It left us with the coppery taste of adrenaline in the mouth and some pride of achievement.

The day turned out hot, with temperatures well above 100 degrees. It was necessary to slow the horses' eager homeward pace to keep them from overheating and lathering. Much more frequently than was our custom, we pulled up and took a rest of ten, sometimes twenty minutes.

We were impressed by the number of chukars we encountered as we traveled the trail alongside the river. This led us to make plans to have a jet boat bring us up the Snake River from Lewiston and drop us off here next fall with our shotguns, dogs, and camping gear for a couple of days of chukar hunting. Not only were the chukars plentiful, but the relatively flat terrain along the river was much better for a wobbly old football knee than the very steep slopes that lay above. Whether or not we came back in the fall—a busy season for wildlife biologists—just the planning and anticipation was a pleasant diversion.

We arrived back at camp some ten hours after our departure, fully satisfied with the results of the very long, full day. After the horses were unsaddled, groomed, and tied to scrubby trees to cool down, a couple of snorts of apple brandy from a bottle miraculously discovered in the bottom of my saddlebag—carried solely in case of snakebite—seemed justified.

We relished our cold supper of canned meat, pinto beans, and crackers and were abed and asleep before full dark. I wondered why I couldn't sleep more than six or seven hours at home on a super mattress before aches and pains and associated aggravations produced a yearning for sunrise. Yet on a trip like this I could sleep ten hours on a thin air mattress, seemingly without stirring. Perhaps it was the cleansing of conscience and the vacating of lingering aggravations that came over me in the wilderness. I struggled to stay awake and listen to the night sounds, which included a coyote chorus. I failed— and in short order.

JUNE 3, 1988

Dawn arrived much cooler and with skies cloudier than those of last evening, a likely preamble to a thunderstorm. We debated staying over in this camp for another day. It was, after all, a comfortable camp with an abundant wood supply, a nearby spring, and good grazing for the horses. The discussion delayed our departure, and we decided that it was now too late to strike out for the trailhead and then home. Not altogether reluctantly, we were "condemned" to a day of fishing for smallmouth bass.

By midmorning the clouds had blown away, and the sun emerged bright and warm in a clearing sky. After lunch and a short nap in the sun, we had one more cup of cowboy coffee—with a "touch of the spirit"—before we set up our fishing rods. Without discussion, Bill headed upriver, leaving me to go downriver. We observed as we parted that we saw no need for us to crowd each other.

I walked downriver to Rush Creek Rapids. These rapids, though less impressive than Wild Sheep Rapids and Granite Rapids, which lay upriver, were considered by experienced rafters of the mighty Snake to be truly first-class whitewater. I sat on a boulder, basked in the sun, and waited to watch rafters and jet boaters navigate the rapids. For well over an hour, no boaters appeared. The roar and the awesome power of the rushing water engrossed me and was entertainment enough.

In the late evening four kayakers, three men and one woman, pulled in just above the rapids to spend the night. I walked down to meet them, and they turned out to be pleasant—what Bill called "yuppie types" from Seattle: two medical doctors, one lawyer, and one stockbroker. It was obvious from their bemused conversational tone that they considered me something of an unkempt rustic. I didn't dispute their impression—after all, maybe it was more accurate than I wanted to admit.

When twilight came, I had not wetted a line. I wondered, why do we have to always be "doing something" when we make our wilderness trips? Why do we forget that the business of recreation—"re-creation" after all—is not merely to do something different but rather to re-create the mind and rejuvenate the spirit? For me, this afternoon was devoted to pure-quill, heavy-duty re-creation.

Things were different with Bill. He was a born, bred, and practiced competitor. He thrived on competition. He arrived back in camp, as usual, with his legal limit of smallmouth bass and a single rainbow trout. The Snake River has the rare attribute of supporting both a warmwater and coldwater fishery—simultaneously. The warmwater fish thrive in the backwaters and eddies where the sun warms the relatively placid water, and the trout thrive in the currents and deep pools of colder water. Sometimes, if one drops the right fly just at the "rip," where the cold current passes a warmwater eddy, a strike may come from either a bass or a trout. "Fishing the rip" made for a game of chance vastly superior, to my mind, to the slot machines down the road in Winnemucca or Reno, Nevada. There is a big difference: we can always make more slot machines and bright lights while the limited number of Snake River eddies disappear with the construction of the hydro dams.

I had clam chowder cooking when Bill arrived in camp with a limit of fish, as I knew he would. I was ready for him. I filleted, deboned, and cut the fish into chunks, fried them in bacon grease, and popped the chunks into the chowder. It was superb, if I did say so myself—which I did. Bill made no effort to dispute my assertion.

After supper, it was time for me to lie quietly in the meadow on my belly with my chin propped on my fists and watch the insects and other little critters within my limited view go about their lives. I was amazed at what went on within six feet of the end of my nose. This evening produced a special treat in the form of a chukar chick, surely not more than two or three days old, that came struggling though the tangle in search of its brood. The chick did not seem to object as I picked it up and tucked it inside my down vest to warm it up. I walked around in circles, gradually increasing the radius, until finally I flushed a chukar hen that put on the time-tested broken-wing act as she fluttered away downslope. Her act indicated that she had either a nest or a brood hidden nearby. Gambling on the brood, I placed the chick under the edge of a pad cactus and backed away. Maybe the chick would connect with the hen and have a new chance to survive and prosper. After all, what is life but a series of chances? It was the best I could do to change the chick's odds.

An hour or so later, the sun dropped below the canyon's rim. As the sunlight faded, I heard a chukar giving forth a brood call. I imagined—hoped was more like it—that my chick had rallied to the call and gained another chance to make it another day. I liked the thought and held on to it until sleep came.

JUNE 4, 1988

The new day arrived bright, clear, hot, and fast. We took that as a signal to move camp back to our more favored portion of the Snake River Canyon—somewhere along the bench trail halfway up to the canyon's rim. We made our way up to the bench country via the Sluice Creek Trail. When we reached the bench trail, we turned the horses south toward one of our favorite camps, located just above the trail's crossing of Rough Creek. The travel was easy over this well-engineered and maintained trail, and we arrived at our campsite in midafternoon. Two years ago, we had excavated a flat place here to accommodate our tent. When we departed, we had seeded the tent site with grass seed and replaced the sod back over the fire trench that we had dug. Our handiwork was so successful that it took us several minutes to find our old camp's exact location. I thought to myself, with a bit of pride, now here was an example of no-trace camping at its best!

We had left the warm climes of the lower Snake River Canyon a bit too soon. Bill was taking care of the horses and I was setting up camp when a freshening and surprisingly cold wind foretold the arrival of dark clouds that soon scudded over the canyon's rim. As the tent and rain fly were not yet in place, it was fortunate that no rain accompanied the first gusts. The air seemed pregnant with moisture, and the wind accentuated the effect of colder temperatures, which we reckoned at just above freezing. We spent the evening sitting as close to the fire as the intermittent whipping winds allowed. After dousing the fire, Bill declared "bedtime" while it was still light—unusual for him.

I liked the way wilderness trips simplified and, in turn, clarified things. Our required tasks were simple: get from point A to point B; take care of the horses; set up camp; gather wood and build a fire;

have a drink; cook, eat, and wash dishes; stay warm and dry; catch horses and release horses; sleep. The simple pleasures of a tasty hot meal; a warm fire; and a dry, warm place to sleep became the most pleasurable of experiences.

Back in the "real world," such things are routine and are therefore little pondered and little valued. All those good things come with flicking a switch, turning a faucet's handle or a knob on a stove, and changing the setting on a thermostat. Perhaps the instant comfort and gratification of desires deprives us of really knowing the value of such things. It is essential—for me at least—to periodically return to places and circumstances where being warm and dry and well fed are no sure thing and, therefore, all the more significant and infinitely more appreciated.

It was most satisfying to be warm and secure in the tent while the wind howled outside. But the wind demanded attention, as the air seemed increasingly charged with sound and energy. I remained half-awake and fully conscious of the wind and the popping of the tent, clouds scudding across the moon, and the sound of the horse's bells— and the cessation of the bells when the horses periodically sought shelter. I suspected that most animals suspended their activities on such nights, making themselves a contrast to the motion and sound of the wind.

JUNE 5, 1988

By daylight the wind had dropped down to intermittent whispers in the trees, though the cold gray sky was still with us. As this was "going-out day," we cooked and ate, made our lunches, broke camp, packed up, and were mounted and on our way less than an hour after the sun arrived in camp. After the long windy night the horses were a bit spooky. But at the same time they seemed to sense that we were headed for the trailhead and the waiting trucks—and for home, where the living was easy. They traveled fast and steady and without a break. When we reached the fingered tributaries above Saddle Creek, sightings of elk became commonplace.

A few of the elk cows had calves at heel. Others were obviously ready to give birth, and others almost surely had newborn calves hidden nearby. But many of the cows and yearlings were still in bunches, indicating that the calving had not yet peaked. By the time we started the climb up from the bench trail's crossing at Saddle Creek to Freezeout Saddle, by my count we had seen some 170 elk; Bill made the count closer to 180. This gathering for calving afford-ed a real sight that Bill said took place each year in this place in late May and early June. And seen through a mama elk's eyes, where could there be a better place for such activities? The vegetation that had come in after the burn of 1971 was an ideal mix of succulent forage plants and shrubs to feed the cows and shelter the calves. The terrain was gentle, and water flowed in the creeks. Plus the area was as isolated from human activities as it gets. The few humans that visit are benign pilgrims on a quest for a unique experience and are not in predator mode.

I have come to treasure the bench country in late May and early June when the cow elk gather and there are young calves to be seen. I knew I would always hold these sights and sounds and smells in my mind and heart. And those memories would remain more vivid than any photographs or videotapes with their audio tracks. I can recover these wonderful memories from where they are filed away in my mind whenever I want to. They always provide a sense of priority and order and well-being. And they remind me of who I am, what I do, and why I do what I do. So long as this place exists in anything like its present state, it holds the promise of good to me—and those like me. That is why I deem it important that such places be maintained for others, whether or not I ever return.

We arrived at the horse trucks at midday. I had to admit that the new parking lot was a vast improvement over the old situation. On the other hand, did the USFS's most excellent engineers have to build the parking lot on top of our hunting camp? Maybe that's the eternal cry of the preservationist—did you have to build it over "my" elk camp or "my" swimming hole or "my" trail or "my" fish-ing hole?" Maybe in the grand scheme of things this parking lot was not such a big deal. But one more special place had been lost to "progress." And so the supply of magic places shrinks again and again as civilization grows and as access to facilities for a growing population of recreationists expands. I suppose individual reactions to such actions depend on the way one sees the world. I tried to be philosophical about the damned parking lot: one person's gain is another's loss. I was a bit ashamed of my self-centeredness, but that was what I felt.

CHAPTER 9

COMPETITION EVEN IN THE
WILDERNESS—SHARING THE BOUNTY

L ack of significant rainfall in the mountain West for the previous two months was setting the stage for the worst fire
season across the region since 1910, the year of the infamous "Big Burn" in Idaho and Montana. At the time of this
trip to the Eagle Cap Wilderness, the Summer of Fire had barely begun, and the scattered wildfires burning in the Greater Yellowstone Ecosystem seemed to pose no serious threat—not yet.

JULY 27, 1988

Bill, Bernice, Margaret, and I left for the Eagle Cap just after daylight. Our drive east across the Grande Ronde Valley from La Grande
to Union was beautiful in the early-morning light. However, the
drive from Union through the foothills of the Wallowa Mountains
was marked by several close encounters of the scary kind with loaded
log trucks coming down the steep narrow mountain roads just a little too fast for conditions. For a log truck driver, time is money. We
noted that numerous new logging spur roads had been constructed
off the main road since last year; the *de facto* wilderness continued
to shrink back toward the legally established boundaries of the Eagle
Cap Wilderness. Numerous cars and pickups were parked along the
new roads. Their owners, some with children, were busily engaged in
picking huckleberries.

The parking area at the trailhead at West Eagle Meadows was
crowded with fifteen vehicles. Just starting the long climb to Echo

Lake was a contingent of seventeen Boy Scouts, each carrying a hefty pack, and five adult leaders. Each adult was leading a packhorse carrying the heavier camp gear and food. It seemed a good arrangement for the older, more portly adult leaders and the energetic young scouts, who were showing their *macho* and inexperience by carrying overloaded packs.

As the horses had been saddled, our gear mantied, and the groceries packed in panniers before we left Bill's place, it took us less than a half hour to put the packs on the horses and be on the trail. We passed the Boy Scouts, in their groups of twos and threes, strung out along the trail. They traveled at different paces as determined by their loads, physical condition, size, and age. By the time we reached Echo Lake, we had left the scouts far behind. We made camp a bit over a quarter mile above the head of the lake, leaving the primo camping sites nearer the lake for the scouts.

For the next two hours, we heard periodic whoops of achievement and maybe relief as the scouts straggled in to the edge of the lake, shucked their hiking boots and socks, and hurried to soak their feet in the cold mountain water. Their exuberant yelling, of course, was a violation of the unwritten code of acceptable wilderness conduct. These young men were high on life and their surroundings. Perhaps they were unaware of that aspect of wilderness protocol. Instead of being annoyed, we relished their expressions of exuberance. They had earned their trophy by finishing a long uphill hike with heavy packs on a hot day. After a very brief swim in the cold water of Echo Lake, there was an hour or so of quiet as the scouts and their leaders recouped strength and enthusiasm. An hour later, their triumphant cries were now associated with the occasional landing of a trout.

I wondered if these young men had any idea how fortunate they were to live in a place where they had wilderness at their back door? Did they ever ponder on the reality that they could visit such places at will—and without permission? Not likely. After all, the wilderness was simply there and, so far as they knew, always would be. I wondered if, when they became adults, they would remember this adventure and do their part to preserve such places and opportunities for those who were taking their places. Inevitably, that will be required, as no land preserved from development is ever completely secure in that state. Wars, serious prolonged economic recessions, changing political circumstances, and a burgeoning population inevitably produce new needs and demands to exploit resources, to "bring lands under management." There are few victories for those who fight for wild places and wild things, and no "victories" are final.

As I listened to their shouts reverberate across the lake and bounce off the cliff walls looming above, my own days as a Boy Scout surfaced from the depths of memory. My adventures as a scout took place well over four decades ago in the Cross-Timbers region between Fort Worth and Dallas, Texas. My scouting world was "Texas flat," and all the land within a hundred miles of my home was in private ownership—most complete with "NO TRES-PASSING" signs. A campout for my Boy Scout troop entailed a five- to ten-mile hike via paved and graveled roads out of our little town of Handley to a camp in some friendly person's woodlot or beside a small impoundment where we could fish for stocked perch and channel catfish. The high point of my troop's year was a two-week stint at Worth Ranch Boy Scout Camp, located thirty miles or so west of Fort Worth and consisting of a few square miles of mostly juniper forests on rocky soil too poor to be worth much for anything else. The often-muddy Brazos River ran along one side of the property. For me and my buddies it was a paradise—a veritable wilderness! Looking back, I find it strange how a state as large and rich as Texas could have been, in reality, so small and so constraining. That world was circumscribed by the ever-increasing thousands upon thousands of miles of property lines marked by fences, often ten-foot-high "deer-proof" fences constructed to confine wildlife and exclude trespassers. And "No Trespassing" signs meant exactly what they said.

Until I signed up to work with the USFS in West Virginia at the age of thirty-two, I had only dreamed of the huge expanses of forests and lakes on public lands, whose boundaries were marked with signs welcoming the owners, the people of the United States. Behind those signs, I could wander where I pleased without begging permission. I could even hunt and fish without paying a "trespass fee" for the privilege. Those new circumstances seemed a genuine wonderment, and I have never forgotten that feeling.

In spite of the many decades that have passed since I left Texas, I still have the nagging feeling that I should get permission from someone to be there. It is then that I ponder what a wondrous heritage the national forests are for folks like me who own no property outside of their house lots. These lands—the great commons—are to be protected, treasured, and passed on to succeeding generations.

As the population increases, the American people will be more and more challenged to maintain those lands in public ownership. Each year, the private lands on the perimeters of the national forests are increasingly marked by signs proclaiming "Private Property—No Trespassing" as people seek their little "place in the country" and exclude others. As decades pass, the national forests will be increasingly surrounded by these tiny fiefdoms—"ranchettes," as they are commonly called. Access for recreation—especially hunting and fishing—will inevitably become more and more commercialized.

Lands inside the boundaries of the national forests will become ever more valuable, and pubic lands will be increasingly subject to pressures to sell or transfer ownership to facilitate exploitation. Some states, noting increasing values, will increasingly covet those lands and make moves to attain ownership or at least management authority. Pressures to sell/divest/exploit our inheritance of public lands for pottage will inevitably increase. Then what? The outcome will always be in question.

As I pondered, darkness arrived, and I heard the scouts singing around their campfire. Some of the songs were the same ones I had sung as a scout forty years earlier. These were fortunate young men, living this special moment. I hoped they would remember and would act to preserve their heritage for their sons and daughters.

JULY 28, 1988

There was a chill in the air at dawn—a contrast to the dog days of summer down below in the valleys. On the slopes above the meadow a mule deer buck, a four-pointer with his antlers in velvet, was grazing in the snow-slide area. If he stays up this high when the hunting season comes, he has a good chance to survive another year and grow even bigger antlers. As I would be hunting elsewhere, I wished him well.

As we sat around the campfire and sipped steaming coffee, Bill and I plotted an imaginary stalk on the big buck. In the end, we concluded that our chances of getting a sure shot at him—the only kind a principled, disciplined hunter should take—lay somewhere between very slim and not much. If it were hunting season, we would damn sure give it a try. An old poker player's admonition came to mind: "no guts, no blue chips."

The tree species that survive and prosper above 7,000 feet evolved over the millennia to withstand strong winds and heavy snow. Limber pines are so flexible that their smaller limbs can actually be tied in knots without breaking. So when they are weighted down with ice and snow and the high winds come, their branches bend rather than break; they spring back to shape to catch the rays of the sun when the warm days come. On steep terrain the trunks of both the limber pine and the subalpine firs sweep downslope (from their roots having been bent with the snow) until they have bulk and the strength to withstand the pressure. Then they grow upward toward the sun to fulfill their destiny. Maybe there is a lesson here, a secret to living and achieving in a harsh environment: bend when it is essential to survival; then, when time and circumstances are right, reach for the sun!

We rode up the trail from Echo Lake, past Traverse Lake, to the pass over into the Minam River drainage. The view from the top of the pass was spectacular. Wilderness stretched out in every direction as far as the eye could see. One of the packhorses had to be repacked, and the effort of boosting the eighty-five-pound packs produced some huffing and puffing. In the thin air at 8,500 feet, it does not take much exertion to cause even a strong man to suck for air.

Just over the summit, we encountered a significant snowdrift burying the trail. We debated whether to attack the drift with the shovel or buck the horses through or retreat the way we had come. But we believed the drift likely covered a switchback in the trail. To miss the switchback and go off the trail could well be a serious, perhaps fatal mistake. Fortunately, when Bill gave the lead horse her head, she picked her way through the drift and negotiated the switchback without missing a step.

Then Meg's horse, Kitty, who was bringing up the rear, balked. This was neither the time nor place for Meg, a relatively inexperienced rider, to dispute the judgment of a recalcitrant horse. With Bill sitting on his mare twenty or so feet directly above her, Meg listened carefully to his firm instructions. She stepped off the horse on the uphill side, tied the reins to the saddle, worked around the mare, took the lead rope, and scrambled up the trail that had been broken through the drift, leading Kitty. If Kitty had pitched a fit and gone over the side, she wouldn't have taken Meg with her. But Kitty deemed this new arrangement a decided improvement and came right along behind Meg without a hitch. There was one thing about Bill Brown—the old horse soldier knew horses!

The trail to Trail Creek dropped 1,600 feet in elevation in five trail miles that switched back and forth across the open granite slope. Some stretches through the boulder fields had been blasted out, and a tread of rocks had been laid down by trail crews. While today's trip covered only eight miles, it included a climb of 1,500 feet and a descent of 1,600 feet and took a bit over four hours to accomplish. Later examination of a detailed topographic map revealed that the distance between our beginning and ending points, as the crow flies, was a bit less than two miles! Where was a straight-flying crow when you needed one? We picked out a camping spot at the edge of a beautiful wet meadow we encountered just at the end of the switchbacks. A spruce-covered knob in the meadow provided plenty of dry wood and flat dry ground for our tents. The meadow itself was covered with green sedges sprinkled with wildflowers. Behind the meadow was the granite slope that we had just descended, gleaming white in the afternoon sun.

Bill set the first shift of horses loose to graze near the stream while I sat cross-legged in the meadow with my senses filled to overflowing. I watched and listened and felt without speaking. Meg's call to supper brought me back into focus. As we ate, a mule deer doe joined the horses in the meadow to graze, hanging around at the edge

of light from the fire until Meg went to bed. I loitered by the dying
fire for another hour, alternately staring into the fire and into the clear
night sky that was alive with stars. As the fire died down to coals and
then to ashes, I became chilled and it was time to head for the tent.
As I lay there in my sleeping bag and waited for sleep to come, the
clanging of the horse bells seemed to be a lullaby, blending in with the
wind whispering in the trees and the night sounds.

JULY 29, 1988

We were on the trail by midmorning and in no hurry, as our objective was the Elk Camp on the Minam River—only three miles down
Trail Creek to the Minam River Trail and then four miles down the
river to just above the mouth of Elk Creek. It was a leisurely sev-
en-mile, two-hour journey.

The trail from the mouth of Trail Creek to the Elk Camp
passed through stands of mature lodgepole pine, white fir, and spruce,
with occasional huge yellow-bellied ponderosa pines and larch sticking up above the canopy. Eight years ago the lodgepole pines were
undergoing an initial attack by an outbreak of mountain pine beetles.
The beetle larvae feed on the cambium layer under the bark, and the
tunnels they leave eventually girdle the tree and cause its death. The
presence of the mountain pine beetle was advertised by the globs of
whitish pitch on the bark.

Now, three years later, the dead and dying stands of lodgepole
pines seemed an example of the proverbial "wrath of God." Well over
half the trees were dead, gray ghosts amid the green. Pitch tubes on
the bark of most of the remaining green trees foretold their almost
certain deaths.

Many of the dead trees had blown down as their decaying roots
gave way, forming jumbled jackstraws of tree trunks. Young spruce
and white fir trees were plentiful and racing the seedling lodgepole
pines for the sunlight. The skeletons of the lodgepole pines lying on
the ground were decaying and would eventually, after many decades,
melt into the forest floor, providing nourishment for the new stands of
trees just poking their heads up through the jackstrawed trunks. And,
thus, death becomes the facilitator of new life.

I wondered, does any living thing ever really die? Or do the elements simply reconstitute themselves and appear in other life forms? Is that not a form of immortality?

A forester focused on the production of wood for use by humans would view this scene, especially the mess of dead trunks, and worry that fire could wipe out the newly developing stand. The forester's job would be to minimize the chance of fire, assure dominance of the desired tree species for the site, manipulate the stand to enhance wood production, and harvest the result to be made into wood products to satisfy human needs. In the event of a fire, young trees would eventually spring forth from the ashes—this time in a stand dominated by lodgepole pines. The process, repeated so many times before, would continue.

I am still learning more about natural ecological processes in my wilderness wanderings than I ever learned from textbooks or from observations of forests managed to maximize wood production, though such experiences were certainly instructive. Human societies need wood—and a lot of it—to sustain economies and provide for human needs. But we also need places to observe and learn from natural processes before we become too limited in our understanding of natural systems and too dependent on knowledge gained from silvicultural manipulations.

In wilderness lies some of our last surviving repositories of the natural process, an ecological treasure house analogous, in some ways, to the great library at Alexandria that was destroyed in a conflagration. The loss of that library shut off *Homo sapiens* from much of the knowledge that had accumulated from earlier civilizations. Only a barbarian could have exulted or been indifferent when the library at Alexandria burned. If we stay on track, succeeding generations will be able to speak well of our civilization in our preservation of wilderness as a library of natural processes.

When we arrived at the very faint trail that marked the turnoff to the Elk Camp, Bill's mare, Manita, with no guidance, turned off the trail and led us on a short journey through dead, downed lodgepole pines so dense that it took nearly a quarter hour for her to pick her way 200 yards or so to the bank of the Minam River. When we rode into the campsite, we encountered a genuine mess—a painful desecration of a beautiful spot.

Since our last visit, the camp had been discovered by slob elk hunters. There was a very large fire ring festooned with dozens of burned cans and broken glass. Deep drainage ditches that had surrounded three large tents had been left unfilled. Three meat poles hung between the trees. Tent poles were scattered helter-skelter. Horses had scraped away the soil and exposed the roots around the trees where they had been tied—evidently day after day. There were hides and bones from several elk. A pile of garbage, including a half-dozen fuel cans and gas canisters, had been scattered about by scavengers.

I saw some anger but mostly pain on Bill's face, much as would be expected upon discovering desecration of a treasured shrine to a dearly beloved. This was just such a place, a shrine of sorts for him. Without comment, we simply dismounted, tied the horses, and went to work to repair the damage. There wasn't much talking in the process.

Bill and various companions had camped in this place, off and on, for four decades and left almost no trace. So had most parties of hunters in the Eagle Cap. Yet there were too many of what Bill called "half-ass hunters" who do not come to such places as this to be one with the wilderness. They come to take, to use selfishly, to "conquer." That is not the pity so much as their not being open to learning the lessons and the code of conduct that wilderness demands and is intended to convey. And then they leave behind their desecrations as a token of their passing and perhaps their contempt—or, just as likely, their abysmal ignorance. Perhaps all of those despicable characteristics come in a single package.

We spent half a day policing up the area and repairing the damage as much as we could before we set up our camp. To get back into the spirit of things, I declared tonight to be "fish night." Fly rods were quickly readied, and we were off on our separate ways to make it so. In little more than an hour of dedicated fishing, I landed some twenty rainbow trout and two Dolly Varden trout. I couldn't remember the legal limit, but two fish per person for supper seemed about right, so I kept the eight largest fish I caught—six rainbows and two Dollies.

While I was fishing, I saw a large battered salmon, more dead than alive, drifting slowly downstream with the current. Patches of scales were missing from the midpoint of its back to the tail, and its fins were tattered. I hoped the dying fish had accomplished what it had come so far from the Pacific Ocean to do: reproduce its kind. It had been on a hazardous 500-mile odyssey journey upstream from the Pacific past fishermen, gill netters, and eleven dams to reach its ancestral spawning grounds here high in the Eagle Cap Wilderness. Such a life force commanded appreciation and respect. I caught myself in the process of a salute—a throwback to my military days, I guess.

When we met back in camp, I asked Bill, "What's the limit?" He replied, "Two per person for supper." That made two of us who didn't know the legal limit but had figured out a commonsense solution. The total of our ignorance produced what is known in northeastern Oregon as a "fish feed"—local parlance for a no-holds-barred gastronomic orgy. In the midst of our fish feed we were joined by a camp doe of the mule deer persuasion, which appeared just in view, off and on, until we doused the fire for bedtime.

JULY 30, 1988

We moved our camp a short distance up Elk Creek to a small meadow just below Tombstone Lake. This was another of our favorite camps in the Wallowa Mountains and certainly one of the more picturesque. A small stream separated the meadow from a huge boulder field at the base of a granite wall that towered above the campsite. The tents and fire were sheltered by a huge lone spruce on a large mound in the middle of the meadow. The "kitchen" was located in a clump of smaller spruce that provided some protection from downslope breezes.

The unlikely appearing stream was first-class habitat for eastern brook trout. True, the overhanging trees prohibited the utilization of standard fly-fishing methods and required the use of a technique we called "dapping," whereby flies were flipped into the pools in front of undercut banks (usually accomplished from a kneeling or sitting position). Though the technique lacked aesthetic appeal, it was nonetheless quite effective. After last night's fish feed, we decided that one fish apiece for hors d'oeuvres would fit tonight's menu. So Bill han-

dled the fishing chores while I took care of gathering wood, cutting it
to appropriate length, and making the fire. In our collective opinion
there was a touch of class inherent in nibbling on high mountain
trout caught within fifty feet of the kitchen and served, with drinks,
well before the main dish of elk stew. From cold stream to frying pan
in fifteen minutes, that was a definition of "fresh" we could understand and appreciate.

Pikas were singing their unique songs in the boulder fields
above camp. Bill declared a contest as to which of us would be the
first to spot a pika through our binoculars. The game ended in a draw
at sundown—zero for all players. Two camp does joined the party
just as the sun disappeared behind the ridge. I imagined they enjoyed
watching us as much as we enjoyed watching them. Bill's dog, trained
not to bark at or chase deer, trembled as she watched the does. The
mule deer returned the favor by not bounding away in their characteristic pronging gait. One deer discovered the dry dog food in the
vestibule to Bill's tent and merrily chomped away. This was too much
for the dog to bear, however, and she protested with a barking charge
that drove the deer into the spruce thicket for the moment.

Bill and Bernice retired to their tent with the arrival of full
darkness. Meg and I sat up and huddled together close to the fire.
This was a night for stargazing. The sky was clear, and the nearly full
moon would not rise for some time yet. As the sunlight faded on the
granite cliffs, the stars emerged—one by one and then in a swarm,
their collective brilliance increasing with their numbers. The dropping temperatures on the granite face above or perhaps an animal of
some sort loosened an occasional rock that gathered other rocks for
a communal race to lower places. The clattering of the falling rocks
in the clear air was distinct in the silence. We could hear the wings
of bats as they swooped back and forth over the creek in pursuit of
their daily bread. An hour later, we were blessed with the soft sound
of a passing owl that we did not see. Camp deer, probably several,
returned. We could hear their footsteps and occasionally see a glint
of the fire reflected in an eye. Listening intently and simply feeling in
the still darkness brought to the surface an awareness and sensitivity
lacking when the eyes are the predominant source of information.

We had a new gadget along that my USFS crew used in our research, a night scope, which allowed us, literally, to see in the dark. Somehow that offended me, though I used the technology. Darkness was among the last mysteries, masking things that we could only guess at and hypothesize about. The night had always belonged to the animals. Fortunately, such gadgets are very expensive and apt to remain in the bag of tricks used by researchers and the military. Being able to see in the dark somehow seemed like cheating. I knew I would get over it, just as I did when we first began to use radio-tracking collars in big game studies.

JULY 31, 1988

Just at daylight I was awakened by several mule deer "just doing their thing" around the tent. Last night's camp doe, identifiable by a spot of missing hair on her neck, returned to visit and brought some friends along—two forked-horn bucks and four does. It seemed that, so far as the deer were concerned, we were the best show in town. I knew, as a scientist and a student of animal behavior, that I was guilty of anthropomorphism, a deadly professional sin, but I didn't care. We returned the compliment.

Using my binoculars, I could make out two elk—a cow and her calf—on the granite slopes above camp. They stared down in our direction from time to time when one of us made rattling sounds as we replenished the coffee in our tin cups. They seemed to consider us as benign and temporary intruders in their wilderness world. They could well learn, come hunting season, that "benign" is apt to be an intermittent thing and that humans suddenly morphed into the most deadly of predators who could deal death from a distance of several hundred yards. Predatory instincts rose in my chest, and I caught myself considering just how I would aim my hunting rifle—a Winchester .30-06 with a Weaver four-power scope—to kill the cow. My mental computer ground in the pertinent data: distance (twilight exaggerates distance), uphill shot, steady left-to-right breeze. I picked out a spot where I would sit, wrap the rifle's sling around my left arm, and brace the rifle over a boulder to ensure a steadied shot.

My rifle, residing at home in my gun cabinet, was sighted in to deliver a 150-grain bullet two inches high at 100 yards, be "spot on" target at 200 yards, and five inches or so low at 300 yards. I estimated the distance, in this case, to be about 400 yards. If so, the bullet would strike some eighteen inches below the point of aim. I considered the breeze to be too slight to alter the bullet's flight path significantly. I took a deep breath and slowly let out half. I brought the crosshairs to bear six inches over the top of the cow's shoulder. Then the long controlled squeeze of the trigger hand and finger commenced. Almost as a surprise, the rifle slammed into my shoulder, and the report echoed and re-echoed in the cirque—somehow it seemed louder than the original report, which was partially lost in the recoil. The cow spun and headed upslope. Within 100 yards she stopped, staggered, and then dropped. My internalized mini-drama of imagination had come to an end. I dropped my binoculars to my chest and looked at Bill. He was intently watching the cow through his binoculars. I suspected he knew what I had been thinking. I asked, "Where would you hold?"

He replied, "Just five or six inches over the top of the shoulder—the wind wouldn't matter that much." He had been working through the same mental exercise. We were both practicing for the fall hunt. In fact, we were always practicing for the fall hunt. I was relieved that we had come to nearly the same answer. How many dedicated hunters play out such games in their minds when seeing a big game animal, flushing a grouse, or watching waterfowl overhead? Mental practice when things are calm and unhurried pays off when such decisions must be made quickly, decisions that can have deadly consequences. Of course, both of us considered the elk in question too far away for a responsible hunter to risk a shot.

Bill and I made up the packs, saddled the horses, and loaded the packhorses while the women made breakfast and lunches. We were on the trail an hour after sunrise. Once we were lined out down the trail, the horses traveled steadily. The integration of a new gelding into the string was complete, and the arguments over hierarchical arrangements had seemingly been settled, at least for the moment.

We were riding easy with the lead ropes under our legs—i.e., the packhorse's lead rope was looped over the saddle horn and the rope's end tucked under the leg. This allows the rope to slide if there is a "pullback" by the packhorse and gives the rider time to reach back and grab the rope. The expression "rope under the leg" meant traveling, by whatever means, in a relaxed manner with no expectation of difficulty. Oddly, the expression is rarely used except to describe the state of calm just before some "blow-up" or other.

Leading one or several packhorses correctly is somewhat akin to riding two or more horses at the same time. It rivets the rider's attention to the horses, leaving little time for what Bill called "golly lagging." Today was different. The entire string of horses performed flawlessly and the lead ropes never tightened. That provided opportunities for all hands to appreciate the view of Diamond Lake and Tombstone Lake as the horses carried us up the mountain, switchback after switchback, and the lakes below seemed to become smaller and smaller.

Once through the pass just above Tombstone Lake, we descended into the East Eagle Creek drainage. Across the canyon we saw a beautiful cascading waterfall formed by the stream emitting from Echo Lake. None in the party knew the name of the waterfall— or even if it had a name.

During the lunch break, I looked at the maps retrieved from my saddlebags (three different vintages) and determined that the cascade was not noted on any of the maps! Somehow that seemed appropriate. It was, after all, only one splendor among many. Besides, things that have names on maps draw more attention than those that remain nameless. Drawing attention to natural wonders often works against their conservation—hence our own code names for our campsites. Those who really care come to know such places and bestow their own pet names, thereby rendering such places something of a personal possession to be used most carefully and shared only with friends.

The horses seemed to know the trucks were waiting down below and picked up their pace. After all, at the trailhead they would be relieved of their burdens and, upon arrival home, their saddles. "Free lunches" of alfalfa hay waited. The horses always seemed eager to depart for a trip into the wilderness and then, days later, equally eager to return home. I suppose it's the same with their human companions. For those who love wilderness as well as life in the "real world," there is a synergy in spending time in both, making the sum of the parts—a total life—more rewarding and exciting.

I held on to that thought as we drove down the dusty logging roads toward home past the laid-out timber harvest areas that signaled the conversion of "untamed forest" to a managed state. In that managed state the forests would produce, hopefully on a sustained basis, wood to satisfy human needs and, if appropriately done, habitats for wildlife and hunters. My job in the real world of USFS research was to provide knowledge to make that transition. Though I loved the wilderness, I considered that a worthy enterprise and my calling.

I pondered as we rode along without conversation. It seemed strange that, as a society, we place such low priority on the proper management of renewable natural resources. We spend but a tiny fraction of our national wealth on such matters compared with the huge fraction spent on engines of war and social programs. My working visits to those parts of the Third World where natural resources had long been taken for granted and abused and forests turned to barren mountains and deserts quickly revealed to me what was important. Such places are poor now and, in too many cases, getting worse. Now it matters little what revolution or religion holds sway at any moment in time.

Where are the mighty conquerors and the empires that rose and fell? They are gone, never to return. The shriveled and shrinking forests, the blowing soil, and the eroded hills are monuments to that reality.

In the end, the management of renewable natural resources provides the basis upon which all civilizations exist—and perhaps rise and fall. With those resource bases intact, many things are possible. Without that base, those who live in such environs face deepening problems and diminished likelihood of improvements. These are not new ideas. The "father" and first chief of the USFS, Gifford Pinchot, put that concept in clear focus in the early twentieth century while perhaps not yet realizing the value of lands that would come to be maintained as wilderness. That was the role and the contribution of such as John Muir and Aldo Leopold and the emerging disciplines and disciples that they influenced. Today's USFS chiefs must be champions of both wilderness and the wise use of the national forests to produce both goods and services.

I believe that the natural resources management organizations in place in the United States and Canada are awaiting a renaissance in the "wise use" movement that lies—in the minds of the hopeful—only as far away as the next election, the next shift in political opinion, the next recession and recovery, or the emergence of new charismatic leaders with a feel for the value of natural resources and their careful husbandry, coupled with a love for and fascination with the ways of nature. It has been a long time, a bit over a century, since President Theodore Roosevelt and his trusty sidekick Gifford Pinchot held sway.

Maybe others like them will emerge at opportune "magic moments." But waiting for a messiah is a foolish waste of time. The job for talented, dedicated conservationists is to hold on, prepare, and work to produce shining moments of opportunity and then capitalize on those opportunities by seizing the day. The struggle for conservation becomes one of holding on to gains while awaiting and perhaps helping to create the next opportunity in conservation. Progress in conservation has not come about, to borrow a forester's way of speaking about timber yields, as a matter of "non-declining even-flow" of improvement. Historically, such improvement comes in fits and starts. *Carpe diem!*

As in any human endeavor, there are ebbs and flows in the business of conservation. A dictionary definition of "conservation" is "the planned management of a natural resource to prevent exploitation, destruction, or neglect." Those concerned with the conservation of renewable natural resources that do not recognize the inevitability of such ebbs and flows are doomed to alternating fits of euphoria and despair. Mature marathon runners in the conservation game remain focused on the long term, with their eyes on the prize. They recognize that the struggles for conservation are the ultimate game that will determine the fate of the earth and its creatures. Secure in this knowledge, dedicated conservationists can watch the ebbs and flows of power, including political power and wealth, with a somewhat dispassionate eye. Those are, after all, minor league games of only fleeting significance. At the end of one's turn on the playing field, it is well to ask, "Is it better to have made and lost fortunes or to have worked to insure the continued productivity of the good earth?" I have known the answer since my youth, when it was instilled in me by my grandfather, Big Dad. To each his own.

The steady pace of the horses brought us to the trailhead without incident. In the near distance, we could clearly hear the chainsaws and logging machines at work. It was time to leave behind what was once the norm, some of which is preserved for the moment in the National Wilderness Preservation System, made possible by the Wilderness Act of 1964. Now it was time to return to the challenges of creating and cultivating what was to come—forests and grasslands perpetually productive of wood, meat, fiber, fish and wildlife, water, and recreation, as required by the Organic Administration Act of 1897 and modified by the Multiple-Use Sustained-Yield Act of 1960.

Therein resides a most worthy challenge—maybe the ultimate challenge for our species. Therefore, I was not put off by the sounds or the activity of the first step in the conversion of *de facto* wilderness into managed forests. After all, such seemed inevitable and even necessary. Yet the sounds of the saws and the logging machinery reminded me of the most important of long-term challenges for our species: sustainable husbandry of renewable natural resources. After all, if we fail in that endeavor, the keystone of civilization crumbles. I was, as always, grateful for the contrast of the wilderness from whence we emerged. It was instructive, humbling, and challenging.

When I saw our trucks through the trees, I could feel a change and imagined a voice saying, "Welcome back to the real world." Or was it the "real world" after all? Maybe we were leaving what was left of the "real world." Once the horses were loaded into the truck and trailer, they exhibited an eagerness—emphasized by a few swift kicks to the wall of their compartment—to commence the return to their pasture and barn. I, too, felt eager to get back to the day-to-day business of conservation and the amenities of civilization. The process of conservation was both my profession—my bread and butter—and my avocation. That was, for me, a combination hard to beat. I felt most fortunate and eager to reenter the fray.

CHAPTER 10

IF NOT GROUSE, WE'LL SETTLE FOR BROOK TROUT

The time had come for what Bill and I called our "annual grouse hunt"—emphasis on *annual*—which entails a week-long trip into the Snake River Canyon, Hells Canyon. But this was not the year for me to make such a trip. The chief of the USFS had told me that I could not be out of touch for so long, as much of the federally administered wild lands in the Rocky Mountain West seemed to be on fire—the most expansive outbreak of wildfires in nearly a century. Firefighting resources, for obvious political and economic reasons, had been focused on the wildfires in the area of the iconic Yellowstone National Park. Closer to my home in northeastern Oregon, there was a wildfire covering over 100,000 acres in the Snake River Canyon country along the Oregon-Idaho border. Obviously, this was not a good time to pursue the wily grouse in those environs, so Bill and I opted instead for a four-day trip into the Elkhorn Mountains just across the Grande Ronde Valley from our home in La Grande.

OCTOBER 1, 1988

Bill, Bernice, Meg, and I loaded up our horses and accoutrements and drove from La Grande south toward Baker City and then turned off the highway and away from the Snake River Canyon into the

Elkhorns. The sun, its appearance and size hugely magnified by the smoke, seemed to hang in the sky—huge and angry red. Even this far away from the fires, the smoke was heavy and irritating to throats and eyes.

As we gained elevation and the smoke became less and less of an irritation, our chances for a pleasant trip began to improve. We traveled the Skyline Trail from Anthony Lakes to where it intersected the trail to Dutch Flat and turned off. We arrived at our Dutch Flat campsite well before dark, leaving us time to fish the narrow stream that meandered across the meadow.

The stream varied from four to six feet wide and was incised three to four feet into the meadow floor. Our legal limits for fish in the creel (twenty six- to eight-inch eastern brook trout each) were quickly and easily caught. Bill told me that these high-elevation streams and lakes were devoid of game fish until they were stocked with eastern brooks in the early part of the twentieth century. The fish, through a cooperative venture of the USFS and the Oregon Department of Fish and Wildlife, had been hauled into this high country in milk cans lashed onto packhorses and mules and dumped into the streams. Such an action would likely be deemed an environmental travesty in today's world.

After supper, with my tummy well filled with eastern brook trout, I lay flat on my back on a manty tarp and contemplated the environmental impact assessments, the legal appeals, and so forth that would be required to accomplish such a thing in this day and time. Somehow I was glad that this particular "bucket biology" job got done in this special place when it did. If it was an ecological travesty, it was one that I could live with. I wondered what the public reaction would be to a proposal to eradicate this fishery and return it to its natural state?

Supper was prepared on a Coleman stove, as the fire risk was much too elevated to permit an open fire. As we finished our supper, the sun was setting—a brilliant orange as the sun's rays cut through the smoky haze. The smoke particles seemed to trap and hold the sunlight, and the sky in the west glowed with the same red as the fires that produced the smoke. The absence of a campfire dictated an early bedtime, as colder temperatures come quickly at this elevation with the disappearance of the sun.

As I lay in my sleeping bag awaiting sleep, I contemplated the social utility of fire—the interactions and bonding that have taken place around countless fires on countless nights over years and centuries, back to when mankind was first able to utilize fire. This night, the escape to the wilderness was not the same without an open fire.

OCTOBER 2, 1988

As I crawled out of the tent clad only in my long johns and unlaced boots, I saw Bill pumping air into the fuel chamber of the gasoline stove. My mood immediately improved, knowing that hot coffee was on the way. While Mr. Coleman's stoves have their place, they lack the aesthetic appeal of an open fire. And the blue flames from gas stoves don't give off much light. As we stood in the darkness sipping coffee, my mind returned to the social implications of fire. I made a pledge to myself to spend more evenings this coming winter watching flickering flames and glowing coals in our wood stove at home and thinking more profoundly about such matters.

The lingering low-lying smoke from the distant forest fires performed one of its magic tricks, and the sky glowed spectacularly with the rising of the sun. The open flat and the surrounding timbered slopes were, for a magic few minutes, awash in an eerie reddish orange glow. My mind rushed back to childhood and the way the world looked when I viewed it through the orange cellophane wrappers around jawbreaker candies.

As the rising sun cleared the skyline, viewing it through the smoke made it appear as a huge red-orange ball several times its ordinary size. As it rose higher in sky, the strange colors disappeared, and the size of the sun returned to normal.

The women were still asleep, and it suddenly seemed like a sterling idea to surprise them by catching enough eastern brookies for breakfast. Actually, neither Bill nor I relished fish for breakfast, and we didn't know what the ladies might think. On the other hand, we adored catching fish for breakfast! That was enough. Life is filled with trade-offs, conscious and unconscious.

To our disappointment, the eastern brook trout did not exhibit the ravenous appetites they had displayed last evening. Perhaps the frost that covered the ground and the much colder temperatures had something to do with that. The insects, so plentiful last evening, were now immobilized by the cold. Likely the fish had figured that out as they showed no interest in our carefully proffered flies—zero, *nada*, none.

We hoped that the coming of the sun would warm the insects, encourage them to fly, and perchance land in the small stream to become food for the fishes. Our wait for the onset of the fishes' appetites became increasingly pleasant as the sun simultaneously warmed the internal juices of the insects and the blood of the fishermen—in our case, abetted by cups of steaming coffee.

Suddenly, as if on signal, the insects began to fly, and the fish, in turn, begin to rise, infrequently at first and then ever more quickly and often. Now was the time for fly fishermen to seize the moment. Bill and I separated ourselves by several hundred yards. Before we crept toward the stream, we negotiated an agreement as to how many fish each of us would catch.

In less than twenty minutes, Bill whistled to get my attention and signaled that he had caught his allotted number of fish. At that point, I needed just one more fish to meet my target and rectified that shortcoming on my very next cast. When we met up, as was his wont, Bill reminded me that he had caught his limit before I caught mine.

Bernice was sitting by the Coleman stove drinking coffee when we arrived with our fish, cleaned and ready for the skillet. I didn't think Bernice liked fish for breakfast either, but she loved to see Bill animated, and providing fish for breakfast inevitably produced such a state in Bill. She praised our skills as fishermen and poured us some fresh coffee. I am sometimes bemused by the attention and praise women gave to their menfolk of whatever age—little boys to old men—and the prideful response and compliance it produces. It may work the same in reverse, but discerning the games that others play is much easier for me than recognizing those I employ.

Meg smelled the fish frying and emerged from the tent. Somehow, she could sleep quite soundly atop a thin pad on the ground for ten hours and love it. And she really liked fish—or fresh-killed game—for breakfast! As usual, she was beautiful without a hair out of place. She even smelled good. I scratched my beard and wondered, how did she manage that?

While the women were washing dishes, Bill and I looked up from our third cup of coffee to see two young men, replete with fishing equipment, walking down the trail from Dutch Flat Lake, which is nestled in a cirque some two and a half miles above our camp. The two would-be fishermen had been camped at the lake for several days and had found the fishing "poor to middling." They decided that they were going to follow the stream until they came to "some water with fish in it."

We wished them luck and watched as they traveled across Dutch Flat, occasionally jumping over the small incised stream as they went. They disappeared from our sight in the trees a mile or so downstream. Bill smiled, noting, "Those young fellows spent the last half hour jumping back and forth over more fish than they could eat in a month. I guess we could have told them about the fishing. But, on the other hand, they didn't ask. And probably we wouldn't have told them anyway. Good fishing spots, like all really worthwhile things, should be discovered through individual efforts or as the gift of a valued friend."

Sometimes the old bastard actually talked like that, and sometimes, like now, it seemed good wisdom.

So our "secret" fishing place remained a secret, at least as far as those two pilgrims were concerned. At the moment, the secondary trail down to Dutch Flat from the main Skyline Trail was something of a real bitch, barely passable for horses and damned unpleasant—and a little dangerous—for backpackers. As a result, the area where we were camped got relatively little human use. It was obvious from the survey stakes and ribbons tied to bushes and trees that a new trail would soon be constructed down from the Skyline Trail into Dutch Flat. These newly constructed and reconstructed trails are a wonderment when compared with the old trails that simply came into existence from use by sheep outfits, hunters, USFS personnel, and a few recreationists. They are readily recognized by their gentle grades and avoidance of rock slides, bogs, and gullies except when absolutely necessary and certainly serve the general public better than the trails they replace. There was a dark side to each additional step toward "taming" of the wilderness. Such improvements would open such places as Dutch Flat to many more people. More use in such sensitive higher-elevation environments would almost inevitably lead to deterioration, and that deterioration would, in turn, lead to more stringent regulation of human use. How was that not an example of a vicious circle?

Still, the USFS recreation managers were doing their job and doing it well. But restrictions on human use lay just over the rise and with those regulations—and their enforcement—would come a diminution of the "wild" in wilderness. Maybe that will not matter all that much over the very long term. One era—and its people with their evolving morays unique to time, place, and circumstance—inevitably passes away, to be replaced by another cohort of pilgrims replete with different desires, objectives, expectations, and standards. That's just the way it is, has always been, and will be. Perhaps that is as it should be, but the rapidly changing times make me uneasy somehow.

Speaking strictly for myself, I doubted that I would appreciate visiting Dutch Flat nearly so much when I might see smoke from a dozen campfires and hear the voices of those seated around those fires. Then it will be necessary to picket the horses instead of letting them run free with bells clattering. Or maybe by then horses and mules will be banned and open fires will be prohibited. Then I won't return—such circumstances would simply be too painful or, more than likely, I will have passed on to my reward. I felt that it was better to hold on to cherished memories than deal with undesired but inevitable change. But, to be fair, the people gathered around those future campfires will most likely be as thrilled by their experiences as I have been with mine. And maybe those future visitors wouldn't like it the way it is now. Certainly there will be many more of them.

OCTOBER 3, 1988

A half hour after sunrise, we finished eating breakfast, cleaned up the dishes, buttoned up the camp, and saddled the horses. We were on our way up to Dutch Flat Lake to try the fishing. I suspected that this morning's expedition was just an excuse for Bill to ride up to the lake. During the ride, I pondered why we seemed to need to fabricate excuses to seek out the wild places. Why don't we just go because the spirit moves us—and admit it?

The fish at Dutch Flat Lake seemed fewer but larger than those in the stream we fished yesterday. But I was satiated with eating fish—even catching fish. Lying in lush deep grass and dozing in the sun, albeit a sun shining through a smoky haze, took precedence over fishing. Bill, being Bill, fished and turned back the fish he caught while most certainly keeping score.

We met back in camp at sundown and were through with supper by dark. After the dishes were washed and put away, we sat cross-legged around the Coleman stove without speaking as the sun dropped behind the ridgeline to the west. The blue flame on the Coleman stove was a poor substitute for a good stand-around fire, but it was far better than total darkness.

After a while, my companions silently left the circle for bed until I was left alone as the temperature dropped and the night chill came on. I was alone with my musings. There was no sound save for the persistent hissing of the stove and lantern. It was a time for reverie and journal tending, which, in my case, tend to be the same thing.

The reverie faded slowly into a deep sleep, lulled by the hiss of the lantern. The hiss diminished as the air, which had been compressed by exactly thirty strokes of the plunger, was exhausted. The cessation of the hiss from the lamp awakened me. It was full dark now and my companions were asleep in their tents.

I was cold and stiff. When I raised my head and looked up, I felt the almost physical jolt of seeing a sky so filled with stars that it seemed I could reach up and gather them to me by the handfuls. A shift in the wind had temporarily blown the smoke away. Still half asleep, my reflex was to reach out, with fingers spread on both hands, and touch the stars. It was a magic moment. I didn't want it to end, though I was almost painfully cold and stiff. I was in awe—and at peace.

I rose, stretched the stiffness away, went to my tent, and carefully and quietly extracted my down sleeping bag. I fetched two manty tarps from atop the saddles and sought out a soft place in the grass to make a bed. I took off my boots. In a moment, the sleeping bag and tarps enfolded me, and it seemed that the stars and the night belonged to me alone.

OCTOBER 4, 1988

Just at dawn, I opened my eyes to a blazing red sky in the east. The wind had shifted once again, bringing back the smoke to remind us that the fires in the Snake River country were still active. I lay there snug in my sleeping bag and visualized the firefighters, adorned in their yellow hard hats and fire-retardant yellow Nomex shirts and trooping single file out of their fire camps on their way back up to the fire lines. They would be quite tired by now with hacking coughs and suffering from the smoke from too many back-to-back days on the fire line.

Lying there warm and snug, I wondered what it would be like to be part of a firefighting effort. I would never know, as USFS research personnel are called upon only in dire circumstances. I had dreamed of being many things in my life, but being a wild-land firefighter wasn't high on that list.

Somehow, I felt that researchers dealing with matters of an ecological nature but having little exposure to wildfires might have something to regret or at least muse about. The firefighting tradition has been a vital component of the glue that binds the remarkable USFS fraternity. When USFS people gather and, perhaps, their inherent reserve is loosened by a touch of bourbon and branch water, the talk is likely to turn to this or that firefighting episode. As I listened to such talk and watched the storyteller's eyes, I could feel the bonds tighten in the group. Their eyes lighted up and sparkled, and I could hear the tenor of their voices change. From wild-land firefighting experiences emerged a brotherhood.

I wondered why this almost magic fellowship persisted long after their days of service on the fire lines had come to an end. Was it the danger? Certainly, that was part of it. But there was more to it than that. Perhaps fighting a wildfire afforded simplification and clarity relative to both purpose and mission. On the fire lines, there is no confusion as to purpose. The fire was the enemy—evil incarnate. The mission is clear: put the fire out. Resources were available. The fire boss was in control. There were no environmental impact statements, no public hearings, no appeals, no going to court, and no second-guessing—at least not until the danger was past. Firefighting provided one of those rare moments in the management of wild lands when everything related to the job at hand was crystal clear—if only for a moment.

The horses grazing at the far end of the flat suddenly wheeled and began a flat-out race to camp. It was a sight to behold and hear as the seven horses thundered on, leaping the narrow creek time after time as they crossed its meandering path. The bells on two of the horses clanged wildly and their hooves thundered. As they hurtled toward camp, I imagined the feeling that infantry must have felt as they faced a cavalry charge. The horses flashed by and circled back through the frost-encrusted grass and slid to a stop before us. Clouds of moisture-laden breath bellowed rhythmically from their nostrils.

They were so beautiful, so strong, and so alive! And for a magic moment so was I. It seemed strange that the only time I was viscerally aware of being alive was in moments like this and in places such as this. To be alive and to fully appreciate that wonderment is far too rare an experience. Perhaps it is essential to be "totally in tune" for that feeling to burst through the layers of calluses on our souls that come from the constant frictions produced by civilization—or maybe just living. I saw Bill standing stock-still in the tree line, watching. What was he thinking and feeling? I thought I knew, but we wouldn't discuss it. Sometimes feelings are best just felt.

Without a vote, we decided that we had enjoyed enough fishing for this trip. Today was reserved for a ride to a mountain lake some ten miles away by trail. Once we made the climb on a too-steep trail from Dutch Flat to the Skyline Trail, the newly engineered trail we intersected became relatively gentle, and it became easy going down the spine of the Elkhorn Range and around the slopes that slanted down to the headwaters of the North Fork of the John Day River. This area had been recently added to the National Wilderness System, a campaign in which Bill had played a significant role despite his increasing age, limited resources, and waning energy and influence. Where the trail crossed the ridge that marked the beginning of the valley of the North Fork of the John Day River, he reigned in Keno. I dismounted and walked up beside him. He sat quietly in his old McClellan saddle looking over this latest addition to the wilderness system. After a while, he simply nodded as a small grin tugged at the corners of his mouth. It was obvious that he felt proud in this too-rare moment of profound satisfaction, and it showed. That satisfaction was well earned, and I nodded my understanding. He nodded back in acknowledgment and quickly looked away. The moment would have only been diminished by words.

We rode across the wilderness boundary on a newly constructed trail, much of it blasted from solid granite rock and built to dead-level specifications around the top of the valley. The old trail could be seen down below, twisting and turning, climbing and falling. Then up ahead we could see Nip-and-Tuck Pass, a narrow slot crossing the boulder-strewn ridge.

Bill told me the pass got its name during the last Indian uprising in this part of the world, when a Bannock raiding party made an escape from the Baker Valley, closely pursued by a contingent of the U.S. Cavalry. It was, evidently, "nip and tuck" as to whether the pursuing troops would bring the Bannocks to bay before they crossed through the pass and escaped. The Bannock warriors won the race to the pass and left a rearguard of young warriors behind that held back the soldiers until their getaway was complete.

As we rode into the slot, I tried to visualize the situation as the rearguard of warriors took up positions where they could be partially protected and delay their pursuers. That delay would allow the weary horses and riders of the main party to make their escape down the steep slope and into the scrubby timber below. The young warriors must have felt very much alone, choking down their fear and filled with a sense of responsibility as they scrambled for positions.

My contemplation was suddenly interrupted when the horses shied simultaneously as one, two, three, four mountain bikes came roaring up through the slot toward us. The yellow helmets and shiny stretch garments worn by the riders shone in the sunlight, as did their aluminum-framed bikes. Whatever the horses deemed these apparitions to be, they didn't like what they heard and saw. Their upset abated when the bike riders stopped, stood upright, and spoke. That gave the horses a chance to understand that these apparitions were merely humans.

I wondered what the Bannocks' rearguard and the pursuing cavalry would have thought of this situation. Even today trail bikes and their riders seem grotesquely out of place in such a place as this, to me at least. Maybe, I thought, Bill and I and the horses were the ones out of place. The word "anachronism" came to mind. I had to admit that sometimes I wanted to hold the world still, at least in such a place as this. But I couldn't do that, and I knew it.

We rode on up to the lake and freed the horses of their saddles and bridles, put on hobbles, and loosed them to graze. We lay on our backs in the grass, tilted our sweat-stained gray Stetsons over our eyes, and enjoyed the sun's warmth. Then we sat up and enjoyed a most wonderful "gourmet" lunch of sardines, crackers, and onions—a veritable feast and most pleasant respite. Fish were rising in the lake to add to the moment. Even when we had no intention of fishing and no wherewithal to fish, the mere possibility quickened both pulses and senses.

On the ride back to camp, I visualized the pass as the blue-clad cavalry troopers in pursuit of the Bannock warriors might have perceived it. A successful direct assault would have been impossible. The only way for the soldiers to gain advantageous positions would be to flank the ambush party and fire down on them from above. That would have taken considerable time to get into position—enough time for the Bannocks, both the main party and those in the rear guard, to get away. Was that serendipity or a brilliant strategy? The answer rested with the teller of tales—the Bannock warriors and the soldiers, who surely saw things through different eyes.

As our horses scrambled up the trail with the packhorses behind, I pondered the stakes and ribbons stretching across the slope, marking the location of the new trail soon to be. Perhaps it would be completed if and when we came this way again. And just as likely we would encounter more mountain bikes and smell their exhaust and hear the throb of two-stroke gasoline engines.

I turned and looked back over my shoulder down at Dutch Flat Lake. I remembered the solitude and the eastern brooks that abounded in the lake. I tucked the image away in the filing cabinet of my mind where it will stay safe and unchanged. I doubted that I would ever return. Sometimes it is better to lock away a memory and let go of a place.

Federal policies relative to wildfires have changed over time. After the Big Burn in Idaho and Montana in 1910, fire prevention and control became a primary duty of the fledgling USFS. When William Greeley became the third chief of the USFS in 1920, fire prevention, carried out primarily to protect trees until they could be harvested, became the agency's overriding mission. Some said that the USFS became the "fire service" in the process. In 1935 the USFS instituted the "10 o'clock rule"—any wildfire spotted was to be extinguished by 10 o'clock the following morning, a goal that was frequently impossible to achieve. Over time, the use of more sophisticated and more expensive firefighting techniques, such as the deployment of air tankers and helicopters, escalated until costs for fire suppression were, in some years, half of the USFS budget. Then in the summer and early fall of 1988, massive wildfires raged in the Greater Yellowstone Ecosystem. When the onset of winter brought an end to the fires, 1.2 millions acres had burned over in spite of suppression efforts costing $140 million. In 1995, as Chief of the USFS, I would declare that, depending on circumstances, some fires would be fought and some would be allowed to burn under close observation. An era had come to an end.

CHAPTER 11

RIDING OUT FRONT IS DIFFERENT FROM TRAILING BEHIND

After chairing an interagency team to propose a management plan for old-growth forests on federal lands (the habitat of the imperiled northern spotted owl), I was the focus of intense and often negative attention, and I simply could not deal with incessantly jangling telephone any longer. Over the course of the previous nights I had awakened several times from deep sleep, gasping for air, in a cold sweat. Was it an anxiety attack? That seemed likely, but I was no "head shrinker." But, by God, I knew a surefire cure. In the Snake River country there was a vast, open retreat of wilderness just waiting. Therein resided solitude enough for me to heal up, get back on the horse, and think my way through things.

A call to Bill verified that he was ready for a week-long pack trip, which, according to his reckoning, he could begin as early as the next day. Of course, he would have to forego attendance at a step-daughter's wedding. But he didn't want to miss what might be his last trip into the Snake River Canyon. He said, "I'm seventy-five years old—first things first." Now, I thought, there was a courageous man.

I placed a call to the USFS's Washington office to let everyone know that I would be in the Snake River Canyon for the next week and therefore out of touch. I was instructed to take a two-way radio with me. Of course, radio reception in the Snake River country was notoriously poor, but there was nothing I could do about that.

JUNE 10, 1990

Bill and I stopped at the café in Imnaha for lunch. As was usual for this establishment, the conversation was interesting, and the food—well, not so much. But the price was right and the beer ice-cold. A young man came in to ask about the condition of the road up to Hat Point at the edge of the USFS's Snake River National Recreation Area. The waitress told him that she had been told that the road was impassable—or close to it—due to recent rains and lack of maintenance. The pilgrim was not discouraged and asked how to find the road. She told him. Then he asked when the new road would be completed up to the top. She didn't know. He allowed as how he thought there should be some information about the recreation area in Imnaha. She grunted. I agreed—silently.

There was a move afoot in the environmental communities in Oregon, Idaho, and Washington to transfer management of the federal lands in the Snake River Canyon from the Forest Service to the National Park Service. Though I didn't like the idea, it was not hard to see why folks might be disappointed in its current management—or the lack thereof.

We departed for the trailhead. By early afternoon, we had the gear loaded on the horses and were on the trail. Bill, as usual, was riding in the lead. He set a pace suitable for fat, out-of-shape horses and equally out-of-shape men. The horses had not been ridden or packed since last November's elk season. Such inactivity was not good for the horses or their riders. But we had plenty of time and our purpose—and my need—was to simply "be away." That seemed much more significant than proving to ourselves that we could cover twenty or thirty miles over tough terrain in a single day.

Somehow, I had never felt really free when we entered the Snake River Canyon via this route until we crossed over Freezeout Saddle between the Imnaha and Saddle Creek drainages. We encountered a foot or more of snow along the north side of Freezeout Saddle, where we stopped at the summit to tighten cinches. We adjusted the britchens across the horses' rumps to keep the packs and saddles from ending up around the horses' necks during the steep 3,000-foot descent into Saddle Creek, which emptied into the Snake River. A slow,

Bill Brown and his horse Keno, Snake River Canyon, 1990.

steady, cold rain set in with a little sleet thrown in for seasoning. We donned our slickers and hat covers, mounted up, and continued our "great getaway."

We rode the bench trail that ran the length of the canyon halfway between the top of the canyon and the river. When we came to Saddle Creek, it was obvious that a band of sheep had passed through the country only a few days earlier. The grass had been cropped close, and there were sheep tracks and shiny black sheep droppings everywhere. The herders were moving the sheep at an appropriate pace, and the grazing was within acceptable limits as set by the USFS. But the sheep grazing came at a price. The cow elk that commonly gathered in the old Saddle Creek Burn for calving around the first week of June had been displaced, at least temporarily, by the passage of the sheep. I wondered if the range conservationist for the Wallowa-Whitman National Forest and the Oregon Department of Fish and Wildlife biologists had talked about that likelihood or were even aware of the situation. I jotted down a note to call the supervisor of the Wallowa-Whitman when we got back to civilization.

The rain and sleet had stopped by the time we arrived at our intended campsite on upper Saddle Creek. So far as we could tell, no one had used the camp since we had been here last September. The stack of firewood under an old flat-topped ponderosa pine was as we had left it—neatly stacked and dry. There was water running in the usually dry stream bed within fifty yards of camp. That combination makes for an "easy camp." It wasn't long before a stew was bubbling over the fire. We sat back and sipped our cocktails of Tang and 190-proof grain alcohol and watched the shadows climb the canyon walls across the river in Idaho as the sun dropped in the western sky. I felt the seven months of strain from formulating possible habitat management strategies for the northern spotted owls begin to slip away.

When twilight came, I was suddenly so incredibly sleepy that I felt as if I had been slipped a mickey. I excused myself from dishwashing, crawled into the tent, kicked off my boots, and pulled my sleeping bag over my shoulders. From somewhere upslope, I heard a canyon wren singing a farewell to the sun. As the shadows reached the very top of the canyon wall across the river in Idaho, I slipped into the sleep of the emotionally exhausted.

JUNE 11, 1990

The clatter of horse bells near the tent awakened me. It was full daylight. When I checked my watch, I couldn't believe I had actually enjoyed twelve hours of uninterrupted hard-core sleep. Bill had groomed the horses and had been sitting by the fire sipping coffee for over four hours, waiting for me to crawl out of the tent. It was not like him to let me or anyone else in his company sleep in after first light. In Bill's book, such indulgence was not only slothful—it did not meet the expectations of an officer in the "Old Army's" horse-drawn artillery. But on this morning he had made an exception, realizing that I was flat-ass exhausted, mentally and spiritually if not physically.

After noting the dropping temperatures and the black clouds scudding across the sky from the west that obscured the top of the canyon, we decided to make our next camp where Saddle Creek emptied into the Snake River. That would be some 2,000 feet or so lower in elevation and, we hoped, twenty or thirty degrees warmer. The trail along Saddle Creek was one of the easier of the trails down from the bench country to the Snake River and, therefore, a favorite route for backpackers. We usually avoided camping at the mouth of Saddle Creek because of the likelihood of encountering backpackers who might not enjoy the proximity of our horses and the horse bells.

We preferred to have, or at least be able to pretend to have, the Snake River country to ourselves. We encountered two groups of backpackers along the trail. One of the hikers asked us if we knew the outcome of the last two playoff games in the National Basketball Association finals. I'm not sure Bill knew who was playing—and wouldn't admit it if he did. I knew who was playing but couldn't remember who had won, most likely the result of simply not giving a damn. It made for a rather one-sided conversation.

At the mouth of Saddle Creek, we encountered a group of horse packers encamped in our traditional camping place. Oddly, I felt as if they were trespassing on our territory. After passing the time of day, we did a "to the rear march" back up Saddle Creek for about a mile and set up a camp under a trio of hackberry trees. There was a cache of firewood under the trees and two cow elk skulls (but no other bones) nearby. "Two Skulls Camp" was added to our list of charmingly identified campsites. There was a method in our madness: we could mention the place in our conversations, and the names didn't mean a damn thing to anybody else.

No sooner had we put up the tent and rain fly than the long-expected rain began to patter on the taut nylon. It rained steadily for some four hours. There was something satisfying—even enjoyable—about making camp in the rain, provided that the camp was set up before it rained, dry wood was available, the fire was shielded by the fly, and all the rainproof items proved indeed to be rainproof. We were sitting under the fly sipping coffee and watching the rain run off our hat brims when a very wet, bedraggled pilgrim, sans rain gear of any kind, came walking down the Snake River Trail carrying a daypack and a rock hammer. We invited him in out of the rain and offered him a cup of coffee.

He was a geology student from Vermont who was spending the summer working for a U.S. Geological Service team helping to prepare a geological guidebook for the Snake River country. He seemed curious about us—who we were and what we were doing—and asked a lot of questions. Bill was pleased to supply him with answers—sometimes related to the questions and sometimes not. Our visitor was entertained, but so was Bill. It was an equitable trade.

I spent my time watching the rivulets of rainwater make their way across the translucent rain fly to drip into the dish pans we had set out to catch the runoff. Lulled by the sound of the rain on the taut fly, I pulled my battered Stetson over my eyes and drifted off to sleep.

I was awakened quite suddenly by a dog's cold nose in my ear, a wet lick on my face, and a female voice yelling, "Orlando, stop it!" Yet another pilgrim had arrived. This one was a wildlife biology student from the University of Washington working under Dr. Gordon Orians, a professional acquaintance of ours. She was looking for an area where she could study something or other about magpies.

To me, the Snake River country seemed a very unlikely place to study magpies. But I kept that opinion to myself. After all, most of the wildlife biologists I had ever known well were a bit eccentric; certainly most of my close acquaintances would include me in that category. The more I thought about it, though, the more I could understand why one would want to study magpies in the Snake River Canyon. It might be a unique habitat—and even a little short on magpies—but the canyon is truly a "wonderment" and a hell of an adventure.

After she wandered off down the trail in search of magpies, Bill and I spent a quiet evening alternately reading and staring into the fire. Ordinarily, Bill was a talker. But this night he sensed my mood, and we sat quietly, occasionally feeding sticks into the fire and listening to the off-and-on drumming of raindrops on the fly. The tattoo of rain above me never failed to sooth my spirit.

JUNE 12, 1990

We saddled the horses, packed up, and rode back up the Saddle Creek Trail to the juncture with the Bench Trail and turned north. Bill and I had traveled this trail together many times, but everything seemed new and different every time. Each turn in the trail, each creek crossing, each ridge reminded us of something that had happened there—or nearby—on a past trip. Here we had seen a black bear and there a cougar. On this ridge I killed an elk, on that switchback we rolled a horse, and so on. We noted changes since we had ridden through last: a favorite snag that had fallen and left a hole against the sky, bones from a dead elk kill that had now been scattered by scavengers, new pine seedlings in an old burn, the fire pits that we had dug and covered on past visits and now couldn't find—"no-trace camping" at its best.

This was "our country," Bill's and mine—his first and now ours. It has belonged to others over the past several thousand years or more and will belong to others waiting to be born. It belongs to each person and each clan in its own special way, defined by experience—a sturgeon caught here, a camp made there, a big buck killed or shot at and missed. Our campsites were named after experiences—"Three Bears," "Two Skulls," "Elk," "Big Deer," "Two Rattler," "Fish," and "Run Away" were among the names.

Experiences are always new and often special to those doing the experiencing, even if experienced many times before by others.

The fulfilling of desire for new experiences is one means of harvesting the zest from life. Yet the failure to recognize that most experiences are but the repeated experiences of others has produced tragedy for generations of *Homo sapiens*—and for the land. Why do we find it so difficult to learn from, profit from, and avoid others' mistakes? There is good wisdom in the observation that "he who does not learn from the past is doomed to repeat it."

We had been on the trail some five hours when we came upon a place between Rough Creek and Saddle Creek where we had camped several times before. There was plenty of daylight left for us to move on for another hour or so before setting up camp. But Bill made it clear that here was where he wanted to camp—offering no explanation as to his reasons.

It was becoming obvious to me that he had in mind very particular places where he wanted to camp on this trip. Once we set up our camps, he told me the stories he associated with those places. Some of the stories were tales he had heard from others, some came from his experiences before we traveled the wilderness together, while others dealt with experiences that we shared. He had said several times on this trip that this was his last trip into the Snake River Canyon. Of course, he had said that during every one of our trips for the last five years.

But this time I began to believe that he might really mean it. It was clear that it was important to him that I listen carefully—and re-member—what he had to say. He meant it to be a special legacy from him to me. It was not a new concept or a totally new thought for me.

Two years earlier my father, Scranton Boulware Thomas, suf-fered a heart attack—from which six months later—he somewhat recovered. Last spring, when I visited him at the old homeplace in Handley, Texas, he talked incessantly about our family and its histo-ry. He told me anecdotes, showed me old family pictures, and took me to visit the graves of my grandparents—paternal and maternal—and of my mother. We spent two days visiting places on the old farm between Fort Worth and Dallas where my father was raised. It was now owned by a real estate developer and was in the process of being divided into "ranchettes" and swallowed up by the inexorable spread of the Dallas–Fort Worth Metroplex. At each special spot, he told me the stories of what had happened there. These were his special places—and mine.

To him, it was important for me to be reminded, to know, and to care about those places and events—and to remember. I sensed then that this was my last time with my father. He knew that as well as I did, that his end lay just ahead in the fog. Those stories—and a shotgun and some of his carpentry and plumbing tools—were the sum total of my inheritance. It was more than enough. The stories were what counted most. He dropped dead at his dinner table last fall.

Now it came to me clearly that Bill felt that the end for him lay just around the corner—if not the end of his life, the end of his time in the wilderness. For him, those two things were very nearly the same. Now there were things he wanted to tell me and show me, things he wanted me to remember.

He talked and I listened. I asked no questions and only nodded from to time to time to let him know that I was listening—and, more important, understood what he was doing. Though I had heard many of the stories before, I found myself wishing that I had a tape recorder. I thought about taking notes but was afraid it might distract Bill from what he wanted to say.

JUNE 13, 1990

Strong winds came and went intermittently during the night. Several grommets ripped loose from the blue nylon tarp that served as our rain fly. I went out barefooted in the storm several times to secure the flapping tarp. During one excursion I not only secured the fly but found a rattlesnake in the process. I had never felt so barefooted in my life. Fortunately, the snake and I were both too cold and sluggish to make a fuss. We retreated in opposite directions—no harm, no foul. When I crawled back into my sleeping bag, I was aware of the taste of copper in my mouth and wondered if rattlesnakes also experienced adrenaline highs. If so, I thought I knew of at least one rattler that would be tasting copper for a while.

The winds brought back the low-hanging dark clouds that prompted our decision to pack up camp and follow the Sluice Creek

Trail to the flats along the Snake River. The trail from the bench country down to the river was steep and difficult—too steep and too poorly maintained to be considered either safe for travel by foot or horseback. The good news was that not many pilgrims traveled this trail, left over from pre-USFS days.

Along the way, we noted red plastic flags festooning trees and shrubs and occasional grade stakes signaling that the USFS would be constructing a new trail to current standards. Without a doubt, it would be a trail relatively safe for dudes. The Snake River Canyon was, after all, designated as a National Recreation Area. A trail built to USFS specifications meant that, as time passed, more and more people would "discover" Sluice Creek, the Sluice Creek Trail, and the bench country, to which the reconstructed trail would afford much easier and safer access. Whether that was good or bad was in the eye of the beholder.

Just as we rode out of the timber along the creek and emerged onto to the drier treeless lower slopes of the canyon, we flushed out a beautiful cinnamon-colored black bear that made its escape straight down the long ridge toward the river. The bear made a beautiful sight as it bounded down the slope. Each time its front feet jarred onto the ground, a ripple went through its hide and hair and the sun played off its shiny coat. We now had a name for this place: Cinnamon Bear Ridge. Over the past thousands of years bears had undoubtedly run down that ridge, even one with a cinnamon-colored coat. And one or more such incidents had been witnessed by a human of one persuasion or another. But that was then; this was now. Now this place had a special meaning for Bill and me—and therefore was accorded a name. Perhaps the name will stick when and if we tell others about what we saw on Cinnamon Bear Ridge. But after due consideration I decided I wouldn't tell anybody. It didn't really matter. This was our special experience. We shared that moment and would remember. That seemed enough.

By the time we reached our Sluice Creek camp, the clouds had given way to clear skies, and the cold temperatures were left behind up along the bench trail in exchange for the warmth of lower elevations down along the Snake River. As we rode into our campsite, we flushed some fifty chukars—nine or ten adults and the rest young of various sizes. Bill called it "chukar kindergarten."

Then, without warning, all four horses shied off the trail and danced around wide-eyed in response to some terrible threat not immediately obvious to us. I finally spied the trouble: a gray-phased ruffed grouse in full aggressive display with neck feathers erect, chest out, wings drooped and fluttering, and issuing whirring sounds as it "charged" the closest horse.

It was one of the much-dreaded but rarely encountered "attack grouse" in full aggressive display. While I thought these feints by the grouse hilarious, the lead horses took it altogether seriously. Then the grouse broke off her "attack" and ran off the trail, feigning injury and issuing plaintive cries. We finally convinced the horses that it was marginally safe to proceed on down the trail. They seemed to retain the vision and fear of the grouse for a good ten minutes, giving a wide berth to anything that could possibly turn out to be, or even conceal, such ferocious creatures.

When we reached our campsite, an old homesteader's place overlooking the river, we found things just as we had left them last September. After camp was set up and the horses cared for, we spent a lazy afternoon each "doing our thing." Bill had packed along a set of pruning shears for the express purpose of removing the deadwood from several scraggly old apricot trees and a single prune plum at this old homestead. The fruit trees were possibly five or six decades old— or more. I watched as my friend, the "old mountain man," spend several hours carefully pruning the fruit trees. And then he thinned the still-green fruit crop to ease the strain on the trees. He pronounced that he "chose to know" that these trees will be there a while longer, producing fruits to be plucked by fellow wilderness aficionados— surely not including him—in Septembers to come. And just as surely the trees would be visited by the mule deer, elk, and bears when there were no humans about. Such hopes and visions of things to come were incentive enough for Bill as he continued his pruning chores.

JUNE 14, 1990

Daylight brought with it an array of birdsong. The birds' songs mixed with the clanging of horse bells when Bill unsnapped the halters of the horses tied on the picket line and they raced to the bunchgrass-covered slopes below our camp. Chukars were calling, seemingly from every direction. I could also hear mourning doves, a long-tailed chat, canyon wrens, the buzz of a hummingbird, and other songs that I could not identify due to a combination of my ineptitude and increasing deafness. If anything would entice me to wear hearing aids, it would be to enhance my ability to hear birds' songs.

It was only two hours after daylight, and it was already uncomfortably warm, even though the sun had not yet appeared over the canyon's eastern lip. It would get much hotter, and we knew it. Bill had the coffee ready and we sipped what seemed an elixir from tin cups, being careful not to burn our lips. We sat quietly, without talking, and waited for the sun. As the direct sunlight arrived in our campsite at the bottom of the canyon, the birdsongs became less frequent, and the infamous heat of Hells Canyon began to build. After the breakfast dishes were washed, we spoke for the first time this day. Bill asked, "Well, what do you want to do today?"

I replied, "I'm thinking of moseying downriver," emphasizing the "mosey" part.

He smiled and nodded, "Fine, I'll go upriver." After all, we didn't want to crowd each other in the vastness of the Snake River Canyon. We parted company.

I walked downriver to Rush Creek Rapids and found myself a perch from which I could watch as the jet boats and the rafters negotiated the rapids. It was relatively cool down near the water in the shade of the giant ponderosa pines. It was a good place to doze and daydream, write in my journal, and watch the occasional boats pass. Mostly, I just wanted to be alone with my thoughts and feelings.

Through my 7×35 Bausch and Lomb binoculars, I studied the faces of the "dudes" in the jet boats and rafts as they passed. Though some seemed to intently study the scenery, none gave any indication that they saw me studying them. Some who passed by, not more than thirty yards from were I sat, seemed to stare right at me but not know that I was there. By midafternoon, I was even waving discreetly at each passing boat but elicited no responses. How true it is that we often look but do not see.

As the sun dipped below the canyon wall on the Oregon side, the birdsongs became more and more frequent. The flies that had been so maddening off and on during the day disappeared, and the crepuscular mosquitoes emerged. I stood, stretched, dabbed on a little mosquito dope, and set out for camp. Just after I crossed over Sluice Creek, jumping from rock to rock to keep my boots dry, and came up out of the creek bed, I saw Bill coming along the trail from the opposite direction. He was still over a mile away.

By the time Bill arrived in camp, I had a fire going and a spring-cool "Tang and lab"—"lab" being 190-proof "laboratory-grade" alcohol—waiting for him. He plopped down on his previously constructed "easy chair"—pack boards leaned against up a hackberry tree, with his bedroll for a seat—took a deep swallow, and pronounced, "Now, partner, that was one fine day." So it was indeed. And it wasn't over yet. There was eating and staring into the fire pending.

JUNE 15, 1990

In lieu of moving on from this favored camp, we decided that our mutual honor, which dictated that we do something rather than just lounge around camp, would be satisfied by taking a ride up Pony Creek to the divide with Sand Creek. This trail was rarely used except by sheepherders. It was an easy trail except for a half-mile stretch that was steep enough to put us on foot leading the horses.

As Bill described it, "Whoever pioneered this trail didn't waste a lot of mountain putting in the switchbacks." Unlike most of the side canyons in the Snake River country, which are V-shaped, the bottom portions of Pony Creek are a bit over 200 feet wide, relatively flat, and populated by scattered hackberry trees. The areas along the side streams are densely populated with a mixture of alder, cottonwood, brambles, and shrubs—mostly ninebark and ocean spray, with a copious intermixing of poison oak. In fact, Pony Creek Canyon supports the most luxuriant growth of poison oak that I have ever seen anywhere, reaching heights of over twelve feet in places. As I am violently allergic to poison oak, I rode with my hands clutching the reins and held head high when we rode through such patches.

As we rode along Pony Creek for about three miles, we saw four mule deer does with two fawns and eleven pairs of chukars with young in tow. As we rode along, we hatched a plot to have a boat bring us and our gear up from Lewiston to the mouth of Sluice Creek next fall and drop us off for several days of chukar hunting. All the while, I was musing about how I could manage to stay out of the poison oak in the process of such a hunt. For damned sure, there was no way I would walk down this section of the trail. The situation made me itch all over just to look at it, and thinking about it made things worse.

It was a hard climb for the horses from the edge of the Snake River back up to the bench trail. We made frequent stops to let the horses blow and cool down. We arrived at the ridge above Pony Creek at midday and took a long lunch break to allow the horses a long breather. Through our binoculars we could make out numerous elk beds in the luxuriant grasses along the ridgeline. We spotted three cow elk and a calf in the shade of a rock on the adjacent ridge, maybe three-quarters of a mile away. The elk looked in our direction when we mounted and resumed our climb. As we got closer, they finally left the only shade for a mile in any direction and crossed over the ridge, putting us out of sight—and maybe out of mind.

It was another mile-and-a-half ride up the ridgeline to the Bench Trail. The elk trails that contoured around the canyon side were so heavily used that we took a wrong turn at one juncture—assuming the elk trail was the main trail—and came to a huge downed ponderosa pine that lay across the trail. Just on the other side of the tree, the trail led into a side canyon at a much steeper incline than even a Basque sheepherder would attempt. We very carefully dismounted, eased around our mounts on the uphill side, and turned them around. The trick was repeated with each of the packhorses. It was a tense moment, but the horses behaved as "mountain horses" should, and we led them back up the way we had come.

Upon regaining the bench trail, we turned south toward Freeze-out Saddle with the intent of camping at the site of Jack's Cabin. We had not camped there for at least five years, and things had changed in our absence. On our last visit, it was obvious that sheepherders had camped there regularly.

Now the signs indicated that it had been years since they or anyone else had used the camp. All that was left of Jack's Cabin was the dug-out flat ground and the remnants of several notched logs at one corner. Jack surely had a taste for magnificent scenery. The view was spectacular even for the Snake River Canyon, where such views are common.

The Seven Devils Mountains, their peaks still swathed in snow, glistened in the sunlight across the Snake River in Idaho. Shadows crept up the far side of the canyon as the sun sank lower in the western sky. A ruffed grouse was drumming, off and on, close to where we sat on our horses. In fact, it was so close that we could hear its low vocalizations between the episodes of drumming. I had never heard that sound before and was fascinated.

Supper was late. Our time leading up to the dinner hour had been spent just looking and listening—feeling and being—instead of making a fire and preparing food. A brief shower on the Idaho side arrived coincident with last light. Then the most spectacular rainbow that I had ever seen appeared for a very brief time before it dimmed and was extinguished as the sun dropped below the canyon's rim. We sat for a while in the darkness and watched the fire burn down to coals before dousing it and heading for the tents. I lay wide awake for what seemed a long time simply savoring the day.

JUNE 16, 1990

We consumed our last onion last night. With one onion allotted for each day of a trip, it was our traditional signal that the time had come to head for home. Bill insisted that it was a poor wilderness trip that included disagreements toward the end of the trip as to what day it was. The old onion trick put an end to such disputes.

As we rode along the bench trail, I pondered why it was so much more difficult for the lead rider—especially with packhorses in tow—than for those who plodded along behind. The lead rider had to be alert and sitting tight in the saddle as the lead horse seemed to have an evolution-imposed duty to be on the lookout for boogers, maybe even "big hairy bad-ass boogers." I surmised that, in a lead horse's mind, charred stumps could morph into grizzly bears or something equally terrible and dangerous. Rocks were also regarded with suspicion—was a cougar hiding there? Soft ground was to be gingerly tested and downed logs to be carefully examined before stepping over. The horses that followed, however, paid scant attention to much of anything and followed along without hesitation. Maybe they assumed that if the boogers didn't get the lead horse, they would not be a danger to those horses that blithely followed. Some horses do well out front, and some never do. We called the two or three horses in our string that were comfortable leading a pack string our "out-in-front horses."

Horses are not so different from people in that regard. There are "out-in-front" people who, just like the horses, remain supremely confident and calm, and if and when something spooky looms up in the trail, they deal with it. And there are "trail-behind" people who follow placidly wherever they are led. When Bill gave me horse lessons, he emphasized that horses were not all that different from people in their individualized ways. The trick was to "get in the horse's head"—i.e., think like a horse.

Riding into the Saddle Creek drainage, we began to see more and more elk as we went along. It was difficult to estimate their numbers as they emerged from, disappeared into, and reemerged from cover. But a reasonable estimate was from fifty to sixty adults. A number of the cows were followed closely by two- to three-week-old calves. Both cows and calves watched us attentively as we rode by at a distance of fifty or so yards. Perhaps the cows were reluctant to run away and out of sight. Adult cow elk can cover a lot of territory in a very short period of time, and they may have feared that their calves would not be able to keep up. Or maybe they sensed that we meant them no harm on this fine June day.

The rest of our trip out of the canyon was uneventful—if you consider it uneventful to travel easy on fine horses, without a hitch, through what surely deserves the description of "God's country."

CHAPTER 12

"YOU GOTTA KNOW WHAT'S ENOUGH"

I f ever I had truly *needed* to slip away into the wilderness, it was now. The political uproar over my committee's management plan for protecting the northern spotted owl's habitat continued to build, and those of us who had developed the recommendations were on the hot seat.

AUGUST 31, 1990

As Bill, Meg, and I saddled horses, sorted out equipment, and made up the packs in the dawn light, I kept fighting down the feeling that I should cancel this trip to the Eagle Cap. Maybe I should stay behind to defend the honor and integrity of my team of scientists.

Bill, a survivor of many intense wildlife management skirmishes over his forty-year career and one of the first wildlife biologists to be derisively identified by some as a "combat biologist," had not spoken more than a short sentence or two all morning. Now he sat down for a break on the bumper of my horse trailer, leaned forward on his knees, interlocked his fingers, and stared at the ground. He was thinking very carefully about what he wanted to say. I took a seat on the tailgate of the old Ford pickup and waited. Finally he spoke.

"Stay home if you think you should. But if I were you, I'd head for the hills to protect myself. You're tired and short-tempered, and it shows. To make things worse, you're dispirited, and you're letting the bastards wear you down. Plus, you're getting angrier and more paranoid by the day. And that can lead to saying and doing things that can come back to haunt you. And worst of all, you're beginning to feel sorry for yourself. You're vulnerable, and that's too bad because a lot of your associates and a lot of forest critters have a lot riding on you and your team. Worst of all, you don't even realize your miserable state of mind. But you're full grown and reasonably bright, so do what you think you need to do."

After a few minutes of quiet, I stood up and resumed packing with my ego and festering self-pity significantly diluted. Bill was right. This was not my first rodeo, after all.

Bill, Meg, and I unloaded the horses at the North Catherine Creek trailhead, directly east across the Grande Ronde Valley from La Grande. As the horses were already saddled, it took less than a half hour to adjust saddles, tighten the cinches, put on the packs, mount up, and start our ride up to Burger Pass. This late in the season, the horses were in good physical condition and climbed steadily without needing a break. The first two miles of the trail followed an old sheep driveway up a ridgeline. Over the past half century, herds of sheep had essentially denuded the ridgeline of vegetation.

The volcanic ash deposited by the explosion of Mount Mazama centuries earlier was stirred up and billowed from under the horses' hooves. Riding through the dust with bandanas tied over our noses and mouths was not pleasant. I wondered about the horses as they snorted occasionally to clear their nostrils. In my efforts to ignore the dust, I kept thinking of the dip I would take late this afternoon in the clear, cold Minam River. It was an eagerly anticipated pleasure as grit ground between my teeth and grated under my eyelids.

Then, at long last, we turned off the old stock driveway onto a newly constructed trail that climbed at a steady six percent grade toward Burger Pass. In a couple of hours, we gained enough elevation to allow us to look over the vast tree-covered foothills to the jagged peaks of the Elkhorn Mountains across Baker Valley to the south. With the emergence of the broad vistas, my personal problems seemed to wither.

My ego also seemed to shrink proportionally with the increase in elevation and the distance from civilization. When the astronauts stood on the moon and looked back on the good earth, they must have been profoundly changed—at least for a moment. If I had my way, I would spend much of my time bringing "big" men to high places in the wilderness and watch egos—mine and theirs—shrivel to appropriate size.

When we reached Burger Pass, we dismounted to stretch our legs and adjust saddles, britchens, and packs for the downhill. As far as we could see, mountains and valleys stretched out in every direction. Off to the south, there were hundreds of miles of logging roads visible, and the forested hillsides gave the appearance of a crazily skewed chessboard with clearcuts and blocks of still-forested areas providing the contrasts. Farther away yet, we could see valleys filled with groomed fields, occasional farm buildings, and even a small city.

But when I squinted, I could see things as I perceived them to have been two centuries earlier. Off to the north were rugged granite mountains separated by steep valleys with clear, cold streams in the bottoms. That was where we were headed—where I truly needed to go and never more so than now. Standing safely at the edge of the wilderness, I could admit to that, at least to myself.

Our descent into the drainage cut by the Minam River was via the recently reconstructed Elk Creek Trail. I had mixed emotions about such new trails. They would be much easier on people, horses, and the land. But almost anyone will be able to traverse the new trails. No longer will they be used primarily by hunters and fishers and other sojourners who are tough enough to walk the relatively primitive trails with heavy packs or those with good mountain horses and the experience and the will to take some risks.

But times and things change. I had to admit to myself that such changes were likely for the better. Those who remembered the rigors and the tests afforded by the old trails would soon fade away, and a new experience would be judged as good as or better than what had been before. I recognized my feelings were strangely elitist and wasn't proud of it, but that was how I felt. I knew I should adjust to new circumstances. And I would adjust. But not today. Tomorrow maybe.

We reached our old Elk Camp only to discover a really first-class mess left by the hunters who had camped here last, likely during last elk season. To call them "slob hunters" would have been too kind.

Sheets of black plastic that had waterproofed the roof of a tent were scattered about. Tent poles were left where they were discarded when the hunters broke camp. A pile of garbage included bottles and cans, aluminum foil, and toilet paper. The latrine ditch had been left open. I was sick-mad, as if some stupid, uncaring bastards had trashed my home—my personal space. The place would be clean and in order when we left. It would give us a chance to do some good, at least in our own eyes, by caring for something we loved and cherished as being, in a way, our very own.

Bill was too old and experienced with such desecrations to be angry or sad. He simply took it in stride, making no comment as we went about cleaning up the mess and putting things in order. The man had developed calluses on his soul that provided him some protection.

SEPTEMBER 1, 1990

We sat close to the fire at dawn, waiting for the three horses that had been turned loose to graze for a couple of hours to come back to camp. Having lost a day of fishing in cleaning up the camp, we decided not to move camp after only one night, as we had originally planned. Rather, we would spend today fishing off and on as the spirit moved us.

Once the breakfast dishes were washed and tucked away and the early-morning chill left with the rising sun, it would be time to "wet a fly," as Bill put it. The warmth that came with the new day's sun in the canyon bottom stirred insects into flights that sometimes ended in inadvertent water landings. That, in turn, provided meals for the fish. The appearance of tell-tale circles in the still waters let us know when the trout were in a mood for feeding. We were eager to cast our offerings upon the waters.

For some four hours, I fished my way slowly upstream on the rocky bed of the Minam River. Bill said that he had never seen the river lower in more than forty years. Though the flow was but a large trickle, the deep pools were still there, and the fish could be seen idling in the crystal-clear waters. A perfect cast with the perfect fly put some of those fish to rest amid the wet wild onion leaves in the burlap sack tied to my belt.

The sunlight cut through the trees like hundreds of spotlights, large and small. My casts were as near perfect as I could make them. The dry flies landed and drifted just so across the sun-dappled pools. But the fish exhibited no interest in my carefully presented offerings. Not a single fish rose to my flies. Oddly, I didn't care. The fish would be there another day. Or maybe this afternoon. Or, if not then, early tomorrow. But I felt there would never be another day as perfect as this one, just when I needed such a day the most. It was a blessed day, a gift that deserved recognition as such.

Just below the last pool that I intended to use to practice my casting, I encountered—at a respectable distance of fifty to sixty yards—a young black bear making a meal of a spawned-out salmon. Just to be on the safe side, I loosened the strap that secured my .45 caliber Colt pistol in its shoulder holster under my left arm. Seemingly, the young bear and I had become aware of each other at the same moment and simultaneously concluded that we represented no threat to each other. The bear resumed its meal, and I watched until the cold water began to numb my feet and ankles and inspired me to scramble up and sit on a huge rock in midstream. At that point, the bear had enough of me and retreated into the alders, leaving what was left of the salmon for the impatiently waiting magpies. The magpies quickly accepted the bear's unintended invitation to dinner. I snapped the strap that secured the pistol in its holster.

I warmed up as I sat on the rock in the full sunlight with the stream swirling by on both sides. The warmth lulled me into a doze that came and went without dreams. When the sun dipped behind the trees and shadows covered my perch, the upstream breeze was too cold for comfort. Reluctantly I stepped into the cold water, crossed the stream, climbed the bank, and worked my way back through the lodgepole thicket to camp.

It was a slow journey. Most of the lodgepole pines in the stand had been killed by an outbreak of mountain pine beetles five or so years earlier. The dead trees, toppled by winds from various directions, formed a jumble that made me imagine a game of pickup sticks played by giants. A new lodgepole forest was emerging from the tangle, with some of the trees already approaching three feet in height. I could tell from tracks and pellet groups that elk and deer grazed here frequently in this seemingly impenetrable jumble of downed tree trunks.

Bill and I arrived in camp at about the same time. Meg, a book in her lap, was seated on a pile of folded manty tarps and leaning against a log, sleeping in the late-afternoon sun. Well, I thought, we each enjoy our wilderness journeys in our individual ways. Bill had two very small fish in his possession. Ever competitive, he queried me as to my success. When I signaled "zero" with thumb and forefinger touching, he seemed relieved. I made a mental note to ask for some fishing advice when we were sitting around the fire tonight. He likes to offer advice, and I can use all the good advice I can get.

SEPTEMBER 2, 1990

We packed up and moved our camp to just above where Sturgill Creek joins the North Minam River, a place known to us as Sturgill Camp or Three Buck Camp. Today seemed a good day for a supper based on yet-to-be acquired ruffed grouse. So as we rode down the trail, Bill allowed Blitz, his shorthaired pointer, to patrol the forest along the sides of the trail. We had not traveled a quarter mile when she went down on point and I could see "supper" on the ground, not ten feet in front of her, moving slowly through the huckleberry shrubs—three adult ruffed grouse.

Fortunately for our supper plans, grouse in the wilderness—at least this wilderness—seldom see people who might do them harm. The grouse waited, almost patiently, as I dismounted, pulled my over-and-under Charles Daley 20-gauge shotgun from its leather scabbard, and eased forward around the pack string.

The first grouse that I intended to turn into supper stopped and stretched its neck to look back at the dog—a big mistake. At the shotgun's report, the second grouse flew up and across the trail—two for the pot. The third bird squatted and, quite mistakenly, gave me time to reload. Then, as Bill signaled Blitz forward, the grouse rose straight up and flew straight down the trail—three for the pot and one apiece for supper.

Three more grouse flew up into the trees and seemed to watch curiously as Blitz gathered up their demised brethren and deposited

*Bill and Jack at Sturgill Camp, or Three Buck Camp, on the
North Minam River, Eagle Cap Wilderness, 1990.*

them at my feet. Luckily for the grouse in the trees, we now had adequate grouse for supper. The grouse sat in the tree thirty yards off the trail, craning their necks as I mounted my mare and we rode on down the trail.

The ride back to Three Buck Camp was uneventful but immensely enjoyable. The horses moved along the newly refurbished trail at a steady five miles per hour with the packs riding easy. It was a time for reflection. There was no place I would rather be, and on top of that, we had a grouse apiece for supper as well as onions and bacon with which to cook them.

SEPTEMBER 3, 1990

We decided that, no matter how good or bad the fishing, it was to be trout for supper tonight. So it was decided, and so it would be done. There were two places where we might catch the trout. One was 200 yards from camp in either Sturgill Creek or the Minam River. Or we could travel some seven miles and climb 2,000 feet in elevation to reach Green Lake. We put the question to a vote. Green Lake won in a two-to-zero landslide, with Meg abstaining. Carrying out this mandate would entail a fourteen-mile round trip, but of course the effort would make the fish—which we would surely catch—that much more delectable.

When we arrived at Green Lake in the early afternoon, fish were rising on the mirrored surface of the lake, loosing the pent-up competitor that lay just below the surface of Bill's psyche. He decided that we should let lunch wait so he could set up his fishing outfit and get to the rising fish ASAP.

He wanted to catch the first fish, the most fish, the biggest fish, and the last fish. On the other hand, I couldn't care less who caught what, when, where, or how many. My less competitive nature made it possible for us to be compatible hunting and fishing partners. I was savoring my grouse meat sandwich when I heard Bill's call of "fish on." Well, I thought, good for you!

My secret desire was to catch a nap in the meadow. But if we were to have a bounty of trout for supper, my presence would be required lakeside with fishing tackle. The fish were indeed rising—some slapping the water—all across the still surface of the lake.

But every rising fish seemed about five feet farther than I could place a fly. Surely, I thought, there were fish closer that were not rising. Persistence paid off. Both Bill and I hooked, played, and landed a fish now and again. The fish were plump and almost identical in size—about a foot long. The colors of the spawning eastern brooks were vivid but faded quickly as death entailed a transition from a symbol of a beautiful wild place to a succulent morsel. The obtaining, the journey, was everything. In the end, a sandwich was just a sandwich—or was it?

The legal limit was ten fish per licensed fisherman, but we decided that six small fish apiece would be adequate for supper for the three of us. There was a time when Bill and I would have fished until we caught a limit in order to prove something, but in my increasing age I could ask, "prove what to whom and why?" To be mature enough to know what is enough—of not only fish but everything—was a blessing that comes to the fortunate along with age.

A colleague that I often fished with when I was stationed in Morgantown, West Virginia, told me a story that made this point. It seemed that prior to World War II, mountain folk in Appalachia collected ginseng root and sold it to the local general store to obtain enough cash to buy shoes, shotgun shells, a pair of overalls, and so forth. When the United Stares entered the war in late 1941, there was a sudden increase in demand for ginseng root. A young economist working for the War Department knew just how to meet that increased demand—triple the going rate for ginseng root. His logic was impeccable—triple the price and get three times the amount of ginseng root.

But to the surprise of all, only one-third as much ginseng root showed up at the buyers. It was a head scratcher, so the economist set out to find out the reason for this unexplained departure from tested economic principles. It took only one interview to get the answer. The patriarch of the family, whose cabin was at the head of the hollow, said, when interviewed, "We only needed enough cash money to buy what we couldn't make or grow for ourselves. It only took a third as long as it used to for us to get what we needed. Why would we work longer or harder than that?"

The economist said, "But you could have made three times the money you made in the past with the same amount of effort. Why didn't you do that?" The old mountaineer looked puzzled. "Son, you've got to know what enough is or you can't ever get there. And you'll wreck yourself and your family just trying." Six fish apiece was enough.

SEPTEMBER 4, 1990

We rode down the trail from Green Lake to the Minam River and made camp just downstream from the mouth of Elk Creek. From there, we could reach the trailhead tomorrow in an easy day's ride, load up the horses, and be home in the late afternoon.

Along the trail we saw several groups of grouse—adult females with their young. We let them be. We had already enjoyed our much-anticipated supper of ruffed grouse and our meal of fresh-caught trout. The day was sufficient unto itself. After all, we knew what was enough.

SEPTEMBER 5, 1990

In riding up the Elk Creek Trail and over Burger Pass, we stopped several times to scout out a campsite for the upcoming deer season. We found a beautiful spot in an island of big grand firs in a big wet meadow that would likely be dry in the fall. It was at just the right elevation to allow us to hunt—from camp and on foot—the big mule deer bucks that sometimes lingered along the timber line in late fall. As a bonus, the scenery was magnificent.

The peaks of the Wallowa Mountains stood out across the Minam River drainage. And there was more deer sign around than we had seen on the entire trip up to this point. It was a good indication that one or both of us just might slay a wily buck, although that didn't really matter in the larger scheme of things. The companionship and the hunt would be enough.

CHAPTER 13

GREEN PASTURES AND STILL WATERS

I had not been back to La Grande since Meg's funeral. After an absence of six months, La Grande seemed so slow-paced, calm, polite, and quiet in contrast to my new life in Washington, D.C. I was winding up some business in eastern Oregon following an emotionally difficult trip to Glenwood Springs, Colorado, where on July 6 fourteen firefighters had died in a blowup of a wildfire on Storm King Mountain. The losses weighed heavily on my mind, and intolerable events seemed to be piling up. I felt very alone and increasingly sorry for myself. Then it came to me that Meg would have had little or no patience with my attitude. In her own sweet way she would have booted me in the ass and told me to "get back on the horse." So with wilderness so close, I declared myself on "annual leave" from my USFS job and joined Bill on a horse trip into the Eagle Cap Wilderness in the Wallowa Mountains.

JULY 21, 1994

I went into the Safeway store to buy the supplies for our trip and was stopped by a good many people who welcomed me, expressed their heartfelt condolences about Meg's passing, and asked, "How the hell are you?" For the first time since Meg and I left La Grande for

Washington, I was overtaken by a wave of homesickness, buffered by a reassuring feeling that, after all, I did belong somewhere.

I felt out of place in Washington and was not entirely comfortable as chief of the USFS. I had been a wildlife biologist—a field biologist and a research scientist—for thirty-seven years but the "head cheese" for some 35,000 employees for only a year. Those feelings were suddenly much magnified now that I was back in La Grande, my more natural habitat. For part of the day, I fought down the wild urge to place a call to the secretary of agriculture and resign as chief.

But I knew, deep down, that Meg would not have been proud of me for even entertaining such thoughts—which were nothing more than hiding from responsibility, duty, and reality. The final lines of a Robert Frost poem came to mind and brought my daydreaming to an end:

> The woods are lovely, dark and deep,
> But I have promises to keep,
> And miles to go before I sleep,
> And miles to go before I sleep.

That was the simple fact of the matter. I still had "miles to go before I sleep."

Bill was waiting for me at his house with the horses saddled and loaded in the horse trucks, the camping gear wrapped up in the manties, and the panniers open and waiting for the groceries. We were lashing the packs on the horses at the trailhead at Moss Springs by midmorning.

When we reached Red's Horse Ranch, I recalled the first time I had ridden into Red's. In 1973 I was acting as a member of a Wilderness Review Team made up of USFS personnel and biologists from the Oregon Department of Fish and Wildlife. The Wallowa-Whitman National Forest had recently taken over Red's, and commercial operations had been shut down. A seasonal USFS hand watched over things and dealt with backpackers and horse outfits that came through the place. The buildings and fences were falling into disrepair.

The windsock on a pole at the edge of the grass airstrip was in similarly sad condition. As we rode through the place, I had a feeling of emptiness. There were no livestock and no equipment in sight. Grass was growing unkempt in the yards and on the old runway. Though we neither saw nor heard anyone, there was laundry hanging from a clothesline, indicating that the caretaker was somewhere about.

Now, some twenty years after my first of many visits to Red's, the only difference I could see as we rode across the airstrip was that the flag of the Confederate States of America was missing; it was originally flown, I was informed, by the owner/operator as a symbol of defiance of the federal government and the USFS in particular. The flag of a squashed rebellion had been replaced, at long last, with the flag of the United States of America. But the outlook for Red's Horse Ranch remained the same—there was no way it could ever be a paying proposition.

The USFS purchased the place for some cash and a land trade adding up to about $1.4 million, which was, in my opinion at least, way more than a fair price. There had been considerable pushback from some local folks who didn't want to lose the tourist attraction or who simply didn't want the USFS to own any more land in Wallowa County. Red's heirs, who were more than willing sellers, took on the complainers, fearful that they would queer the pending deal.

The USFS had been supported by many others in efforts to eliminate inholdings within the newly expanded boundaries of the Eagle Cap Wilderness. Operating a dude ranch deep inside the Eagle Cap Wilderness was clearly incompatible with the intent of the Wilderness Act. The USFS had been queried by many, including members of Congress, as to what the agency would do with the property. Would it be operated as a concession? Used as an administrative site? Maintained as a "historic" site? Or burned down to return it to "wilderness" condition, a place "untrammeled by man?"

Though I didn't know what the answer should be, I found it difficult to see how operating a resort or routinely using the adjacent landing strip could be in keeping with the spirit of the Wilderness Act, though there were landing strips in several other Wilderness Areas that I knew of. It was likely that, whatever the supervisor of the Wallowa-Whitman National Forest decided; it would be controversial, immediately appealed, and might well end up on the desk of the chief of the USFS—my desk at the moment. So I reminded myself to ask questions while expressing no opinions that might come back to haunt me—and the USFS.

We camped at the meadow that had been formed behind the old splash dam on the Minam River. Meg and I had camped here on her last horse trip with me into the Eagle Cap Wilderness. As we sat around the campfire and talked, I remembered how beautiful Meg had been—and I was certainly not the only one who thought that—and how full of life. She retained that special beauty in spite of suffering from cancer. She always took on life as a great adventure and maintained that attitude all the way to the end, insisting that I take the job of USFS chief in Washington, D.C., though it meant she would surely die far removed from friends and family. She explained that she was never far from friends and family in her heart and mind—and that was what counted.

As evening settled in, I breathed deeply and let myself be enveloped in the magic of the wilderness. The stresses and strains of being the new USFS chief seemed to dissipate. I could hear the river, the hum of insects, the very slight breeze in the trees, the crackle of the fire, the birds' songs, and the horse bells.

Three camp does came to the edge of our camp. One had a torn ear that flopped at a crazy angle. I had seen her here at this camp before—was it last year or the year before that? Then, just at sundown, two hobbled horses that were grazing in the meadow came to attention and stared into the trees across the Minam River. We saw three cow elk and three calves emerge from the dark timber to graze at the edge of the meadow along the cut bank. We watched them for close to an hour before they disappeared in the gathering darkness.

When it was time to go to bed, I walked out into the meadow, spread a manty tarp on the ground, rolled out my bedroll, and covered it with another tarp. A generous application of "bug dope" took care of the mosquitoes—for the moment. It was especially important to me on this night to see the stars. As I lay there on my back with my hands behind my head, staring up at the sky, it came to me that I had not seen the stars in six months. There are no stars visible from where I lived—alone now—in a condominium in Rosslyn, Virginia. The stars there, even on a clear night, are obscured by lights and smog, and I intended to take advantage of this too-rare opportunity to do some serious stargazing. But I was dead asleep before the stars had emerged in all their glory. I did not waken until I smelled coffee boiling. For the first time in several weeks I had not dreamed of the fourteen firefighters who had perished fighting the wildfire at Storm King Mountain.

The new day came clear and cool. My feather jacket, which had been stuffed into the sack that contained my down sleeping bag, felt good as we sat around the fire, ate our fried Spam and eggs, and sipped steaming coffee. Talk seemed superfluous. The camp does returned and hung around in the edge of the trees.

We left camp via horseback and traveled upstream along the Minam River on a well-laid and well-tended trail, seeing trout rising in the river, a bald eagle soaring, six elk fording the river, and the tracks of a mountain lion and a black bear. When we arrived at our Three Buck Camp, it appeared that no one else had camped here since we did so in the middle of last summer. The cache of cut-to-length wood for the sheepherder stove was as we had left it, hidden under the protection of a large spruce. Grass stood tall and ungrazed by horses in the small clearing in the lodgepole stand. There was a dug-out spring within ten yards of the fireplace. The fishing for small eastern brook trout on this stretch of river had always been outstanding. We would see about that.

Bill and I—sometimes accompanied by our wives—had camped here at least forty nights over the past twenty years. I took pride in observing that most passersby never identified the place as a suitable camping spot. We practiced as close to "leave no trace" camping as was possible, save for the woodpile that was well hidden and would end up as ashes—now sooner rather than later.

I liked revisiting the same old camps. There was a feeling of "home" based on collective memories. I knew the pools in the river. I knew behind just what boulder a carefully cast bucktail coachman might well elicit a strike from a trout lying there and waiting for the current to deliver a meal of a floating insect.

We supped on trout battered in cornmeal, salt, and pepper and fried in bacon grease, with a pan of biscuits cooked in a reflector oven and thin-sliced sweet onions on the side—Bill called it "wilderness ambrosia." It seemed the best of all possible meals, and at that moment perception was indeed reality. Better yet, there was no need to dress for dinner—hands and faces splashed clean in the cold river water would do.

Again I arranged my bed in the middle of the meadow with the expectation of seeing the sky awash with stars. But not long after the stars began to emerge in the darkening sky, sleep sneaked up on me. Sometime in the night, when I awakened to answer a call from nature, the moon was full and the meadow was awash in what seemed the brightest moonlight I had ever seen. Owls were calling from several different directions. When I sat up and threw off the sleeping bag and manty tarp, I saw three elk in the moonlight grazing in the meadow with the three horses Bill had left untied. Now the moon was so bright that even the brightest stars were barely visible. I was not disappointed in my decision to sleep out in the open.

My mind and soul were totally at peace. I dreamed of the many pleasant times spent in this camp. I could visualize Meg walking through the meadow, three forked-horn mule deer hanging from a meat pole tied between two lodgepole pines, fish flashing in the late-afternoon sun as they broke water in striking at a fly, and the laughter that came easily around the campfire. Such magic places produce feelings in me of a special kind of "ownership"—not in fee title but in spirit. We the People do hold title, of course, to the Eagle Cap Wilderness in the Wallowa-Whitman National Forest—at least for now.

That circumstance, as I pondered on it, seemed a very special and wonderful thing. This place, and all the places like it, belonged to me simply because I was a citizen/resident of the United States—those now alive and those yet to be born. And that would remain so as long as we, and they, treasure these places and do what is necessary to hold on to and care for them. That, I knew, was no sure thing. There would be an increasing struggle as to whether We the People should own such increasingly valuable treasure. Would it not be better to turn such places into the more tangible and better understood and appreciated treasure of another kind—"money" and "jobs" and "tax revenues?" Would not the states, which are "closer to the people," be more rational stewards than the federal government?

Bill and I, the great prognosticators that we deemed ourselves to be, thought that such a challenge was certain to arise more frequently and more forcefully as natural resources per capita dwindled, populations increased, and the public debt inexorably grew. Would the time come when We the People would essentially sell this wonderful inheritance—unique in all the world—for pottage? Perhaps it was the affinity for special places on the national forests that motivated some citizens to protest against clear-cut logging and the associated access roads in places on federal lands that were special to them. I could understand how those folks feel. I know how I would feel—and likely react—if, during our next trip, I encountered stakes along the trail into Three Buck Camp and paint on selected trees, indicating the pending arrival of a new USFS road and, ultimately, the cutting of the marked trees.

Nearly every section of national forest that has not yet been logged evokes very strong concerns among people who recognize the special qualities of those places, qualities that, to their way of thinking, would be negatively impacted by road building and logging and subsequent management for the production of timber. Why are such feelings so very strong? Likely, I thought, individuals treasure these places because of their personal experiences in and associations with such special places. If so, when they struggle to protect special places, it might be concluded that they struggle to protect themselves—or their images of themselves.

Bill and I silently watched the campfire crumble into ashes, listening to the night sounds, lost in our individual thoughts.

JULY 22, 1994

We had intended to ride up to Green Lake today to sample the fishing and see some beautiful country in the process. But somehow we just never got around to getting started and spent the day eating, drinking coffee, sporadically napping in the shade, shooting the bull, watching the horses graze in the meadow, and—in my case—catching up on my journal.

I had not done a good job of journal tending during my first six months in Washington. Looking back on that lapse, I could blame the constant physical and emotional exhaustion. When coupled with a lack of time to simply think and contemplate what was going on around me, journal tending suffered. I regretted that.

In retrospect, that had probably been a serious mistake. So many of the decisions I had made and actions I had taken demanded careful consideration and postpartum rumination. I needed to consider what went right and what went wrong—and why. How else could I understand how to do my new job better? In order to improve my performance, I wished I could look back on journals kept by my predecessors for insights and guidance. On the other hand, I had been advised against being too diligent in keeping a journal, as it could come back to bite me if it were subpoenaed in a legal dispute.

As a research scientist, I was most comfortable with a process of decision making that was methodical, logical, subject to peer review, published, analyzed, debated, criticized, and synthesized. Now the process of decision making involved being briefed by staff, accepting or rejecting staff recommendations, or asking for more information. Such took place several times a day. By the end of the business week, decisions made on Monday had faded into memory by Friday night, even before they were executed. And tomorrow was another day with more decisions pending.

The disappearance of the sun behind the ridge and the fading light made writing in my journal difficult and then impossible. At dark I heard a ruffed grouse drumming and the sound of horse bells as Bill caught the horses that had been loosed to graze and led them into camp. He tied the horses to the picket lines, took their bells off, and put them on the two horses that he was turning loose for their turn to graze and drink. The horses took off for the meadow at a run, kicking their heels in the air. Bill had taught me that, in any string of horses, each horse has a special companion—a buddy. One of the ways Bill managed our string was to make sure that he understood those relationships and took advantage of them. He never turned two close buddies loose to graze at the same time on the theory that the free horse would not stray far from its tied buddy. When appetites were satiated, it was not unusual to see the two buddies—one tied and one free—standing head to head. Understanding horse—and human—behavior was Bill's forte.

Light was fading now—and quickly. I heard a ruffed grouse doing its last drumming of the day. It got cooler fast as the sun went down behind the ridge. It was time to stoke up the fire and have a "sundowner," an expression for a cup of brandy that Bill had picked up on safari in Kenya. I put on my down jacket and began preparing supper. I was thinking what a very good day it was to be alive—and to be in this very special place with a very special friend and colleague.

Bill was sitting on a folded manty tarp and leaning back on a pack board braced against a lodgepole pine. Out of the clear blue sky he quoted a passage from Psalms, "He maketh me to lie down in green pastures; he leadeth me beside the still waters; he restoreth my soul." I smiled and nodded. He continued with another quote from Psalms, "Thou shalt not be afraid for the terror by night; nor for the arrow that flieth by day." I was thinking similar thoughts but not in such eloquent terms.

Sometimes the crotchety old bastard amazed me with what came out of his mouth—quotes from the Holy Bible, Shakespeare, Aldo Leopold, Keats, Browning, and Will Rogers, not to mention the comic strip characters Elmer Fudd and Blondie Bumstead. He much preferred to be known by his carefully cultivated and maintained image of a rugged outdoorsman, no-nonsense wildlife biologist of the old school, grizzled old horse soldier, and stern commander of his "troops."

Only a very few close friends knew him as a "closet intellectual" and incessant reader. He was not a traditional religionist while being something of biblical scholar. He told me once that, in his youth, he spent several seasons alone manning fire lookouts (his dad worked for the Oregon Forestry Department) in the backcountry of western Oregon with nothing to read but a King James version of the Bible. He had an amazing talent for remembering much of what he had read and frequently quoted from those readings. For the next several hours, conversation was limited, as such seemed merely intrusive and a detraction from the magic of the wilderness. I drifted off to sleep staring into the campfire. When I was awakened by the cold of the deepening night, my friend had gone to bed, leaving me alone curled up next to the coals. My sleeping bag was calling.

JULY 23, 1994

We spent most of our second day at Three Buck Camp doing little more than eating, sleeping in the shade, sitting around the fire drinking coffee, making a few halfhearted efforts in pursuit of the wily trout, and wrangling horses—turning some loose and tying up others. In midafternoon we packed up our outfit and moved on down the trail to the main Minam River and another of our favorite camps. This camp too was filled with magic memories. There were memories of fish (likely bigger and more plentiful in memory than in reality) enticed to our flies and then made into meals (surely more delectable in memory than in reality). We reminisced about elk we had seen grazing in the old burn across the river. I remembered lying on a manty tarp and watching the stars, often with Meg resting her head on my shoulder. In the darkness there was no need to hide or even wipe away the tears.

A contest broke out as to who would be the first to spot a shooting star or maybe a satellite. In the meantime we listened to the night sounds—oh, the memories. This whole trip, for me, had been one of reverie. I pondered if I was moving into a time of life where I was more and more sustained by memories of good things and good times gone by than looking forward. Was the past becoming more compelling and demanding of attention than the new and undone? Or was it that I needed to touch the past, remember how good it had been, and then build on that and move on? I desperately wanted that to be the case and fought the urge to dwell in the past, though at the moment it seemed a much better place.

Our trip from Three Buck Camp to our new camp in the Big Burn took only about three hours. When we rode into the Big Burn, the sky was clear and the wind still, and we guessed the temperature to be near 100 degrees. Our shirts were sweated through. Whatever the temperature, it was most assuredly "pretty damned hot."

After unpacking and unsaddling the horses and setting up camp, we took a two-purpose dip in the river: to wash off the sweat

Inspecting ambitious beaver activity in the Big Burn,
Eagle Cap Wilderness, 1994.

and grime and to soak away the heat. We found a place where the river's flow bounced off a rock face and incised a deep pool. The water was clear and almost too cold for skinny dipping. It took me several minutes and at least three tries to ease into the water up to my waist. Then, after several deep breaths and a 1-2-3 count to steel myself, I went completely under. When I surfaced and gasped for air, I deemed the experience "bracing." I forced myself to stay in the water up to my neck as long as I could stand it.

This form of "wilderness air conditioning" worked wonders and helped us to beat the heat for several hours until the body's propensity to bring its temperature up to normal won out. Two more such cool-off sessions seemed appropriate as the day wore on. Yet our antics did not seem to alter the behavior of the trout, as Bill and I both were able to land three nice rainbow trout apiece in between our dips in the pool. As we already had enjoyed two meals of trout on this trip, we behaved as gentlemen fly-fishers should and caught and released our fish in a style we thought becoming. That, I admitted, went against my grain, as I was more of a catch-'em-and-eat-'em kind of guy. It was a good thing to periodically revert to a hunter-gatherer mode.

As it had so many times on such trips, little marvels of life came to mind. There were so many species—ranging from single-celled organisms to vertebrates of many sizes to fit every niche. In their totality they both exploited and maintained the ecosystems of which they were part and parcel. From where I sat on a log by a huge beaver-gnawed tree, I could see dozens of life forms each making its living in some special way. There were both mule deer and elk tracks in the sand along the river and signs of their grazing the sedges growing along the bank.

This flat in the bend of the river had been home to a family of beavers for the twenty years that I had known the place. It had been rendered something of a beaver paradise by the stretches of alders along the banks. The current was too variable—and too strong when in flood in the spring—to allow either beaver dams or beaver houses to withstand the currents. So the resourceful beavers exercised their "plan B" and dug out dens in the riverbank. The remains of several old beaver dens were discernible in the cut bank on the outside of the bend in the river. The activities of the beavers either didn't provide enough wear on their ever-growing teeth to keep pace with their growth, which was my logical surmise as a wildlife biologist, or some of the beavers were simply overachievers, gnawing away at trees that were some thirty-six inches or more in diameter at breast height. That was my more winsome idea.

I spent a considerable amount of my time on these trips musing on one thing or another. In this case, my musing was engendered by the stumps of several trees on the flat more than fourteen inches in diameter some two feet off the ground—the height at which the beavers gnaw off trees. There was one larger-diameter tree close to the river that a seriously ambitious beaver was gnawing away on at the moment. I sat down and contemplated the tree for some time and marveled at the beaver's ability and patience to undertake such a task. What the hell was the beaver going to do with a tree of that size once it was down? Well, I thought, maybe it's the branches of the downed tree that the beaver was after. If that were so, how had the beaver figured that out?

One of the horses that were feeding on a sandbar in the river used his long tail to whisk away a horsefly sucking blood from his shoulder. A mosquito sucked blood from a crease in the knuckle of my middle finger. I could see and even hear spruce budworms feeding on the foliage of a branch hanging down close to my face. I noted the pitch tubes on a lodgepole pine, indicating the presence of a mountain pine beetle beneath the bark; its tunneling through the cambium layer would eventually doom the tree.

A fish jumped clear out of the water in the pool in the process of consuming an insect that came to rest on the surface. A kingfisher dove from its perch to take a small fish—perhaps the same fish that just broke the surface of the pond. I saw where a black bear had traveled along the sandbar and had torn open a rotting log, likely in search of insects. There were birds feeding around me—some in the canopy, some on the tree trunks, and some on the ground. I heard small stirrings in the leaves, and though I could not see them, I knew that there were chipmunks and pine squirrels about. A goshawk darted across the opening in the canopy afforded by the river; I guessed it

would sooner or later take a pine squirrel or chipmunk that was scur-
rying about in the litter in search of a snack. And in that litter were
insects and worms and fungi and bacteria.

Schoolchildren are taught about the "web of life" that I was
contemplating—but without this laboratory. On this fine day it plea-
sured me to make my own observations and consider them—one more
time—as new knowledge leading to improved understanding. The
wilderness was a well-appointed classroom always awaiting students.
Life seemed, at that moment, to be so simple and yet so complex and
so wondrous. We know enough now to be able to contemplate and
develop an appreciation for life's complexity and to understand that
we *Homo sapiens* exist only as a part of that overall system. I had visited and worked among many native peoples—in North America and
in India, Pakistan, South America, Israel, and Africa—who smiled at
my "science" and my observations. They intimated that their forefa-
thers had always known such things. They seemed to politely ask, by
way of knowing smiles, "What took you so long?"

In a few days I would be back in my office in Washington, D.C.,
with a view of the Washington Monument from my office window.
I would be freshly barbered, dressed in a three-piece suit fresh from
the cleaners, making decisions that would influence how these relationships played out over hundreds of thousands of acres of national
forests. In guiding, making, or approving such decisions, there were
dilemmas for a scientist turned administrator. The scientist is trained
to be aware of complexities, some barely guessed at, that would come
to bear on the future of forest lands and rangelands. Yet the pragmatic administrator knows and understands that burgeoning human
populations must and will exploit resources to attain the "good life."
Caution in the absence of complete knowledge—the "precautionary
principle"—will be, in the face of inexorably increasing demands,
ever more difficult to apply.

Dale Robertson, my predecessor as USFS chief, pronounced
"ecosystem management" to be the new approach for managing the
national forests. Chief Robertson's decision was based upon the stated
purpose of the Endangered Species Act: "conservation of ecosystems
upon which threatened or endangered species may depend." Admit-

tedly a rather grandiose and presumptive term, "ecosystem management" will require the maintenance of ecosystem functions and forms while manipulating those systems to sustainably produce needed goods and services. His pronouncement raised a rather frightening question: "Just how the hell do we go about doing that?" And is this really possible? Yet increasing human populations with increasing demands dictate that we try. It seemed to me that, in that trying, "humbleness while learning" would be an appropriate mantra.

As managers of renewable natural resources, we *Homo sapiens* have, for all of our recorded history, been too certain of our knowledge, too confident in the correctness of our positions, too confident in our abilities, and too arrogant to listen to other voices expressing other views and begging for caution. The scientist in me says to consider all of our approaches and actions to be experiments, to be consistently evaluated and tweaked into new experiments in management. The process, of course, involves a never-ending experiment marked by myriad mid-course corrections. That is what our species has done since we stood up on two feet and began to speak and develop, record, and pass on experience and knowledge.

Now USFS leaders and others must come to grips with constantly adjusting our ongoing and accumulating management experiments. That necessity is complicated by erosion in public confidence, approval, and support. There is, after all, such a thing as "political science" to consider in addition to the biological and ecological sciences, including the "dismal science" of economics. We seem unable to learn and adjust rapidly enough from our mistakes and setbacks to develop new approaches to facilitate a leadership role in conservation. In trying to adjust, we became so enamored of process—sometimes to the detriment of substance—that we severely damaged our ability to lead and adjust. The rapidly emerging specter of climate change and global warming exacerbates that emerging understanding.

Do professionals in the business of managing natural resources still have a significant role in defining how, when, and where natural resources are exploited and simultaneously conserved? Or do we merely produce information, conduct and report upon research, formulate potential courses of action, and then seek to capture the illusive ghost of public consensus, not to mention blessing by often fickle courts? The "public"—even those individuals who are informed enough to have well-grounded opinions—seems destined to be more or less evenly divided on every issue. Who, then, will lead? Who, then, can lead? Should such leadership be the responsibility and the role of "experts" in the integrated "science" of ecosystem management—which includes people?

My musings ended as waning light made writing in my journal impossible. The emergence of crepuscular mosquitoes prompted me to head for camp and dig out the mosquito dope buried somewhere in my saddlebags. Applying the repellent would allow me to lie out in the meadow and study the stars, which seemed not only desirable but overwhelmingly important.

JULY 24, 1994

Our ride back to the "real world" went without untoward incident. As always, I felt better for the respite provided by the retreat to the wilderness. Such trips—immersions, really—have never failed to "restore my soul." I had once more been blessed to be able to retreat to "the hills from which cometh my strength." Once more, the wilderness had not failed me.

There is beauty in the word "recreation" or "re-creation." It seems a shame that now most common meaning of the word is to "have fun." The original meaning, the one that appeals most to me, was to create anew, to refresh strength and spirit. For me, there was no other "re-creational" experience that could match a retreat into the wilderness. The beauty and the philosophical implications of a "re-creational" experience are not trivial matters. In our society, still strongly influenced by puritanical thought, "having fun" is considered somehow trivial—unless, of course, there is money to be made.

Having an experience that fosters re-creation of purpose, zeal, and faith is much more than simply having a good time. For people like me, it is a necessity. Without periodic re-creation, there is danger of diminished spirit, purpose, confidence, belief, and effectiveness.

I was trying, in every way that I knew, to produce a sense of "re-creation" in the people of the USFS relative to managing wilderness and recreation areas. That was best done, I thought, by producing a clear vision of the agency's heritage and its destiny. After all, to quote Proverbs, "Where there is no vision, the people perish." I felt it was essential for leadership at every level to experience an ongoing re-creation of the agency's purpose and mission. Nominal leaders, who are by definition transitory, can take the lead only for a brief time. Then each person must deal with his or her own ongoing re-creation.

On the ride out to the trailhead, I felt ready to go back to my temporary post in Washington and reengage—to try again. I knew I would never escape the nagging sense of responsibility for the deaths of the firefighters at Storm King Mountain. However, those losses were now in perspective. If those young people could routinely face danger—and even death—in carrying out their mission, how could those who, at the very worst, face the vicissitudes of the political fray flinch from duty or despair of progress?

CHAPTER 14

WILDERNESS AND A
SUMMER OF DISCONTENT

I had scheduled a week-long escape from my duties in Washington, but large ongoing wildfires in Idaho and Montana necessitated a change in plans. Now I was in Boise, Idaho, where I had attended briefings relative to the salvage of burned timber at the Boise National Forest. Being so close to my old home in La Grande, Oregon, presented an unexpected opportunity for a wilderness escape, one too good to pass up. I called Bill in La Grande, apologized for the short notice, and asked if the two of us could possibly head for the Eagle Cap Wilderness the next morning. He didn't hesitate in saying yes. I hung up the phone, called my secretary in Washington, and declared myself to be on leave. I rented a car in Boise, and in less than an hour I was driving west on Interstate 84 headed for La Grande. I had pain in my soul and wilderness on my mind.

SEPTEMBER 2, 1994

I arrived at Bill's house just outside La Grande by midmorning. Bless his heart, he had everything—including the tucker—ready for our short getaway. After my first two trips into the Eagle Cap with Bill back in 1975, I had never trusted him again with buying groceries for such a trip. His menu was apt to be bacon and eggs, saltines, sardines, bologna, canned corned beef, rat cheese, peanut butter, grape jelly, and cheap whiskey. Let's just say that Bill was a minimalist when it came to camp grub. I was relieved when I saw that he had adhered to the grocery list that my secretary had dictated to him over the phone.

As pressing professional duties had limited my wilderness get-away to only three nights, we opted for a destination that was one of our best-kept secrets—Dutch Flat Lake in the nearby Elkhorn Mountains. It took only one long hour of driving from Bill's place to get to the trailhead. Once there, all we had to do was unload the horses, tighten cinches and bridle the saddle horses, and lash on the manty packs and the panniers with attendant top packs—a thirty-minute job. We were on the trail in no time flat with only seven trail miles to Dutch Flat lying ahead. With each mile on the trail, I felt the weight almost magically lifting from my mind and soul until there was only the wilderness.

The trail alongside Dutch Flat Creek had been imposed many decades before by USFS trail crews over an old sheepherder's trail. It was obviously of low priority for maintenance. With tight budgets, more heavily traveled trails came first. Dutch Flat Lake, perched just under the crest of the ridge, was reached via a trail that meandered along the ridgeline. Dutch Flat, located several miles down Dutch Flat Creek from the lake, was a mostly marshy flat ground with a narrow incised stream meandering through it at a depth of three to five feet.

On past visits we had found fishing for eastern brook trout in the meandering stream quite exceptional in terms of the number of fish easily caught if not in terms of their size. This spot was not within a Wilderness Area, and some of those who tilted toward conspiracy theories suspected that the long-standing omission was because the area's ski industry had at one time coveted that landscape. There was no more lonesome, yet easily accessible spot in the surrounding mountains. We deemed the place close enough to "wilderness" to serve our purposes. As we rode along, I made up my mind that it was time to try again for formal designation as "capital W" Wilderness.

We had no sooner arrived at our campsite, dropped the packs, and put up the tents and kitchen fly when a brief but intense thun-

Dutch Flat, Elkhorn Mountains, 1994.

derstorm suddenly towered up and broke over the Elkhorns. The storm included several brief episodes of hail that seemed to come down in sheets, accompanied by a significant drop in temperature. When the storm passed, almost as suddenly as it had appeared, the ground was covered with a layer of buckshot-size ice pellets that took several hours to melt away. We were cold and a little damp, which made a stand-around fire seem a sterling idea. However, Bill informed me that just yesterday the supervisor of the Wallowa-Whitman National Forest had declared a fire closure due to the extreme fire danger.

Judging from what we had seen on the ride in, that action was certainly appropriate—even a bit overdue. And the storm we had just experienced was likely an isolated event. But we couldn't help but shake our heads and laugh as I pumped up the Coleman stove to make some coffee. Hot coffee mixed with a touch of brandy was judged essential to lessen the chances of our catching cold or even pneumonia. Heaven forbid!

Bill, reasonably enough, wanted to ignore the fire closure and build a warming fire. I voted an overriding no, considering how very embarrassing it would be for the chief of the USFS to get a ticket—or even an ass-chewing—for violating a fire closure order. So we had to tough it out without a stand-around fire. An hour earlier we had been stripped down to our T-shirts and sweating as we set up camp. Now we were digging into the manty packs to retrieve down vests, wool jackets, and wool caps.

Within a couple of hours, the gusting winds subsided to a slight breeze and the sun reappeared in an open sky. The insects, rejuvenated by the warm sun, were buzzing about and making a discernible hum—good news for the waiting fish. I pondered the strange set of circumstances as I set up my fly rod and walked down to the stream, the hailstones crunching underfoot.

Dutch Flat was festooned with elk droppings—what wildlife biologists call pellet groups. They were stuck together in globs instead of being separate pellets, the more common state at this time of year. This "poop condition," jokingly referred to as a technical term by wildlife biologists, was likely due to consumption of abundant suc-

culent grasses and forbs that covered the naturally subirrigated flat.
The year to date had been unusually dry in a series of dry years. The
ground vegetation on the uplands was sparse and mostly cured out.
From the sign, quite a lot of elk had concentrated on this flat for the
easy pickings. Abundant succulent food on gentle terrain requires little expenditure of energy per unit of nutrition obtained, leading to
rapid weight gain. Whatever fat reserves the cow elk can build up
before calving will often make the difference in whether a cow will be
able to carry a calf to term and then whether cow and calf will make
it through the coming summer and winter.

As I was fly-fishing along the meandering stream, I encountered
old elk beds in the sedges at every twist and turn. Several times I lay
down in an elk bed and imagined—and smelled—the elk that lay
here yesterday or maybe just last night. I surmised that it was a mature
cow elk as I made out the much smaller bed of what I believed to have
been her calf nearby. I knew that the cow's early fall coat would have
begun to show reddish and shiny in the sun as she chewed her cud
and, off and on, nodded away to sleep.

In the distance I heard two widely separated bull elk bugling.
It was too early for the cows to pay much attention to such things.
But the mature cows harbored developing "eggs" in their ovaries that
would, in days or weeks, descend through their fallopian tubes, and
estrus would begin. Then those bugling sounds would have more
meaning. The sexually mature females, estrus pending, would gather
into small groups, encouraged by the mature bulls as a prelude to
mating. Males would check their readiness for copulation with regu-
larity, sensing—through behavior and odor—when a cow would accept the bull's ardor. And once more life would begin again.

With an adequate number of mature bulls, most of the females
would be successfully bred in their first estrus and the calves would be
born the next spring at the most optimum time for their survival and
prosperity. Most calves would be born in a "flood" of new calves that
would, to some extent, overwhelm the ability of their predators—
bears and cougars (wolves in the old days)—to significantly reduce
their numbers before they became increasingly fleet of foot and more
and more apt to survive.

If breeding was not successful the first time around, those cows would come into estrus again in twenty-eight or so days. A successful breeding would result in a calf born a month later than the first cohort of calves. That would make late-born calves more prone to predation as they entered winter in less vigorous condition than those calves born "on time." That, in turn, would make the calf less likely to survive a harsh winter. So mentally I wished all the cows an early, successful breeding. I heard the bulls in the timber on the hillside bugling again and, once, thrashing a convenient small tree. I laughed to myself when I imagined that the bull's exuberance was in response to my best wishes.

The sky was clearing now and the sun warming. I dozed and dreamed of past visits to this special place. I dreamed of Meg snuggled up close, her head on my shoulder, as I leaned back against the trunk of the downed spruce that marked one side of the camp. A fire was burning in front of us. I could see the firelight gleaming in her brown eyes and could feel her warmth as she snuggled closer to fend off the chill that came as the sun sank below the horizon. My dream seemed so very real. It was in these old familiar places that she emerged full blown from my core, vibrantly alive again if only for a fleeting moment. She was always alive in my memory and dreams, but these encounters were especially vivid.

Just then, one of the grazing horses ran up to me with its bell clanging, stirring me from my half-asleep dream that I reluctantly relinquished. It was time to get on with the serious business of catching enough fish for supper. The stream was narrow, not wider than six or seven feet, and the thriving streamside vegetation hid the surface of the water from my view. My most effective technique was to approach the stream at a right angle and cast from far enough away that the fish could not see me or my shadow. The trick was to drop the fly—a black gnat proved to be today's best bet—into the narrow gap of open water. Dropping a black gnat onto the stream's surface was not easy considering that the wind was blowing off and on. If my cast overshot its mark, the retrieval of the line and fly through the grasses scared the fish. A too-short cast, of course, was futile. I spent considerable time unhooking my lures from the vegetation.

However, when all went according to plan and the fly paused in the air and dropped gently onto the surface of the stream, there was a moment of anxious anticipation of a strike—which was the outcome almost as often as not. It took me less than an hour to catch more than enough fish for supper. In the process, I caught and released a half-dozen trout that I judged to be shy of eating size. It was a new style of fly-fishing for me—but, hey, whatever works! I took some pride in adjusting to the circumstances but quickly dismissed the thought of selling the story to a fly-fishing magazine. There was nothing pretty about it. And, frankly, I wouldn't have wanted to listen to Bill's critique.

The eastern brook trout were in full color with bright orange bellies and orange, yellow, and greenish white spots on the upper sides and back. Once the fish were dead, their eyes quickly lost their luster and the vibrant colors faded to a grayish green. In life there was color, vibrancy, and electricity—in death, a faded dull stillness. Yet when coated with cornmeal and spices and fried crisp, the dull-colored fish were transformed into the finest of meals, something much more than bodily sustenance. Thus went my meandering exercise in philosophy as I sat in the sun alongside the meandering stream, easing my conscience over the death of the beautiful creatures as I prepared them for the frying pan.

I wondered if other predators higher up the line marveled at the beauty of their prey. Or did they simply do what their instincts compelled them to do: kill and devour and thereby live another day? I guessed not. Maybe that was the significant difference between humans and other predators—the ability to see the beauty in their prey and wonder at the complexities of life. Of course, many humans do not acknowledge themselves as top predators, able to overcome their lack of physical attributes by the development of tools and cunning combined with accumulated knowledge that gets passed between generations. They pretend that the meat they consume simply comes in plastic-wrapped packages from the corner grocery. They hire others to do their hunting and gathering.

There is great loss in that process, as they develop no appreciation or empathy for those animals that they cause to be killed and prepared for consumption—and that they "harvest" from the cold cases at the market. They do not understand what they do in that process because they really don't want to know. As a result, too many hold no reverence or affinity for the land that, in the end analysis, is the source of all that sustains them.

I have come to believe that it is good thing to periodically return—some might say regress—to a state where the flesh one eats comes from animals killed and prepared for consumption by one's own hand. And from where the vegetable matter consumed is likewise gathered and prepared. Then, for that moment, the "hunter-gatherer," by proxy, becomes a part of the ecosystem in both action, mind, and grateful recognition.

Many decades ago now, I learned from my Big Dad that hunting and fishing and gathering were ritual acts—though he didn't call them that—of communion, renewal, and re-creation. In the case of those whose ties to such things have been severed by several generations of residing in cubicles, whose feet have trod only artificial surfaces, and whose contacts with nature are made up of vicarious experiences in movie theatres and in front of television sets, a dramatically important "something" is missing from both mind and soul.

But was that merely my fantasy, a biased and twisted view of reality? Perhaps Aldo Leopold said it best and most succinctly: "There are those who can live without wild things and those that cannot." I knew full well that I was no Aldo Leopold, but I considered myself in his latter category.

Back in camp, Bill and I wrapped up in our bedrolls and watched the day fade into night after the sun dropped below the ridgeline. It suddenly became much colder. Thanks to the fire closure order, we had no open fire to stare into. There was nothing to do but to relive the day as it disappeared into memory and then sleep.

SEPTEMBER 3, 1994

I slept soundly without being conscious of any dreams. It was the sort of sleep that blessedly comes to the emotionally exhausted. The last several months had been a blur of events—struggles over budgets, fights with political appointees over personnel assignments and wild-fire suppression issues, funerals and memorial services, investigations and speeches, grillings by congressional committees, and deteriorating health.

But now, lying flat on my back at Dutch Flat and staring into the sky, I felt free and relieved of the pressures of all of those things. I knew the reprieve was only temporary, and yet it seemed all the sweeter and more precious for that.

At dawn, we stepped out of the trees into the open meadow to greet the warmth of the new day's sun. We enjoyed several cups of boiled coffee—cowboy coffee—which, in my well-tested opinion, is the very best kind, especially when sipped from a tin cup in a place such as this. I sat and soaked up the sun until near midmorning when I picked up my fishing gear and made my way upstream to explore the stream in another higher-up meadow that showed on my map but that I had never visited.

Sure enough, as was nearly always true, the map was correct. It seemed likely to me that there were fish residing in the meandering stream that had never seen an artificial fly or felt the tremors from the feet of a fisherman easing along the on the bank. At least, that was what I wanted to believe—so I did.

For some reason, I was not eager to make my first cast. I lay down on my side in an elk bed, soaked up the morning sun, and went to sleep with a bandana over my face to both ward off flies and sun-burn. I could almost feel the weariness leave my body and seep into the ground. Lying in that slight depression in the lush sedges, I felt no air movement and the sun seemed deliciously warm and soothing. When I rolled over onto my back and removed the bandana, I looked up at a clear blue cloudless sky—the clouds had fled to elsewhere or perhaps merely dissipated. There was no sound save for the intermittent buzz of insects and the whispers of the occasional gentle breezes in the trees that surrounded the meadow.

I mused on how rare such an experience was in today's world. Surrounded by near silence, I tried to remember the rush that is Washington, D.C.—the traffic, sidewalks filled with people hurrying off somewhere to accomplish some important task or other, sounds of aircraft overhead, smells of exhaust, honking horns, food smells from street vendors' carts. I tried, but I could not bring the accompanying images to mind. They were overwhelmed by the here and now, which was nothing and everything—the warmth of the sun, smells of crushed ground cover, insects whirring, birds of several kinds singing, and breezes whispering in the spruce trees. Those simple things flooded my senses and left no room for anything else. Feeling without thinking was cathartic—medicine for the soul.

I ate my lunch, a sandwich made with leftovers from last night's fish fry garnished with wild onions gathered from the meadow. Bread and mayonnaise were courtesy of the supermarket in La Grande. On my way back to camp, I came across several saplings that had been almost stripped of both bark and needles by a bull elk raking the poor young trees with his antlers, recently freed from the skin and hair that had covered the bony growth until the sudden seasonal surge of testosterone cut off the blood supply. From far up-slope I heard a bull elk bugle. Maybe it was the same bull that had vanquished the young conifer in a warmup bout for the rut. Wild-life biologists have explanations for why bull elk do such things: declaring their territories, removing the last of the skin that covered the antlers as they grew, preparing for potential combat with other bulls. But maybe the bulls did it simply because they were healthy, strong, virile, full of piss and vinegar, and, quite literally, "horny." "Hey, tree! Take that!"

When I walked into camp, I scanned the surrounding area through my binoculars and saw Bill and Blitz at the other end of the meadow. It took me a while to figure out what Bill was doing. He was fishing—but not for the purpose of providing supper. There were numerous small ponds in the meadow that had been created when the meandering stream cut off a meander, leaving an isolated body of water. They might be called "oxbow mini-ponds." They were too deep for successful spawning and therefore lacked reproducing resident fish. At least, that seemed to be the case when we first camped here fifteen years ago earlier and fished the stream and the ponds.

I finally figured out that Bill was transplanting the too-small-to-eat fish he had caught to those small ponds. He told me later that, after stocking, he fished the ponds on a two-year rotation. The stocked fish, given reduced competition, grew rapidly and reached a larger size than the average fish in the stream. He took great delight in his clever fish management, which seemed to work as described.

More important, it provided Bill an excuse for another day of fishing after our appetites for fish had been satiated. As Big Dad once told me, "Son, unless there's a very good reason, never piss on another man's parade." This was Bill's parade and I had no reason to comment.

Fall was already in the air at this elevation, and I always appreciated the preview of what was coming to the valleys in a month or so. Fall had always been my favorite season, but this year it seemed dour and foreboding.

After supper was done and clean-up was completed, Bill and his dog retired to the tent while I stayed out and watched the cold, dark clouds moving across the top of the ridge and the wind moaning through the flagged spruces along the ridgeline. I felt cold and profoundly lonely. How lucky I was to have had these brief few days in the wilderness. A bit reluctantly, I felt myself ready to reengage.

SEPTEMBER 4, 1994

We left our camp in the Elkhorns at first light and headed for the trailhead. Then it was on to La Grande. The early start was to allow me time to get a haircut before leaving town. After all, chiefs of the USFS should look presentable, and I was about to return to active duty. My old barber gave me a haircut on the house, and after leaving the barber shop I wandered across La Grande's Main Street—in the middle of the block—without concern for being run over, getting a ticket for jaywalking, or being yelled at by an irate motorist. This was La Grande after all—small-town eastern Oregon. I encountered the same old lunch crowd at the Elkhorn Cafe, almost as if they had been sitting there since I left for Washington some nine months ago. It all seemed so familiar and comfortable. After lunch, I paid a visit to the USFS's Range and Wildlife Habitat Laboratory, where I had been the chief research wildlife biologist for two decades. For a couple of hours, it seemed like dear old times. It came to me that here I belonged, and here I longed to stay. But it was a dream and I knew it.

Then I checked on my old home on Main Street, now rented to one of the lab's employees. It had been Meg's and my home for two decades. I parked at the curb, and as I studied the house and the gardens for the better part of an hour, memories washed over me. In my mind's eye, I could see every one of my family who had lived or visited in that house come and go through the front door. I could even see every one of our family pets—all now buried in the "wild" slope behind the house—playing in the yard. Then, to my dismay, I realized that I simply would not be able to bring myself to enter the house. There were too many ghosts there—mostly good ones, but ghosts nonetheless. As I drove away, tears streaming down my face, I wondered if I could ever enter that house again.

I was scheduled to retire from the USFS in less than two years and planned to return here to live. Down deep, I didn't believe my dream of doing that would be fulfilled. Recognizing that impending truth did not improve my mood. Washington was, after all, the "real world" for me now, and it was waiting.

CHAPTER 15

THE WENAHA-TUCANNON WILDERNESS, BILL BROWN'S PRIDE

I was able to escape Washington for a short horse trip with Bill into the Wenaha-Tucannon Wilderness in the Blue Mountains of northeastern Oregon and southeastern Washington. Bill called this particular Wilderness Area "his wilderness." It seemed a shame to many of us who were privy to the backstory that it had not been christened the Will H. Brown Wilderness. He was the Oregon Department of Fish and Wildlife's regional supervisor for northeast Oregon when the agency purchased the Wenaha Game Management Area, and he was a prime mover in the behind-the-scenes organizing force that led to the establishment of the Wenaha-Tucannon Wilderness Area on the Umatilla National Forest, despite the determined opposition of the forest's supervisor and many others in the USFS.

JUNE 20, 1995

Bill and I left La Grande an hour before first light and proceeded to Troy, Oregon, at the juncture of the Grande Ronde and Wenaha Rivers. We left Bill's horse truck at the headquarters of the Oregon Department of Fish and Wildlife's Wenaha Game Management Area. Bill and I were mounted, and each led a single a packhorse.

Livestock grazing had been excluded from the Wenaha Game Management Area for nearly thirty years. Compared with the adjoining private lands, the results were obvious in terms of dramatically improved range conditions. The open, gentle slopes were dominated by bluebunch wheatgrass and Idaho fescue. The bunchgrasses seemed to ripple in the intermittent breezes, much as waves on a lake. The recovery of the climax perennial vegetation on these slopes, which had been denuded by overgrazing by sheep and cattle year after year and decade after decade, seemed just short of a minor miracle. Results were better than the most optimistic projections made at the time by range specialists, a testament to the area's recuperative powers.

As if to boldly underline the story of recovery, we encountered twenty-seven Rocky Mountain bighorn sheep scattered along the rocky outcrops that loomed above us as we rode. Likely there were others that we did not see. The sheep seemed as curious about us as we were about them. They appeared, disappeared, and reappeared—singly and in small groups—along the lip of the rocky outcrop that loomed above the trail. Finally, they looked down at us, all twenty-seven bighorns arrayed in more or less of a row. We pulled up our horses and stared back at the sheep for a few minutes. It was a grand sight that I would likely never forget.

I thought Bill sat a little taller in his old saddle as we rode away. I could understand why. Sometimes doggedly persistent efforts in wildlife conservation pay off. And then in the wildlife business you have to hang on tight to the gains, knowing that there are no victories that are final—a lesson too often forgotten.

As we rode on down the trail—in the way of wildlife biologists who seem compelled to count and classify all the animals they encounter—we argued about the exact number, sex, and age of the bunch of wild sheep we had come upon. He was bucking the political tides when he had ordered the removal of livestock from the area's badly overgrazed slopes above Troy.

And it was Bill, against the advice and opposition of naysayers in and out of the Oregon Department of Fish and Wildlife and the USFS, who spearheaded the reintroduction of long-absent bighorn sheep. That initial band had multiplied and spread throughout the canyon and into the Grande Ronde River drainage.

He professed great respect for the USFS professionals that he had jousted with over the establishment of the Wenaha-Tucannon

Wilderness. He recognized that they just saw things through different lenses. On the other hand, few sang Bill's praises. That may have
been just the way he wanted it. After all, his *modus operandi* was to
work behind the scenes and largely through others. Fame, or noto-
riety, in the business of fish and wildlife biology, falls mostly upon
those who write books and articles, make frequent presentations,
teach in universities, appear on television, testify to legislatures and
Congresses, serve on special committees, receive awards, and are otherwise brought to the public's attention. Yet it is the Bill Browns of the
wildlife conservation business who may well leave the greater legacy
in the form of lands acquired or dedicated, improved management
practices, and the native species returned from exile in remote pockets
of their original range. Their reward lies in knowing "the rest of the
story" that others do not.

All professional wildlife biologists have done their part and will
continue to do so. But in many cases, it will be the Bill Browns who
finally get the job done by hook or by crook. They are highly unlikely
to receive recognition. They are the street fighters, the "combat biologists." Their greater rewards lie in knowing what they strived for
and sometimes achieved. Bill's reward was riding through the Wenaha-Tucannon Wilderness and the Wenaha Game Management Area
knowing, along with his friend and protégé, his role in their establishment and subsequent management. Watching his eyes and listening
carefully to his story made my day.

I detected that it was important to him for me to ride along
with him on this trip—his so-called "last trip"—up the Wenaha
River. It was no less important to me. Each succeeding trip I made
with Bill was increasingly precious. Time was taking its inexorable
toll, and each trip could be our last together. It was increasingly
painful for me to watch Bill struggle to mount Keno, his tall, thoroughbred gelding. When he looked to see if I was watching, I always
managed to have my attention directed elsewhere—the rigging on a
packhorse, my rifle scabbard, the rain slicker tied behind my saddle,
or something off in the distance. I doubted that I fooled him much,
if at all. But I thought he appreciated the courtesy implied. At least
he never called me on it.

After we made camp at Fair View Bar on the Wenaha River, it became obvious that this wilderness experience was going to be different from what I was accustomed to sharing with Bill. After we made camp, some twenty-five members of a hiking club from Seattle straggled in and set up their camp on the other side of the meadow. So much for the code of the wilderness of not setting up camp near another camp. But these pilgrims—most of whom sported the latest fashions in the Eddie Bauer or Filson or Cabela's catalogs—were friendly, polite, and courteous. What they lacked in wilderness experience and etiquette they made up for in enthusiasm. And they liked to socialize. It was my impression that they considered Bill and me as rustics of a sort. I regretted that I didn't have some chewing tobacco in my pocket to complete my costume.

Bill, in between playing "old mountain man" and regaling his audience with stories, blew my cover and let it be known that I was the chief of the USFS. The young people seemed to know little about the history of their national forests or their purposes as established in legislation. They knew even less of the intense struggle that was brewing over the future of those lands. They seemed to simply assume that the national forests would always be there and that they were "sort of like national parks."

From what I saw during our day rides out from our camp at Fair View Bar, the country was much more heavily used by recreationists—nearly all on foot—than other Wilderness Areas that I was familiar with. However, the land-use ethics displayed by the sojourners were commendable. We were treated to an intermittent passing parade of fishermen, Boy Scouts, horsemen, and several kayakers who came down the river. Taken all together, it represented a dramatic increase in use of the area since I first visited this place a decade earlier.

During our rides, we stopped and visited with at least a dozen parties. I conversed at length with each party as to what they thought about the concept of "wilderness" and solicited their thoughts about proper management. They seemed to have an appreciation for the USFS, so such folks were clearly a potential constituency that the agency had not adequately cultivated. They seemed to be part of a "silent majority," part of the middle-of-the-road constituency that will be sorely needed in the immediate future.

This weekend's escape into this very different kind of wilderness experience was an eye-opener. I met and visited with and learned from folks who were wholeheartedly enjoying their national forests and were eager to share their experiences and hopes and dreams. I was struck by their courtesy and their passion for the land, which was, after all, their land. I felt better for having met these special people in this special place and sharing a special time. Not only were the encounters most educational—it was fun. If one strives to be a leader in the conservation arena, it is well to learn from, as well as teach, the citizens that one aspires to lead.

CHAPTER 16

A RETURN TO THE EAGLE CAP—NONE TOO SOON!

Oregon's elk hunting season had arrived—at long last. It seemed to me that five years had passed since last year's elk season. Maybe that was because I felt as if five years' worth of personal and professional stresses and strains had been crowded into a single year. Now for a blessed few days, I was going to escape into the Eagle Cap Wilderness once again. No one except my trusted personal secretary knew exactly where I would be camped and how I might be reached, but to my mind, nothing could happen in my absence that couldn't be handled, perhaps even better, by the very competent second-in-command personnel.

Accompanying Bill and me were Robert "Bob" Nelson, director of the USFS's Wildlife, Fish and Rare Plants division, and Randy Fisher, director of the Oregon Department of Fish and Wildlife.

OCTOBER 23, 1995

Only five of our horses were fit for active duty—two were on medical leave. That meant that Bill and I would ride in with three packhorses carrying the camp gear, our food and possibles, and enough horse feed for a single day. Bob and Randy, toting their hunting packs and rifles, would make the journey on foot. The next day, Bob and Randy would put in a supply of wood, cut to fit the sheepherder stove, while Bill and I made a round trip to the trailhead at Two Pan to pack in an adequate supply of pelleted horse feed.

When Bill and I rode into our campsite, we found some two feet of snow on the flat with an overcast sky promising more of the same. We had considered this place as a potential campsite for a half-dozen years but for some reason had never camped here. The spot was sheltered in a grove of large spruce trees on flat ground and with a "veritable plethora," as Bill described it, of firewood of appropriate diameter for the sheepherder stove. The Lostine River ran less than fifty yards away from where we would build our stand-around fire and put up our tents.

Bill was, as he put it, "a little on the puny side," being a bit shy of full recovery from a bout with pneumonia that had involved a week in the hospital. Yet here he was, eighty-one years old and still feeling the effects of a lung problem, camped at some 7,000-foot elevation and wading around in two feet of snow. That did not seem to me a sterling idea, but Bill had privately said to me that this was likely his last elk hunt and he would rather be here than anywhere else. If he died in his sleeping bag, that just might be to his liking.

I had a big decision to make while on this trip. Should I continue to serve as chief of the USFS? I was approaching my sixty-first birthday. The thirty years I had already spent in the USFS—plus military time—would entitle me to full retirement benefits. And I had several standing job offers from fine universities to join their faculties—with a significant increase in pay. There was no better place to consider my options than the solitude and grandeur of the Eagle Cap Wilderness. This trip would provide me long hours to be alone to ponder, wonder, remember, be in touch with the earth and myself—and then to decide. Now, more than ever before, these retreats into the wilderness had become my touchstone that provided time and space to reconnect and even rediscover who I was and, more important, what I wanted to be. Wilderness provided the blessed silence that allowed the small, still voice buried deep within a chance to be heard—and perhaps heeded.

Such had always been true, and I hoped it would be so again. The clutter and confusion of the everyday striving that goes on down below in the "real world" were simply too loud and clamorous to hear that inner voice. But high in the wilderness the earplugs of ego evaporate in the thin air, and a shrinking of ego comes with staring up the granite faces that loom up above camp in the starlit nights. I had come here once again, maybe for the last time, to listen to what the silence had to say.

I suddenly feel very sleepy and warm and good-tired. My companions are asleep. I can hear Bob and Randy both snoring, one gently and the other, not so much. The candle by which I am writing is guttering out.

OCTOBER 24, 1995

Bill and I made a round trip to the trailhead at Two Pan to pick up an additional 500 pounds of pelleted horse feed. Bill seemed a bit more chipper and full of bull than he was yesterday. Maybe just getting out of town and into the backcountry was good for what ailed him. He was still "too weak in the poop" to saddle the horses or help with the packing. While I could handle that by myself, it seemed very strange not to have him on the off side of the packhorse as I did all the packing. The trip was uneventful, if riding fine, well-trained, well-conditioned horses through such spectacular country on a crisp snowy day can be so described.

The tracks we saw in the trail told a story to those who could decipher the "handwriting"—elk were moving downhill toward their winter ranges; snowshoe hares had crossed between patches of cover; two coyotes had traveled alongside part of the trail, as had a bear that should have been hibernating but wasn't—not just yet. There was also evidence of chipmunks, pine squirrels, flying squirrels, and voles. In two places Bill pointed out where a great horned owl (he thought) had intercepted one of those creatures and made a meal. For those who can read such writings in the snow, there is a fascinating, ever-changing record of some of what has transpired since the last snow. Then the "snow board" is erased by more snow or by thawing. There was nothing new or startling in these writings, but for those who could interpret them, they were always new and fascinating.

Uncertainty, I supposed, was part of life or, just maybe, the spice of life. And here, deep in the wilderness, I was surrounded by life in its broad variety of forms. All life was wrapped up in a giant puzzle whose solution could be addressed only one tiny piece at a time. As my grandfather would say, "Boy, life is a pure wonderment!" He was so right about so many things.

The brief history that had been written in the snow was no different from that written by man on tablets of stone or clay or paper, save in relative terms related to persistence. The history of this place, written in the snow, lasts but an hour, or a day, or a week. That set down by man in various forms may last for many decades, even many centuries. But in the end those records too will pass away, and there is but little difference except the notation that life is forever a wonderment. Each individual of its species lives out its life—be it short or relatively long—generation after generation, century after century, millennia after millennia, and whatever comes after that. It is not only the living that is significant; it is what that living leaves behind.

When alone in the high-elevation wilderness, I have stared for hours at the stars, with my vision unimpeded by neither clouds nor smog. The stars seemed to number in the tens of thousands. How many, I wondered, were home to the ultimate wonderment—life? So far as I know, life on earth is all the life there is. Life, for me, remains the ultimate wonderment. In that recognition resides the wedding of the spiritual and the pragmatic. In the recognition that each individual being—animal and plant—is life and that life supports other life forms lies the embodiment of the rationale of why humans have a spiritual and pragmatic duty to be concerned about such matters as "biodiversity" and "sustainability" and "ecosystem management." There is no better situation in which to ponder such weighty matters as riding fine horses along good trails in the high mountain wilderness.

Time seemed to fly by and we were back in camp with the horse feed by midafternoon. Bill and Randy had enough firewood cut and stacked to last a month. And, in addition, they had a pile of wood that was adequate for several significant stand-around fires if it ever quit snowing long enough to make such seem desirable.

OCTOBER 25, 1995

We awoke to discover that several more inches of soft wet snow had quietly fallen while we slept. The roofs of the tents were sagging under the weight. I knocked the snow off the tents and tightened the stake lines while Bill got a fire going in the sheepherder stove. The sky seemed pregnant with the promise of more snow.

I convinced Bill that, considering his worsening cough, he should stay in camp and let me do the hunting for both of us. He wasn't hard to convince. He said he would build a warming fire, keep it going, guard the coffee pot, and take care of the horses. He promised to be ready with his old sporterized World War II–era 7mm German Mauser should an elk try to make a getaway through camp. He was fully prepared to "defend" both himself and the horses.

My planned hunting route for the day would take me up the Lostine River, up the Minam River Trail past Minam Lake, and then higher yet up to Blue Lake. I had that route in mind despite the likelihood that the snow would get deeper with the increase in elevation. If so, it was almost certain that the elk that had resided in the upper basins would have already set out on their annual migrations toward their wintering grounds where there would be less—or no—snow to interfere with their feeding.

But there was a small chance that a few elk still lingered up around Blue Lake. Besides, for some unexplained reason that had nothing to do with hunting for elk, I felt a real need to look down at Blue Lake just one more time. The basin just below Blue Lake was a longtime favorite spot of mine for encountering both mule deer and elk. And there was an even more compelling reason. I had good memories of killing two magnificent mule deer bucks there in past hunts—and two cow elk.

The climb from Minam Lake to Blue Lake was very tough going through one to two feet of unbroken snow that covered the trail. I was sweating and getting more than a tad pooped when I got to Blue Lake. My sixty-one years and accumulated injuries of an active life were wearing on me. And riding a swivel chair and walking on concrete between taxi rides in the nation's capital at sea level were poor preparation for mountain hunting. By this point, my shirt, heavy sweater, and wool coat were tied onto my hunting pack, and I was wearing only my long underwear on top. As I rested, I cooled down and dried out. I put my heavy sweater and jacket back on and turned my face to the sun and drifted almost immediately into reverie.

A decade or so before, in August, Meg and I had hiked up to Blue Lake from our camp some three miles below on the Minam River. When we finally arrived at the lake, we were hot and sweaty and tired from the climb. A skinny dip seemed in order. But no matter how warm the day and how hot and sweaty we were, the snow-fields above the lake provided a clue as to the water temperature. We were not dissuaded and took what may have been among the briefest skinny dips in recorded history. Later we lay side by side in the early-afternoon sun to dry off and warm up. The special memory of that long-ago moment washed over me and warmed my heart. It seemed so long ago. Was it even real?

I sat looking down at Blue Lake until there was only enough daylight left to get back to camp before pitch darkness caught up with me. I realized that my behavior was more akin to that of a pilgrim seeking solace than to a supposedly dedicated elk hunter. But "Jerusalem" takes different forms for every individual. And that was between me and the mountain. On my way back to camp, I left the established trail and traveled along the lakeshore, enticed by following the tracks of a black bear in the mud along the shoreline. Whimsically, I thought I might track the bear to its place of hibernation and find the bear all tucked in for the winter.

My enthusiasm dimmed when the bear's tracks turned uphill and disappeared under the deepening snow. I wished the bear well in its journey to a den in which to sleep away the winter. Suddenly the daylight was waning fast, and I struck out for camp as fast as conditions permitted. The real chance of falling and busting my ass made appropriate caution a priority over speed. The last time or two that had happened, I noted that I didn't bounce nearly as well as I used to.

Randy, Bob, and I arrived in camp within ten minutes of one another. Bill had the stovepipe of the sheepherder stove glowing red

Bob Nelson, director of the USFS's Fish and Wildlife division, Eagle Cap Wilderness, 1995. Bob was on an elk-hunting trip along the Lostine River with Jack, Bill Brown, and Randy Fischer, director of the Oregon Department of Fish and Wildlife.

and greeted each of us with a tin cup of steaming, stout, boiled coffee laced with a generous "touch of the spirit." After several cups, stories of the day's endeavors flowed ever more freely, all of them replete with adventures and experiences that were enhanced by hunting without any of the distractions associated with finding. All in all, we judged it a great day! The hunters were tired and ready for supper and their bedrolls. We were in our sleeping bags and snoring less than a half hour after the dishes were washed and put away.

As I drifted off to sleep, the sleet that was tapping ever more intensely on the tent flies seemed a lullaby. A feeling of complete satisfaction that came over me as I snuggled into my down sleeping bag and listened to the storm that was building outside the thin tent walls just inches from my head.

Then, sometime in the middle of the night, the tapping of sleet on my tent gave way to the steady drumming of rain—heavy rain, falling on top of two feet of snow that, in turn, rested on frozen ground. A whole lot of water was building up on flat ground—PDQ. Within minutes, the floors of the tents were covered with water.

We quickly concluded that the first order of business was to get our bedrolls off the floor and hanging from the center pole of our tents. The next job was to dig a ditch around the bottom of the tent walls to drain off the water. All hands fell to with whatever tools were available, ranging from a shovel and ax to sheath knives. Fortunately the warmth in the tents over several days had thawed the first few inches of soil, which facilitated the ditching efforts.

After an hour or so, the rain turned to heavy wet snow. We took the tarps that had served as tent floors outside and shook off as much water as we could and brought them back in the tents and suspended them from the ridge poles, along with our sleeping bags. The sheepherder stove was stuffed full of wood and the vent hole opened wide to provide maximum heat. The approach did not return the situation to normal, but there was some improvement.

When we returned to bed after sitting in the impromptu Turkish bath for nearly three hours, there were no puddles on the floor, and our body heat helped to dry our damp sleeping bags somewhat. But the situation was not good for an eighty-one-year-old man recovering from pneumonia. We feared that, come morning, the circumstances would put an end to Bill's hunt.

Shortly after we bedded down for the second time of the night, the camp was wracked by heavy gusts of wind—first from downslope and then from upslope. The sound of the wind gusts was akin to that of an approaching train. From time to time we heard a tree crash to the ground. We hoped the tree was not one to which a horse was tethered. As I lay there and listened, it seemed certain that my tent would come down or, at the very least; the plastic fly over the roof would be ripped away.

Along with first light, the winds died down to a strange stillness. The sagging tent was still standing with, Hallelujah, the fly intact. We had been blessed with more than a little luck in getting through a crazy night of weather with the tents still standing. Then, to add to the excitement, temperatures were dropping precipitously to near zero with the subsidence of the wind. This was a night to be remembered, not necessarily fondly.

OCTOBER 26, 1995

Bill was slow getting started this morning. He said he "felt poorly" and commented that "the air doesn't seem to have much oxygen in it." His face was flushed, his breathing labored, and his skin hot to the touch. I offered to ride out with him to the trailhead so he could drive home in the car brought by Randy and Bob. But he decided to tough it out. When I tried one too many times to dissuade him, he gave me the infamous Bill Brown look, ending the discussion.

Bob and Randy tended to horses, and I had breakfast and lunches ready to go by the time they finished that chore. They didn't dawdle after breakfast. I handed them their lunches, and they were off in pursuit of the wily elk.

An hour later, I had all the still-damp bedrolls hanging from the roof of the cook tent; damp underwear and socks were hung out to dry around the sheepherder stove. The kitchen gear was washed and in order. The stove was chock full of wood and huffing and puffing and glowing red around the base of the stovepipe. Bill, who had hardly stirred all morning, was sitting on a campstool hunkered over the stove nursing a cup of coffee. The stove was surrounded by enough split firewood to keep the fire blazing through the day. The crisis of the moment was over, and there were no more chores to keep me in camp.

Bill assured me that, despite feeling puny, he was alright and would remain in camp in case of an Indian raid or an elk stampede. I shouldered my pack, picked up my featherweight Winchester .30-06, and headed off downriver. I had not gone a quarter mile when I encountered tracks of at least eight elk and took up their trail. The noise of my footsteps in the crusted snow would likely preclude my walking up on an elk within reasonable shooting range. I was really looking for a well-used elk trail that other elk on the way down from the high country might follow.

Right before midday, it began to snow just as I found what I considered a good ambush spot under a trio of spruce trees whose lower branches hung close the ground. The "tent" of spruce provided some protection from the snow, and the ground underneath was essentially bare; the dead fall provided plenty of fuel for a hunter's fire. I gathered wood and settled in to spend the day.

As the hours passed, the air remained still, and the softly falling snow increasingly muffled sounds. The absolutely dead silence became the essence of the time and place. Over the course of nine hours in my tent of spruces I saw no other life with the exception of two gray jays that moved ghostlike in and out of my sight several times during the day. It was a day blessed by emptiness—empty of strife, conflict, passion, and challenge. I needed, perhaps above all things, that emptiness. I burrowed down into the dry duff of spruce needles and lay against the earth and, simply, was. All my tensions seemed to seep away into the spruce needles. Sleep, deep sleep, came and lasted several hours. The day seemed to speed by, and all too soon the sun was sinking below the west canyon wall. The sudden drop in temperature told me it was time to head for camp.

But I had made a decision while I slept in that bed of spruce needles. I had to stay on as chief of the USFS for one simple reason— duty and loyalty to the men and women of the agency. I had asked them to follow me, and they simply would not understand if I were to leave at this critical juncture. More than anything else at this moment, the USFS needed stability—and so did I.

As I slowly worked my way back toward camp, I made out the green-walled cook tent glowing in the darkness from the light of the two-mantle Coleman gas lantern hanging from the center pole. I stood still and listened to the talk and laughter in the high mountain stillness. It had ceased snowing, and the sky was clear and filled with brightly shining stars. Suddenly I was hungry and cold and eager to step out of the cold and into the warmth of the tent—both the warmth from the stove and the lantern and the warmth emanating from the joyful sounds of old friends. It was time to come in from the cold. As I set about preparing supper, I was humming to myself. Bob said, "Well, I see that you've made your decision and I can tell what it is. You've decided to stay on the job."

I asked, "And just how do you know that?"

He replied, "You're laughing and telling jokes."

OCTOBER 27, 1995

Bill had a terrible night, much of it spent sitting on a campstool huddled over the sheepherder stove with his sleeping bag draped over his shoulders and occasionally wracked by fits of coughing. When I told him it was time for him to get down the hill to the trailhead and then home and to a doctor, he agreed, although the decision pained his ego. He viewed it as "a wiener giving in to old age." But he finally had to concede to the eighty-one years that he had lived with exuberance and vigor—and the cumulative peripheral damage associated with that life. I felt then that he would not recover from this most reluctant concession and that this was likely his last elk hunt in the high country. It was my honor to accompany him on his journey.

While I was frying a mess of bacon for breakfast, the skillet got knocked off the stove, spilling hot grease onto my foot. By the time I could remove my camp moccasin and heavy wool sock, two patches of hide the size of a silver dollar came off with the sock, a third-degree burn. I packed the wound with snow, which rendered the pain somewhat less intense. While there was some discussion of whether I should ride out to the trailhead and seek medical attention, I concluded that there really wasn't much a doctor could do that I couldn't do right here in camp. So I cleaned the wound, covered it with antiseptic ointment and a sterile bandage, put on clean socks, and got my foot into an insulated boot.

There was no way I was going to cut short a wilderness trip that I needed so badly, nor was I going to spoil the getaway for my friends. But now I needed to get Bill to the trailhead and to a doctor, so we left camp mounted on our two best saddle horses with Bill's gear on a single packhorse. By this point in the elk-hunting season, the main Minam trail was well compacted by horse traffic, making travel considerably faster and easier than what we had encountered on the trip in. We took no breaks along the way and got to the trailhead at half past noon. Bill was not in good shape, but he insisted that he could drive home on his own. If he was well enough, he said, he would come back for us at the appointed time. If not, he would arrange for someone else to bring his horse truck back to meet us.

I had mixed feelings as I watched Bill drive out of sight down the road. I was relieved that he was headed to the doctor but certain that this was his last wilderness trip. I mantied up the packs and loaded the packhorses with the last 200 pounds of horse feed. It was a lonely trip back up the trail. Something truly dear to me, a significant part of my life, was ending. This was the first time in some twenty-odd years that Bill was not riding ahead of me on the trail, leading the pack string. Our time on the trail together was coming to an end, and I didn't like facing the reality. Even the toughest and most determined are ground down by the burdens imposed by age and accumulated injuries of mind, body, and spirit.

I was filled with admiration for Bill's indomitable spirit. But no matter how tough and determined the players, the game of life sooner or later ends only one way. I hoped that I could do as well when my turn came, perhaps not so very many years ahead. It was a sobering realization. Tears streamed down my checks. As there was no one else to see, I did not bother to wipe them away. Why could I not say to Bill what was in my heart? "Bill, you are one of the few real friends I have had in my life, and I love you. I wanted to be with you, just once more, in the wilderness that you taught me to love and cherish.

I know you feel the same—just one last trip for both our sakes, just one last hunt."

And why could he not say what I knew he was thinking and feeling? "Jack, you are my friend and my adopted son. I have helped you become who you are and what you are still becoming. I showed you the wilderness for the first time. I taught you how to handle horses and a pack string. I showed you the first elk you ever saw. We have shared much. To share my last elk hunt with you is important to me."

By the time I got back to camp and unsaddled, watered, and fed the horses, the pain from my foot was wearing on me. After due consideration, my best bet seemed to be to build a fire in the Sims stove, chew some aspirin, down a generous double shot of Wild Turkey rye whiskey, and lie flat on my back with my foot elevated on a campstool. As there was no one around to hear, I figured that a little moaning and groaning couldn't hurt. I thought it just might make me feel better. It didn't.

Bob and Randy soon came wandering into camp. The temperature had remained well below freezing all day, but there was no wind. The late-afternoon sun was bright and warm on our skin, and our dark wool clothing soaked up the heat from the sun. The three of us sat on campstools around the fire pit and simply enjoying the heat both from the fire and the sun. Bob pointed out a sun dog to the right of the sun. We discussed the phenomenon, which we had all read about or heard about but had never seen. There was one show after another in the late-afternoon sky, including a series of "rainbows" around the sun dog and then around the sun. Then, from the top of the mountain extending to the space between old Sol and his illusionary companion, the rainbows disappeared and there was a wavelike movement of parallel distortions pulsing across the face of the sun dog. The show faded as the sun sank toward the ridgeline. It was indeed a wonderment.

As we watched the show, no one had spoken. Now we were all speaking at once. We wondered if the marvelous show was the privilege of only those in this time and place with the inclination to watch, wonder, and appreciate. We wanted to believe that the show was ours alone—and so we decided and so we believed.

OCTOBER 28, 1995

It had become obvious that I was not going to be able to walk very far. That meant that my hunting for this day would involve doing most of my travel via horseback. Bob wanted to hunt out the upper Minam River drainage. So the two of us rode to the tree line and tied our horses. Bob would work his way down the drainage along the slopes just at the tree line. I hobbled over to locate a good vantage point that just might yield a shot at elk moving down to lower ground with less snow.

I found a good spot out of the wind with a good view that would provide a clear shot should an elk come wandering by. Bob and I agreed that I would meet him, just before dark, with the horses four miles or so down the Minam River. The day passed without me seeing or hearing an elk. But the place provided me great pleasure as I lay out of the wind in the warm sun and treasured the beauty and solitude of the place. Frequently, during the course of the day, Vs of geese and swans passed overhead on their way to their wintering grounds. They "talked" incessantly to their companions as they flew.

As a biologist trained not to anthropomorphize, I supposed that the geese "talked" just to keep in touch and to maintain formation, maximizing their efficiency in flight. Yet I wondered if there was more to their "talking" than biologists would dare acknowledge. Whatever the purpose, the goose music was most pleasant to my ears. One flight of twelve swans made a pass at landing on Minam Lake. But the patch of water in the middle of the lake that remained unfrozen was, I guessed, by now less than a half acre in size. At the last second, the swans pulled up their landing gear, aborted their approach, and flew on to the south. By tomorrow, I thought, Minam Lake will be completely frozen over. The core of winter will have arrived in the high wilderness.

When I figured there was about an hour of daylight left, I mounted up and, leading Bob's horse, rode down the canyon to find my hunting companion. We arrived at the designated rendezvous point almost simultaneously. Daylight quickly faded to pitch darkness as we rode back to camp. When full darkness enveloped us, we gave the horses their heads, knowing they would take us to camp. It was good to see the tent glowing green in the darkness and see sparks and smoke rising from the stovepipe.

The three horses tied in camp began to whinny a welcome a full quarter hour before we arrived in camp. That gave Randy plenty of warning to have the coffee ready. Once in camp, we left the saddles on the horses so that they could cool down gradually while we gratefully accepted the hot coffee Randy handed us. Hot damn! The coffee was flavored with a big dash of rye whiskey—a proper greeting for "hunters home from the hill."

We did not tarry long after supper before we sought our sleeping bags. We faced a full day tomorrow. We had to break camp, saddle and pack the horses, and get to the trailhead at Two Pan by midday.

An early arrival in La Grande would give me a chance to arrange with a realtor to take over management of the rental of my old home. I also wanted to call on some special old friends and colleagues at the research lab that I had headed up for nearly twenty years. And a bittersweet visit to Meg's crypt in the La Grande cemetery was long overdue. Such visits were becoming easier and less painful with the passage of time. Now the memories are more of the good times—especially horseback trips in the wilderness—and less of the pain of her suffering and loss to her family and friends. Her willing sacrifices in going to Washington were a final gift to me. I knew it was a gift that she really wanted to make, even if I sometimes regretted the decision.

OCTOBER 29, 1995

It seemed so very strange to saddle the horses, pack up the camp, and load the pack horses without Bill being in charge or even present. In all the years we had traveled the backcountry together, especially the various Wilderness Areas, this was the very first time I had served as the "head honcho." I knew what to do and had no trepidation about filling that role, yet I didn't like the feeling that the time had finally come for me to take the lead. Bill was not here.

But, by God, he had hung tight as long as his physical capabilities allowed. As I threw the diamond hitch over the panniers and top packs, as he had so carefully taught me, I had a terrible feeling of loss. I sensed the end of something truly precious. Tears were running down my face as I tied off the last diamond hitch. Rob and Randy saw the tears that I had not tried to hide. They said nothing and looked away.

The trip to the trailhead was routine except in one most significant regard. I felt seriously out of place riding in the lead after so many hundreds of miles of seeing Bill riding out front. The role played by the lead rider and his horse are much different from and more important than that of the riders and horses that follow. But I had watched carefully and learned much in the process, anticipating that this day would ultimately come.

We arrived at the trailhead at Two Pan a bit after midday and were delighted to find that Bill was there to meet us with his horse truck. He even seemed chipper, and, in spite of a nasty cough, he looked pretty damned good. After checking the pack string and packs, he seemed both pleased and relieved. I suspected that he had not been totally confident in my abilities as packer and trail boss.

When we arrived at Bill's place, I hurried to clean up and change the dressing on my foot. I had business to take care before my plane left for Washington tomorrow.

I met the realtor and we agreed upon arrangements for her to handle the rental of the house on Main Street. I had not been in the house since Meg and I left for Washington, D.C., and I feared the memories that lay in wait for me there. But when I entered, I found that the house was simply empty. It had become just a house and nothing more. There were no ghosts. She and the boys were not there. But suddenly and finally I knew that I could never come back here to live—not to this house and not to La Grande. And I realized finally that Meg would not have wanted me to. She would have wanted me to simply get on with living—and with as much vigor and enthusiasm as I could muster. The only way I could do that was to let go of the past and move on to whatever future there was left for me.

On the way back to Bill's house, I stopped by the cemetery, which looked out to the east over the Grande Ronde Valley to the Eagle Cap. As I stood there in front of the crypt that held the urn with Meg's ashes, wonderful memories flooded to the surface. There was pain as well, but much less than the last time I stood here. Time may not heal all wounds, but it certainly helps. And I knew that it could not be too long before my ashes would be with hers in the crypt. I would prefer that they be scattered in the forest, perhaps on the Starkey Experimental Forest and Range. But, I thought, if she wanted my ashes here with hers, so be it. A promise, after all, is a promise. Besides, sooner or later, that melding with the good earth would come anyway. Here seemed as good a place for that to happen as any.

Jack on Shadow, heading into the Eagle Cap Wilderness in 1996.

CHAPTER 17

A TRIP TO THE WILDERNESS WITH THE UNDERSECRETARY OF AGRICULTURE—A CHANCE TO SAY THANKS AND GOOD-BYE

On this trip to the Eagle Cap Wilderness, Bill and I were accompanied by my immediate boss, Undersecretary of Agriculture James "Jim" Lyons, and his ten-year-old daughter Elizabeth. This was a trip for Jim and his daughter that I had long promised them both. Now that I knew my tenure as USFS chief would be over at the end of the year, it was time to make good on my promise.

AUGUST 21, 1996

When I arrived in Pendleton, Oregon, courtesy of Horizon Airlines from Portland, Bill was waiting for me at the airport. We loaded my gear into his Ford pickup, which I had I sold to him, along with my three-horse trailer, for one dollar each, when I left La Grande to move to Washington, D.C. Our understanding was that he would sell them back to me for the same price when I returned to La Grande after my tour in Washington was over.

Bill seemed in fine fettle and looked a lot better than he did last fall when we rode out from elk camp to the trailhead after he had declared himself to be a little "puny." He had been right about the puny part: the doctor diagnosed him with double pneumonia and admitted him to the hospital. He was destined for a two-week stay. I suspected that he was a bit irritated not to have died in elk camp. That might have been to his liking, but most decidedly not to mine.

For the next five days in the Eagle Cap, the world would shrink down to what we could see and feel and sense around us. As always, I felt at home in places far beyond the end of the road—in contrast to what I felt in Washington: a tad ill at ease, a little tense, never quite in tune with the environment.

My periodic escapes to wild lands gave me the renewed vigor to face the constant struggle relative to the management and care of those lands. That service was worthy, but there wasn't much enjoyable about it. When I sat behind my desk in Washington, I asked myself such questions as "Now, just why am I doing this?" and "Who needs this?" Yet the answers always became clear when I could escape and steal some time for a trip into the wilderness. The idealized mission of the USFS, "caring for the land and serving people," became real when I stood in a national forest, especially in Wilderness Areas, with time to breathe deep and reflect uninterrupted. On such escapes to the wilderness I allowed myself, indeed, to "lift up mine eyes unto the hills from which cometh my strength."

We had a horse contingent of seven head—the five that Bill and I still owned and two borrowed for the occasion from old friends to whom we had sold or given two of our old string. I was pleasantly surprised at how quickly the skills required to carry out such an "expedition"—saddle the horses, load the horses, drive to the trailhead, unload the horses, pack the horses, mount up, and head off down the trail—returned to me after too many months without practice.

Bundling the gear into manty packs, basket-hitching them on the packhorses, and putting the panniers and top packs on other horses using hitches suited to their purpose returned easily from memory. The packing exercise—especially the diamond hitch—never failed to fascinate any "greenhorns" along on the trip. And there was a certain pride that went along with the exhibition of such archaic skills. As always seemed to happen once we were mounted and on the trail, a sense of relief came over me, engendered by the sudden realization that this was the beginning of an escape from the present into a more innocent time and place.

Bill and I had set up camp at what we called Splash Dam Meadows on the Minam River. At bedtime, everyone retired to the tents except me. I sat near the fire until it died into coals and ashes and it got too dark for me to continue to write. I went into my tent and spread out my bedroll. The entrance flaps were tied back so that I could lie on my back and watch the stars emerge with the deepening darkness, one by one at first and then by the hundreds until they dazzled my eyes and my mind. When the darkness was full and the sky was ablaze with stars, I felt at peace and sleep came quickly. The only noise among the many sounds of the night was the clanging of the bells on the horses that had been set loose to graze. I considered that a lullaby.

AUGUST 22, 1996

It was good to be back in Three Buck Camp on the North Minam River, one of my favorite camps in the Eagle Cap Wilderness. Bill and I, along with various companions, had camped here many times over the past two decades. Many good memories resided here, and I hoped even more good memories were waiting to be made.

Thunderheads built up in the late-afternoon heat, and it seemed wise to erect another tent. Bill and I busied ourselves with that task, along with gathering in and covering a pile of wood for both cooking and warming purposes. I encouraged Jim to take Elizabeth fishing for the eastern brook trout that thrived in the North Minam River.

In spite of our mutual good intentions to wet a hook, Bill and I never managed to make it out of camp and whiled away the day just visiting. Much of our talk centered around the many times that we had made camp in this meadow. Our two "dudes" returned to camp just before sundown with more fish stories than fish, but still with enough fish for supper. Obviously father and daughter had had a fine day, which, after all, was the primary purpose of the trip.

While I was slow-frying the fish so that their flesh could be easily stripped away from the bones and added to the seafood chowder that was beginning to bubble on the grill—a mixture of canned clams, shrimp, oysters, diced potatoes, a can of tomatoes, and onions—I looked up to see that we had been joined by a yearling camp doe. Though I knew better, it would be easy to conclude that the doe had shown up on cue for the express purpose of charming our guests. She spent the last hour of daylight curiously circling the camp, alternately appearing and disappearing. As I was writing in my journal after the others had gone to the tents, I looked up to see the light of the dying fire reflected in her wide-open eyes as she curiously watched from behind a fallen fir that bordered one edge of the campsite. I wondered what she was thinking. Perhaps she found watching us as entertaining as we found watching her.

AUGUST 23, 1996

Jim, Elizabeth, and I left camp an hour after sunup to ride up to Green Lake. We had two purposes in mind—a day ride through beautiful country and a bit of fishing. Bill, for the first time in my memory, opted to stay in camp. When I teasingly asked him if was getting old and tired, he nodded. He said, in so many words, that he simply didn't feel like putting out the effort. I nodded, put my foot in the stirrup, and stepped up on my mare. I thought that maybe he was just off his feed, but down deep I knew better.

The trail had been recently "brushed out" by a USFS trail crew all the way up to North Minam Meadows. The trail from there on up to Green Lake crossed the very upper reaches of North Minam River via a wooden bridge. When I dismounted and checked out the bridge, I deemed it too rotted to risk crossing with the horses. I was surprised that a USFS Wilderness Guard or trail crew had not at least tacked up a warning sign about the condition of the bridge, which I doubted could carry the weight of a pack string. I dismounted, handed Jim the reins of my mare, and searched out a place where we could ford the river more or less safely.

The trail on up to Green Lake had not been refurbished by a trail crew for several years—maybe they didn't trust the bridge any more than we did—and dozens of trees had blown down across the trail. Riders who had preceded us had simply ridden around the downed trees, producing damage and erosion that was magnified with each such excursion. It was obvious that cuts in the budget for infrastructure and trail maintenance were having the anticipated negative impacts. Shamefully, the champions for Wilderness Area designations are not equally effective in assuring appropriate funds for managing those areas.

Once we arrived at Green Lake, our attempts at fly-fishing were hampered by consistent but erratic strong winds. While we were fishing, two young men—who turned out to be juniors in high school—rode in, dismounted, tied their four horses, and walked up. They told us that they were packing in their camp for the black bear hunting season, which would commence the next day. I couldn't help but wonder how many young men of their age would be so perfectly at ease horse-packing twenty miles into a Wilderness Area to go bear hunting. I guessed not many. But, by God, there were at least these young pilgrims. Their independence, skills, and enthusiasm bolstered my spirits.

Shadow, my saddle mare, very much unlike her, became more and more agitated as the day wore on. She was tied to a small spruce and kept dancing around, looking back down the trail, and neighing. Her best buddy was tied up to a picket line back in camp, and she obviously didn't appreciate the separation. When it was time to depart, I was untying her lead rope from the sapling when she pulled back hard, likely with the intent of taking off back down the trail to camp. I grabbed the lead rope with both hands, and she jerked me down flat on my face, though I managed to hold on to the rope. She lost her footing on the granite gravel and went down. I jumped up and ran around a fir tree with the rope. She really pulled back hard at that point, and the rope smashed my knuckles into the tree. I worked on shortening the lead rope until her nose was rammed into the tree. Then I tied off the rope and stepped away. I was almost afraid to pull off my riding gloves, half expecting my hand to emerge minus a fingertip. Two separate counts indicated that I had all my fingers, but my hand was badly bruised. The second bit of good news was that I still had my horse. I left Shadow tied in that uncomfortable position until I was convinced that all thoughts of a rapid solo departure for camp had left her mind.

The trip back to camp was a pure pleasure. Shadow, who had always been hesitant and a little pokey when in the lead, stepped out at a five-mile-per-hour pace. As I had heard Bill say, "Both horses and people both travel a lot faster when they're going where they want to go."

AUGUST 24, 1996

We packed up and got off to a leisurely midmorning start from Three Buck Camp, heading up the Minam River Trail to our "Camp across the River." We bestowed that name on the campsite because we had to ford the river and work our way through a screen of trees along the river's bank that concealed an old burn of some ten acres. Apparently no one else used this beautiful camp, which was richly endowed with good grazing for the horses, handy water, plentiful firewood, and shelter from the wind.

We arrived in midafternoon, erected the kitchen fly, got in plenty of wood, cut it to stove length, stacked it, and covered it with a manty tarp. After considering the clear blue sky and our decided lack of motivation for additional work—plus a building urge to get on with fishing—we didn't erect our tents. I had an excuse, as my left hand was swollen and becoming wonderfully colored in various shades of red, yellow, and blue as the result of yesterday's argument with Shadow. If deemed necessary, we could put up the tents later. Or maybe tomorrow.

The fishing water was running clear. Bill encouraged Jim and Elizabeth to get in a little fishing while he and I finished unloading, unsaddling, and grooming the horses. That done, Bill suggested a short siesta for the older folks—that being the two of us. I offered no argument. At this lower elevation, the temperature was warm, and intermittent breezes whispered in the trees. The only other sounds came from the river running around boulders and the drone of insects. Those sounds combined to give me an insatiable desire for a nap in the shade of the firs that surrounded the camp.

The stalwart fishers were successful and visibly enthused when they came back into camp. Both were definitely catching on to fly-fishing. After I cooked up a fine dinner of fried battered fish, fried potatoes, and fresh sweet onions, I left the dishwashing and cleaning up to Jim and Elizabeth while Bill took care of the horses.

I sipped bourbon, chewed aspirin, and nursed my bruised hand

and fingers, soaking them in the cold river from time to time. As darkness came quickly to the narrow valley, we lay on the manty tarps and greeted the stars as they emerged, too quickly to count. Two owls were calling—a barred owl and a screech owl—back and forth across the river. Their calling continued, off and on, until the sky was awash in stars and sleepytime arrived on the downslope breeze. One by one, we headed for the tents.

AUGUST 25, 1996

Our trip from the Camp across the River to the trailhead at Moss Springs, the loading of the horses and gear, and the haul-out over mountain roads to La Grande went without a hitch. Jim, as assistant packer-in-chief, served admirably in helping Bill with the packing and unpacking, as my right hand was still sore and swollen and not much use in pulling ropes tight. I was the optimist in the group in betting that my hand was only badly bruised and not that some bones were broken.

The Grande Ronde Valley was choked with smoke from a complex of wildfires burning around Tower Mountain, so after we unloaded the horses and unpacked the gear at Bill's place, Jim and I borrowed the old Ford pickup, once mine and now Bill's, and headed out for the USFS Fire Center at the La Grande airport to get an update on the status of the wildfires around the country. The fire situation had worsened since we disappeared into the Eagle Cap Wilderness, and it was time for me to get back to Washington. Vacation, as brief and badly needed as it was, was at an end. The time warp morphed back into real time, and the real world was waiting.

But first I stopped by the cemetery to visit the crypt that held Meg's ashes. These visits were becoming easier now. The first time I visited, the pain that welled up in me resulted in tears streaming down my face and sobbing. But the passage of time does salve wounds—not all but some. My next pilgrimage was to our old home at 206 Main Street in La Grande. I parked at the curb and studied the house and the yard and gardens for the better part of an hour. Memories washed over me. I realized that I was there to say good-bye to my idea of returning here after my service as USFS chief came to an end. I knew now that Thomas Wolfe was right: you can't go home again. It was time to give up on that fantasy and move on. There was a new life—a fresh start at the age of sixty-two—waiting for me in Missoula, Montana.

CHAPTER 18

ONE LAST RETURN TO THE EAGLE CAP WILDERNESS

A fter three and a half years in Washington, D.C., I had a new home, life, bride, and career as a college professor at the University of Montana in Missoula. I had driven from my new home in Florence, Montana, to La Grande, Oregon, for a horse pack trip in the Eagle Cap Wilderness. I was joining up with my old wilderness companion, Bill Brown, and two of our mutual friends, Craig and Karen Veloosing from Spokane. It was my first visit to La Grande in two years, and a lot of water had passed under the bridge. Bill had sold all our old string of horses except for his favorite gelding, Keno. Fortunately, he had sold the horses, pack saddles, horse truck, and trailer to a close mutual friend and had managed to retain "borrowing rights."

JULY 29, 1999

I spent the night at Bill's place with my sleeping pad and sleeping bag laid out on the floor of what passed for his living room. He was clearly very much out of place—and out of character—in his new surroundings. After Bernice died, Bill had sold his old homestead, moved into town, and, as he put it, "set up his last camp" in a small rental house on the "wrong side of the tracks" near the Boise-Cascade lumber mill. But in his typical style he was toughing it out the best he could.

As we sat on the only two chairs in the place—folding lawn chairs—partaking of a dram or two of "good sipping whiskey," he expressed his doubts as to whether he was physically up to a wilderness trip, even one of only a few days' duration. Seeing his physical state, I had to admit that he might well be correct. Maybe we should call the trip off? Bill just grunted, most expressively.

JULY 30, 1999

Bill was up before the sound of the alarm clock and kicked my foot. There were no words spoken. We had our gear ready to go before sunup. He was no longer doubtful—or if he was, he kept it to himself.

We started our trip from the trailhead above the settlement of Cove, located just across the Grande Ronde Valley from La Grande. The drive across the valley to Cove was a trip down memory lane. Seeing Mount Emily and Mount Fanny on the horizon made me feel at home. La Grande was the place that I had lived longer—twenty-one years—than any other place in my life. Margaret and I spent two-thirds of our married lives together and raised our two boys here. Our boys were graduates of La Grande High School, and one was a graduate of Eastern Oregon State College, located in La Grande. In my estimation, the most productive of my professional years were spent here. Margaret's ashes rested here, and there was a place in her crypt waiting for mine.

Despite my new life in Missoula, at the moment I had the feeling of being back home, and it felt so very good. As we packed our gear into the truck and saddled and loaded up the horses, I wondered if the horses remembered me. It shocked me to see the gray hairs in the mane and on the muzzles of my longtime saddle mare, Shadow, and Margaret's gelding "partner." They too were growing old.

I was pleased that my packing and horse-handling skills had remained reasonably intact save for the intricacies of the diamond hitch, which I had never totally mastered. Tying the diamond hitch, slowly and with a few fits and starts, brought back memories as Bill, perhaps for the hundredth time, talked me through the steps. There was one big difference. Bill's hands were now so stiffened and his knuckles so swollen from arthritis as to prohibit him from standing horse left and taking on the role of lead packer. Now he stood horse right and took on the role of assistant packer. I could tell from the expression on his face that the change in our roles was not to his liking.

Our route of travel was familiar: from the trailhead at Cove we took the trail down, across the Eagle Cap Wilderness boundary, to the Little Minam River. Then we rode up the Little Minam to the junction with the Jim White Ridge Trail, which took us up and over the ridge between the Little Minam and Minam Rivers and down to Red's Horse Ranch on the Minam. We turned up the Minam River for a couple of miles to where we made camp. This was the first time I had ridden horseback since knee replacement surgery, and I was much relieved to find that I could mount, dismount, and ride without any significant problems.

Bill and I again traded roles as I unpacked and cared for the horses and Bill gathered firewood and hauled water for the kitchen. Craig, taking over my usual duties, was the cook, and Karen served as assistant cook and handled cleanup. It gave me a strange and uncomfortable feeling to see our routine and roles so completely altered.

By the end of the first evening in camp, we were all a bit better acquainted. Craig, a professional musician, had played with several big-name bands and still put together bands for special occasions. He spoke several languages, including Chinese. He had, on contract, arranged meetings between U.S. delegations and the Russians, Chinese, North Koreans, and others. I got the impression that this was all the information he cared to share and I probed no further. Karen, a Ph.D. in nuclear chemistry, worked for the Department of Defense in Florida.

Long after everyone else was asleep; I lay out in the open on a manty tarp by the fire and entertained myself by making out images in the flames. I conjured up bittersweet memories from their storage bins deep in the recesses of my mind where they patiently waited such opportune moments to escape their confinement.

I wondered, how many times had Bill and I had camped in this spot, often accompanied by one or both of our wives? Now Bernice and Meg had both passed over. Neither Bill nor I could have ever contemplated that those two lovely, vibrant ladies would precede us in death. In those long-ago heady days, we had no doubts that our visits to the wilderness would continue forever. Then one day our trip did not include Bernice when her struggle with Parkinson's disease and then dementia rendered her unable to ride. Two years later, Margaret began an eighteen-month-long losing battle with cancer.

When Bill and I visited the old campsites alone, there were precious memories of good times passed in each place, especially this one. I easily conjured up specters of faces and sounds, most of them involving laughter. I had finally arrived at a place in my heart and soul where the memories were sweeter and less painful. I had long despaired over whether such a time would ever come. But now the replacement of pain with the pleasure of sweet memories seemed a blessed thing.

The fire is dying now, and I can barely see to write. I am not sleepy and feel, for some reason, vibrantly alive and wide awake. I moved back from the fire and stretched out on my back atop my sleeping pad and bag and watched the stars. There were occasional streaks of light from a meteor's flaming end in its long-destined collision with the earth's atmosphere. I wondered how many years—perhaps millions of years—that meteor had traveled through space before the end of existence in a flash of light. How different, really, are the journeys of men and meteors?

We of the species *Homo sapiens* make our journeys in warmth interspersed with moments of passion and then grow old and disappear back into the earth from whence we came. Meteors travel through space, some for unfathomable periods of time, inert and unfeeling. Then at the long-ordained moment, they die in an encounter with another larger body traveling in space. If the larger body they encounter has no atmosphere, they die in a collision without fanfare. Those that encounter earth's atmosphere are granted a "Viking funeral" as they burn brightly in their last moments. Somewhere on the surface of the earth, human beings—probably alone among the earth's creatures—look up in the night sky and salute, or at least note, the death throes of a fellow traveler. In either case, there is a brief flickering of fire and light and then eternal darkness. But there is memory for those who saw and wondered and appreciated the long journey and the brief twinkling at its end.

AUGUST 1, 1999

Compared with standards that Bill and I had established a decade ago, we got a late start. On the other hand, there was no good reason to hurry. It was, after all, only a four- or five-hour trip to Two Buck Camp. Craig and I were handling the horses and the packing. To my amazement, Bill seemed content to sit by the fire, poke the ashes and coals, and watch our efforts—oddly for him—sans criticism or comment. I thought that he must have been biting his tongue. When we arrived at Two Buck Camp, we were relieved to find that the meadow, created by a fire many decades ago, showed no sign of recent use by campers or of grazing by horses. Our horses would have ample grazing for several days.

Once camp was set up, Bill took up his usual spare-time occupation when at Two Buck Camp: clearing the tree seedlings from the meadow. Though he must have known that his chances of ever coming back to this treasured place were next to nil, he wanted to assure that the meadow remained open and productive of feed for horses, elk, and deer. Karen and I worked our way through the trees to the North Minam River for a bit of fly-fishing for eastern brook trout.

We immediately encountered a problem. Due to some recent rains, the water was too high and too swift for good fishing. In addition, my recent knee surgery had left my new artificial knee not quite up to wading around on slick rocks in swift water. Not to be deterred, we worked our way downstream to a stretch where the river widened and the bottom was made up of more sand than rounded rocks. After a half hour of my very best fly-fishing efforts, I could count only a half-dozen strikes—and one measly fish in the bag. We concluded that our time would be better spent with me teaching Karen something about the fundamentals of fly-fishing.

She proved a quick study and had the fundamentals of Professor Thomas's Fly-Fishing 101 course down pat within a half hour or less. She caught a few small brookies while keeping me busy tying on flies to replace the ones that she lost on her back cast in the alders that hung over the stream. For the first time in all the many years that I had fished this "secret spot," I returned to camp without even enough brook trout for hors d'oeuvres.

Bill looked up from his ongoing efforts to clear the meadow of tree seedlings and inquired as to our success. When Karen held up three small brook trout, he snorted something about "pilgrims in the wilderness" and went back to his work. Small piles of seedlings pulled up by their roots were scattered around the meadow. This treasured opening—in close proximity to a fine spring that provided water for the camp—would remain free of trees for another several years and continue to provide grazing for horses, mule deer, and elk.

But if this was indeed Bill's last visit, within ten to twenty years the meadow would be covered with fast-growing, waist-high young trees. In another decade or two after that, those trees would begin to shade out the grasses and forbs. In thirty or forty years, only a very few old-timers would remember this place as a prime camping spot for those traveling on horses. Only the ghosts would remain, and then they too would disappear with the passing of all those with treasured memories of this place. But, I reasoned, for some thirty years, this place had been maintained as a magic camping place by the annual efforts of one old man "paying his dues."

When evening came, there was no hurry to leave the fireside and crawl into our sleeping bags. The conversation around the campfire drifted easily and seamlessly from music and big bands to "horses I have known and loved" and "some, not so much." Oddly, it is possible to establish a strong and lasting rapport with relative strangers in the course of sharing a wilderness experience, sitting around a campfire in its small circle of light and warmth, surrounded by thousands of acres where there is no other light but that emanating from the moon and stars, and listening to the silence and intermittent night sounds.

Likely we would not long remember the eloquent discussions that took place this night when our faces were illuminated by the firelight and our tongues loosened a bit by good sipping whiskey. Maybe that would be a blessing, as the brilliance of tonight's conversation and insights would almost certainly fade in the cold, sober gray of dawn. But the moment itself was everything. One by one, those who sat around the dying fire stood, stretched, and excused themselves. Finally Bill was left alone staring into the fire. I looked out from our tent and wondered what he was thinking, remembering, feeling.

AUGUST 2, 1999

Just after daylight, we sat around the cooking fire enjoying just one more cup of coffee while mulling our plans for the day. Bill went over the options with Craig and Karen and discussed each in detail. I could not help smiling to myself. They likely thought they actually had a choice of the options Bill proposed.

I knew last night where today's journey would take us. I had camped here with Bill at least two dozen times over the years. We always stayed in Two Buck Camp for two nights and then took a day ride up to Green Lake, taking along one packhorse that carried what we needed to cook lunch. The hobbled horses grazed in the meadow around the lake while we caught enough fish for lunch—and enough in our poke for a fish fry back in camp. If all went right, we would be back in Two Buck Camp in time for "cocktails" as the sun dropped behind the ridge.

And, sure enough, after a half hour of conversation, we concluded that the best thing to do was to stay another night at Two Buck Camp and spend this day riding up to Green Lake. The discussion had meandered to its inevitable conclusion. Affording a choice—which was really no choice at all—was important to Bill in making his companions feel important and valued. I wondered if Bill understood his own game. It really didn't matter—it worked every time.

Since our last visit, the old timber bridge over the North Minam had collapsed, having been in a sad, deteriorating state for several years. So we had to find a place where we could ford the river without too much risk. After a mile searching upstream and down, we settled for one where we could "slide" the horses down a steep bank, wade four feet of water, and lunge the horses up the bank on the other side.

It seemed to me that we were taking a significant chance on a "horse wreck." But Trail Boss Bill thought differently, and there was no doubt that he was in charge. It was a thrill, but to everyone's relief the crossing went just fine. The ride on up to Green Lake was a bit tedious, as it had been a few years since a trail crew had cleared trees that had fallen across the trail. Yet the horses handled jumping or traveling around the downed trees without real problems.

When we arrived at the lake, as usual, Bill tied the horses, put his fly rod together, staked out his claim on fishing water, and was the first to have a fly in the water. As I had come to expect, he called out "fish on!" while I was still trying to get my fly rod assembled. The old guy was still competitive—and good enough with horses, fly rod, rifle, and shotgun to get away with it. As I didn't really give a flip as to who caught the first, last, most, or biggest fish, I figured that if being *numero uno* meant something to him—well, that "just tickled me plumb to death." Besides, what the hell could I really do about it? I couldn't best the old bastard if I tried.

The fishing gods smiled on us. Brookies were rising almost continuously. Better yet, they seemed to be hitting whatever flies vaguely resembled a free lunch and seemed especially enamored of the bucktail coachman. Within an hour, a creel check revealed that we had ample fish for both lunch and supper. So catch-and-release protocols governed our fishing for the next couple of hours.

Lunch was made up entirely of trout salted and peppered, rolled in cornmeal, and fried in bacon grease. The fresh fish curled when they hit the hot grease, and Bill proclaimed—for what seemed to be the hundredth time under such circumstances—"When you see fish curl up like that, it means they're really fresh!" The combination of high mountain air, an open cooking fire, and a tummy full of fresh fried trout made for the most wonderful meal and something close to a perfect day. I buried the uncooked fish in a remnant snowbank to keep them cool. Soon all four of us were lying flat on our backs with our hats over our faces to ward off the midday sun. It was siesta time. I was struck by the absolute silence—if one disregarded the occasional birdsong, the whisper of wind in the trees, and the sounds of running water, buzzing insects, and horses stirring. Is there anything in today's world that is in shorter supply than such "silence"? Few people who live their lives in towns and cities ever have the opportunity to know and listen to such silence.

When we all awoke from our siesta, the sun was lowering in the western sky and it was time to head back down the mountain to Two Buck Camp. The horses' pace was fast and steady—no "snorting or farting around," as Bill put it. I suspected that the horses knew full well that, once in camp, they would be freed of saddles, bit, and bridles and loosed to graze, suck cold water from the river, and scratch their backs in the sand/gravel soil. It was a constant tussle to slow their pace to one more comfortable for their riders. Horses and riders alike seemed to be looking forward to an evening in camp. The tents were up, firewood split and stacked, fresh fish on hand, water bags full, and we had canned peaches, dumplings, and canned milk for desert—a combination hard to beat.

The camp was quiet after supper as we sat, watched the fire, and talked quietly as night sounds replaced those of the day. Then gradually the talking ceased and silence reigned. The dying fire provided entertainment enough. After a while, my fellows slipped away to their tents, and I realized that, even now, I didn't want the day to end. Only my heartbeat in my ears, a coyote's wail from off in the distance, and the calls of an owl broke the silence.

AUGUST 3, 1999

After the breakfast dishes were taken care of, there was time to savor one last cup of coffee and begin the ritual discussion as to where our next camp should be established. Bill trotted out the options. As I knew where we were headed, I didn't really listen. We would ride downstream along the North Minam River to its juncture with the main Minam River and then turn upstream to where we would wade across the river to what Bill and I called the Elk Camp.

When we got to the spot where the river ran shallow and the banks were gentle enough to allow a safe crossing, Bill called a halt—as he always did at this point in the journey—and announced with concern in his voice, "I don't know if we ought to try to cross the river. There could come a water spout, and the high water could trap us on the other side for a few days."

That was my cue to sagely observe, "Well, a heavy rain could happen. But what the hell, we have plenty of groceries and an adequate supply of good whiskey. We could wait out the high water if we had to." Then Bill would shrug to indicate that he had warned us of the possibility of a water spout. He turned his horse and led out across the Minam. A water spout was possible, of course, but unlikely. And it was obvious to me that we were going to take the risk—we always had and always would. Was this a "cover my ass" statement or was he thinking out loud? Maybe he was spicing things up a little for the dudes. Tradition!

The cast of actors—save for Bill and me—changed from trip to trip and year to year. But the basic underlying script for this annual trip remained the same. The horses even knew the trees where the picket line would be raised and would go there and stand and wait to be tied when their turn at grazing was over. They knew how to work their way through the trees to the old snow chute where repeated avalanches swept away or flattened the young trees so that the grasses grew in full sunlight, and they knew the way back to camp and the picket line.

Bill had camped here nearly every year—sometimes twice or more—for some forty years. He had hunted elk out of this camp with various companions now departed or too old and stoved up to hunt or even ride the wilderness. He had come here often with his first wife and then with a second wife as she slipped away into the land of mystery created by Alzheimer's. He clearly believed that each trip to this special place would be his last. Here is where he is most comfortable as he repeats the old familiar stories, essentially without variation. I appreciate the sparkle that comes into his eyes and the vibrancy in his voice when he tells the old stories. For Craig and Karen and other pilgrims who have come to this place with Bill, the stories are new and entertaining. Bill thrives on an appreciative audience and is notably happy in his storyteller role. Just watching and listening as he relives the past always gives me pleasure.

Now I am the only one still awake, sitting by the fire and writing in my journal. The fire is dying, and the light from the lantern is waning. I love this camp. A special spirit always seems to reside here. I am blessed to be here for what I now believe to be the very last time. I sense myself gathering into the storage locker of my memory as much of the essence of this special place as possible. Lying on my back in the darkness, my hands with interlaced fingers behind my head, I watched the stars emerging and I reflect on the day.

AUGUST 4, 1999

This morning we discussed travel plans for the day. As I knew he would, Bill announced that we were moving to another favorite camp about halfway between the Elk Camp and the trailhead at Moss Springs. Bill and I called the spot the "Camp across the River" or "Splash Dam Camp." Over the years that splash dam operations took place there, the river deposited enough sandy soil behind the dam to produce a significant meadow. The open, flat, sandy ground in proximity to the river afforded an attractive campsite for hikers and horse parties. By late summer and early fall, it was commonly beat out and dusty from heavy use.

However, unknown to most, there was a beautiful camping spot with abundant feed for the horses just out of sight across the river. A dense stand of white firs along the far riverbank hid a meadow that had been created by a hot wildfire some quarter century or so earlier. Our approach to the "hidden" meadow was a bit tricky, as it was necessary to get down the bank into the river and out on the other side without leaving enough evidence to entice others to follow suit. Sometimes being stingy with information can be well justified. This was, for Bill and me, one of those times and places.

We had not occupied this camp for four or five years and found the meadow densely populated with tiny conifer seedlings. We found a slightly less suitable but still satisfactory camping spot close by. Bill was noticeably weary and low on energy. He sat slightly slumped in his ninety-three-year-old McClellan cavalry saddle and even struggled a bit in lifting the relatively lightweight saddle off his gelding's back. I quickly averted my eyes so that he wouldn't see me watching.

I encouraged him to sit down and allow the rest of us to deal with unpacking and unsaddling the horses and setting up camp. To my great surprise, he made no argument and sat down on a stump and watched as we worked. Uncharacteristically, he even refrained from giving directions or making comments. I watched him out of the corner of my eye and tried to imagine what was going through his mind and maybe churning in his gut. Bill hated his increasing "weakness"—you could see that in his eyes and hear it in his voice.

After a while, Bill gathered firewood while Karen, Craig, and

I set up camp. It was a quiet camp and bedtime came early. I lay awake for several hours and treasured the time to think, remember, and simply feel.

AUGUST 5, 1999

The trip from the Camp across the River to the trailhead at Moss Springs was an easy, pleasant ride; for me, it was flavored with a heavy dose of nostalgia. I remembered those with whom I had shared this ride in the past.

We were greeted at the trailhead by a flat tire on Bill's old horse truck. The volunteer host at the USFS campground had noticed the flat and left us a note on the windshield informing us that he had an electric pump we could use. Bringing the pressure up to standard proved slow going for the small pump, but it finally got the job done. As we still had the trip down the mountain ahead of us, I bought the pump for $25 cash money. We stopped every four or five miles and used the pump to bring the tire back into full round. That routine was irritating but better than replacing an inside tire on a dually on a steep and narrow mountain road. We limped into the service station in Cove and got the tire repaired.

When we got to La Grande and unloaded, unsaddled, groomed, and fed the horses and then unpacked, our conversation was limited to business matters. There was nothing much left to say. Actually there was much to be said, but we simply avoided saying it. It would have been too painful.

Bill Brown with Blitz, Snake River Canyon, 1990.

EPILOGUE

As I write this in October of 2014, my wilderness adventures are at an end. Various injuries accumulated during a vigorous life of now over eighty years have taken their toll, including an ongoing struggle against pancreatic cancer.

But my trips into the wilderness essentially ceased when my partner, Bill Brown, finally had to give in to the vicissitudes of old age and old injuries and moved into an assisted living facility. As I feared—or, maybe for his sake, hoped—he did not survive long in exile from his wilderness and without his horses.

When I visited him from time to time at a nursing home in Spokane, Washington, his eyes would light up when we relived one or another of our horseback trips together, many of them hunting and fishing adventures in various Wilderness Areas. I enjoyed listening to the old stories, told every time in the same words and in the same way. Sitting there in his small room in the nursing home, we were, for just a little while, together again in the high lonesome—just us and our pack string. The horses grazed in the mountain meadows, an elk bugled from the meadow around the cirque lake above camp, trout rose in the streams, and we sat around the fire and watched the setting sun play on the mountaintops.

Bill Brown was a class act to the very end and left a legacy as a pioneering wildlife conservationist. But he could be one ornery son-of-a-bitch when he put his mind to it. It was part of his charm and an aspect of his character. I will be forever grateful that he went out of his way to cultivate my friendship and spent much time and effort into my training and education, especially in the ways and values of wilderness. He saw and cultivated in me potential as a conservationist that I did not perceive in myself.

When I had the honor of speaking at Bill's funeral service in 2012, I fell back on my Texas upbringing for the words I wanted. Among the Texas Rangers—those almost mythical heroes of the Republic of Texas—the highest praise one Ranger could say of another was, "He will do to ride the river with." I said, "Of all the fine people I worked with and played with over my half century of professional life, I would pick Bill Brown to ride the river—or the high lonesome—with."

I still have my model 1906 McClellan cavalry saddle that Bill gave me. It is hanging in my workshop, oiled and ready to go. When I clean it with saddle soap and wipe it down with oil, I think of our horses and the trips into the wilderness. I wonder, what stories could that 108-year-old saddle tell?

I have dozens of photographs of raft trips on the Grande Ronde, Snake, Owyhee, and Deschutes Rivers and the many horse trips into the Eagle Cap, Bob Marshall, and Wenaha-Tucannon Wilderness Areas. I seldom seek those pictures out. I like the pictures stored in my memory better.

Now that my days of traveling into the wilderness, floating down wild rivers, and hunting the old-fashioned way in the outback are over, I think about how much of the zest in my life was due to those experiences. Now my wilderness adventures are confined to dreams and to the telling of tales, perhaps only slightly embellished. It is my hope that the journal entries in this volume might stimulate others to care, and care deeply, about wildlife and wildlife habitats and about the welfare and appropriate management of our national forests and other public lands.

I feel compelled to expound a bit on a special kind of back-country/wilderness experience—whitewater rafting. Unfortunately, I was derelict in keeping up my journals on most such excursions. When I arrived to take over supervision of the USFS's Range and Wildlife Laboratory in La Grande, Oregon, whitewater rafting was a well-established aspect of the social and family life of the researchers stationed at the Forestry Sciences Laboratory in La Grande. At first

A cold, wet day on the Grande Ronde River, 1991.

our equipment was made up of old surplus military life rafts fitted with homemade plywood "rowing decks" where the "store-boughten" oars were mounted, along with one spare. There was a place for ice chests and waterproof gear bags. La Grande was handy to a number of rivers and streams, many of which had stretches in designated Wilderness Areas—or a reasonable facsimile thereto—that could handle raft trips from a half day to nearly a week in length.

As the years passed, running whitewater became more popular, and equipment designed especially for that purpose became available—heavy-duty rafts that could handle "battle damage" from collisions with boulders. Whitewater river rafting became a social event for our lab family, and our flotillas of up to a dozen rafts manned by folks from ages twelve to sixty-five were quite something to see. The ladies each had specialty dishes they prepared in advance for each night's camp. The pies—especially my favorite, apple pie—were to die for.

Oregon, Washington, and Idaho were a rich environment for rafters. Of all my memories of the Pacific Northwest, it may just may be the raft trips—the expanded family raft trips on the Grande Ronde, Minam, Imnaha, Snake, Deschutes, and Ochoco Rivers—that come most frequently to me in my now increasingly fitful dreams. All the players that take the stage in my dreams of river trips are young and vibrant—and so alive. In reality, most of the adults in those dreams have passed over and the "kids" are middle-aged with kids of their own.

I now live near the small unincorporated town of Florence, Montana, located in the valley of the Bitterroot River. Fortunately, a small creek runs through the nine acres of my homestead; the creek and its two ponds add to the remarkable variety of wildlife my wife and I can see from our windows and porches. Included are white-tailed deer and an occasional mule deer, muskrats, beavers, fox squirrels, nesting Canada geese, mallards, pheasants, and wood ducks. A moose even passed through once. A pair of red-tailed hawks routinely nest in the huge cottonwood trees. At night we often hear coyotes singing. The songbirds are varied and plentiful, and many visit our feeders. It is not wilderness, but it will have to do.

I admit to being a bit uncertain about "heaven." But I know what heaven would be for me: simply being able to do it all over again. The good parts of my life overwhelmed the bad. I am grateful and have but few regrets.

It seems that now, after a long hiatus, there is a surge in interest and effort to designate more federal lands as "capital W" Wilderness. I applaud that effort and only hope that those dedicated to the cause of wilderness will be as zealous in assuring that federal land managers have adequate resources and support to manage and protect those lands—those national treasures that will become ever more valuable in a world of increasing human population and increasing exploitation of remaining wild places.

In the end, the best one generation can do for the next is to provide legacies and opportunities to those who follow. Now, as always, the legacy of wilderness passes to a new generation. I trust that generation will do well with its hard-won inheritance.

But, oddly enough, there is a festering movement in some western states to "return the federal lands to the states" for management and/or disposal. Note the play on words. How does one return ownership to the states when they never owned or controlled those lands? Why? Smell the aroma of money in the air and remember the old adage that "money talks and bullshit walks."

I am reminded of Charlton Heston speaking for the National Rifle Association while brandishing a muzzle-loading rifle and proclaiming, "You will get my firearm when you pry it from my cold dead hands!" I don't feel that way about my rifles, but I do feel that way about my national forests, national parks, and other federal public lands. No damned way!

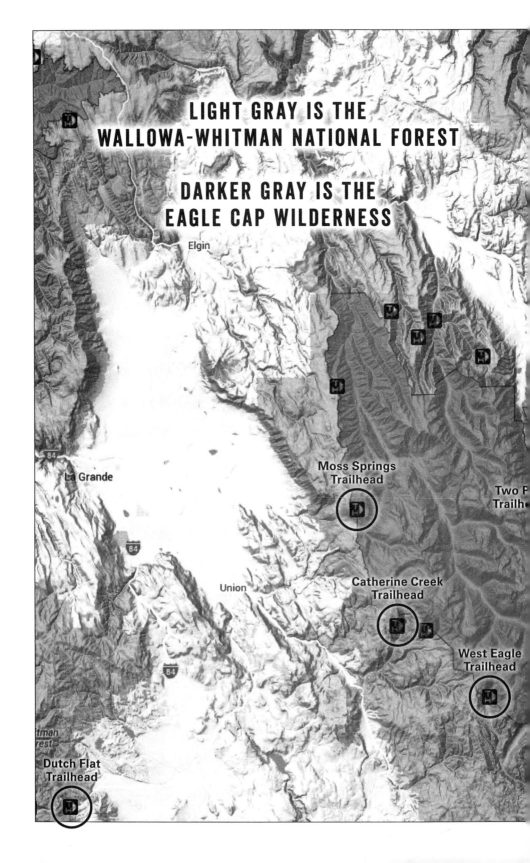

Jack and Shadow taking a break on the trail between Sand Creek and Pony Creek, Hells Canyon, May 1990.

APPENDIX

NATIONAL FOREST WILDERNESS AREAS—A TRY AT IMPROVED MANAGEMENT

AUGUST 26, 1994

Today the USFS hosted a reception in my office to commemorate the thirtieth anniversary of President Lyndon Johnson's signing of the Wilderness Act in 1964. In my short talk I announced several changes in USFS policy relative to the management of Wilderness Areas. It was my desire to exhibit leadership in improving management of Wilderness Areas in the care of the USFS and thereby move that cause forward. The anniversary provided an opportune moment.

It was my intent to establish a new staff director for Wilderness Affairs under the deputy chief for National Forest Systems. Wilderness Affairs had previously been part of the portfolio of the staff director for Recreation. I believed that the value of the Wilderness Areas we managed was much different from and more significant than simply providing a different kind of recreational experience and taking such areas off the table for activities such as construction of roads, logging, and mining.

It was my opinion that the most significant values of Wilderness Areas were the very different recreational and re-creational experiences that they could provide. Just as significant, such areas would inevitably become increasingly valued for providing baselines for ecological research—knowledge that would be increasingly essential to carrying out the USFS's new emphasis on ecosystem management. In addition, the potential philosophical implications should not be underrated as to their effects on our national vision for the management of the public lands. As long as we preserved our nation's Wilderness Areas, a very significant piece of what America once was would continue to exist in a state more or less "untrammeled by man." In such places, in both fantasy and reality, those who care about such things can act out their dreams and glimpse what our ancestors lived and learned—and prospered therefrom.

When I was an undergraduate some forty years ago, we were taught in a class on natural resources policy about the significance of the North American concept of a national parks system to budding conservation efforts all around the world. In the final analysis, the concept of "wilderness" as a land-use classification was an even more radical turning point in how *Homo sapiens* might deal with their rapidly changing environment. In the wilderness concept was embedded an increasingly profound recognition of the value of "untrammeled," ecologically significant areas of adequate enough size to simply continue to exist in that state—i.e., their "existence value" exceeded the "opportunity costs," defined as the economic use values forgone.

Of course, these areas will continue to evolve and change and adjust—no ecosystem can be frozen in either time or place over the very long term. But some lands—like those in Wilderness Areas—can be allowed to make their own adjustments, as they always have, over the millennia. I find it strange that economists evaluate such land-use allocations in economic terms rather than in terms of their ecological, spiritual, and recreational/re-creational values. Unfortunately, such attributes are not fully measurable in terms of the coin of the realm. Yet to a large extent, those are but semantic differences, and it is in such semantics that many of the underlying, sometimes camouflaged values of professions and societies are revealed.

So long as We the People care deeply enough to speak out and enough dedicated citizens are active in the political arena, the Wilderness System has a real chance of remaining intact and, in my opinion, even growing. In that case, We the People will exhibit that we are, and will continue to be, a different kind of nation. The innate value of such places will only increase as the human population inexorably increases, along with rates of exploitation of natural resources to keep pace.

Of course, even those places that are relatively "untrammeled by man" will gradually become ever more "trammeled" to the point of requiring more regulation and management of human uses. That seems an inevitable conundrum that must be recognized and faced, sooner rather than later. Over time, pressures will mount to "develop" such areas so that they may accommodate more and more visitors in greater safety and provide them with more amenities while protecting "wilderness values." There may well be pressures to strip these wild areas of their special legal status so that they may be exploited—sustainably or not—for timber harvests, reservoirs, mining, gas and oil extraction, off-road vehicle use, campgrounds, or other purposes, all involving roads and road maintenance.

I have seen bumper stickers—gateways into the minds of the vehicle's owners—that boldly proclaim "WILDERNESS—LAND OF NO USE," a blatant parody of the USFS's slogan "NATIONAL FORESTS—LAND OF MANY USES." Obviously, these drivers cannot conceive of and therefore appreciate the philosophical, spiritual, ecological values that Wilderness Areas represent for others of a very different persuasion.

When I first saw those bumper stickers and others of similar sentiment, I could not help but think back to my youth, tramping the woods of my grandfather's farm located between Fort Worth and Dallas—all now buried beneath the suburbia of the Metroplex. Big Dad took care to point out to me where so-and-so shot the last black bear out of a tree, where the last white-tailed deer was taken down by dogs, and where the last wild turkey came to a hunter's call. I even knew some of those "last killers"—very old men who were inordinately proud of being so recognized and even honored for their actions. At the same time, I thought I could hear in the voices of the "last killers" their mourning of the passing of an era. Sometimes I thought I could see tears in their eyes and hear a crack in their voices as they puffed their pipes, told their stories, and passed the jug around the campfires. They did not seem to recognize that they had helped to destroy what they loved most.

In those years between 1943 and 1957, I hunted for squirrels, cotton-tailed rabbits, jack rabbits, raccoons, and opossums on Turkey Knob, along Buck Creek and Cougar Creek and Buffalo Wallow. My favorite place to seek out bobwhite quail was on the high ground of

Quail Flats above Village Creek, where an Indian village had once stood in the late 1880s.

Today those are street and place names in the subdivisions that crept across the landscape and spread like a giant amoeba stretching out pseudopods in every direction. How could I complain now? I had put myself through school by building some of those houses and was grateful for the work. But I wondered even then, was there not room for both—vibrant, growing cities and wild and semiwild places? A Wilderness Area designated by an act of Congress was beyond my comprehension or imagination at the time.

Decades later, I was introduced to and came to love and treasure wilderness. It was in such places, for a little while in the last half of the twentieth century, that I could see and experience what much of the United States must have been like "once upon a time." Even as a boy growing up in a place where every piece of property was fenced, I dreamed and even heard rumors that somewhere, maybe far off to the north or west, there were huge swaths of land that belonged to We the People—even people like me. Somewhere out there in my nation were lands that were wild and free and even some without roads and fences—which, in theory at least, would always be so. I was entranced with the idea—what seemed to me an impossible dream. I liked the feelings that the very idea stirred in me. It produced a longing and determination to someday seek out and experience what seemed to be mythical places. I hoped the stories were true.

Now I am much older and well acquainted with the idea of national forests and Wilderness Areas—both in myth and reality. Now, after more than five decades as a conservation professional, I am still in love with the idea. When I am too old or too sick or too crippled up to go into the mountains in the national forests, especially the Wilderness Areas, they will still be there for younger pilgrims—maybe my grandchildren and great-grandchildren in search of their own dreams. I will take pride and solace in knowing that such lands still exist for the young—and those yet to be born. Those precious remaining vestiges of wilderness will be there, just past the ends of the roads, and memories of my visits there with fellow aficionados, many now departed, will remain fresh to arise in the flames from fireplaces and campfires. After all is said and done, perhaps the true value of wilderness is a place for retreat in the present and a creator of dreams and memories.

While most value wilderness for the unique recreational experiences to be had there, such places hold an increasingly important value for ecological research and evolving understanding. The relatively new concept of ecosystem management of the national forests, which has grown out of the requirements of the Endangered Species Act of 1973, demands that management actions be firmly rooted in "good science." One purpose of this act is to provide a means whereby the ecosystems of endangered and threatened species may be conserved.

Wilderness Areas provide essential baseline study areas for the scientific community in its efforts to improve our understanding of ecosystem functions and evolutionary adaptation. Wilderness Areas contain remnants of ecosystems most closely resembling those that evolved to their present states over millennia. Their current ecosystem processes are relatively intact and relatively little manipulated by humans. Such areas provide benchmarks to which more intensely managed forests and rangelands and rivers can be compared, evaluated, and sustained over centuries.

My second pronouncement described a new approach to the administration of Wilderness Areas within the National Forest System. Traditionally, Congresses and presidents designated Wilderness Areas and their boundaries through political processes that have been likened to making sausage. Such processes are better appreciated by savoring the end results while avoiding watching closely what is involved in the process. Wilderness Areas, quite commonly, were simply laid down over maps of existing regions, national forests, and ranger districts, resulting in fractionalized oversight and management. Wilderness Areas seemed to have evolved more as "targets of opportunity" for wilderness aficionados than an overall strategic approach. Perhaps such an approach suited the times. But now it is time to take a more strategic approach to do what is possible to preserve needed examples of ecosystems.

The USFS programs that historically and routinely received the most attention were timber management (especially timber harvest and reforestation), road construction and management, livestock grazing, campgrounds, habitats for fish and wildlife, water quality and quantity, and recreation. Wildernesses Areas, which often overlapped jurisdictional boundaries, seemingly inevitably and by default, became somewhat like orphans to many USFS managers, as they were without organized local constituencies and lacked adequate dedicated sources of funding. After all, the reputation of the USFS with administrations and Congresses did not often turn on how the agency dealt with the management of Wilderness Areas. As a result, these lands of "NO USE" traditionally received relatively little attention and even fewer dedicated resources. The constituents who fought so hard for wilderness designations, by and large, went "missing in action" when it came to assuring adequate resources to protect and adequately manage Wilderness Areas and their uses.

So as a management experiment, I announced that the Frank Church–River of No Return Wilderness Area in central Idaho would be considered a single management entity with a wilderness supervisor of equal rank to a forest supervisor in both grade and authority. The wilderness supervisor would have an adequate budget to contract with the various national forests and ranger districts for services. My intent was to provide a clear signal—through allocation of resources and the elevation of the manager—that the importance of wilderness and its management had been enhanced and was equal to that of multiple-use landscapes. My intended message was that Wilderness Areas were no longer orphans within the USFS.

Unfortunately, I was thwarted by the congressional delegation from Idaho and, I suspected, some undercover internal resistance from within the USFS. And there was no rush to support the idea by those concerned with the welfare of Wilderness Areas. It is well for any administrator of federal lands to remember that changes in the status quo will be resisted and that "turf wars" are with us always.

Simultaneously, I announced that the share of resources being directed to Wilderness Area management would be increased, either by increased appropriations (which I knew was unlikely) or through gradual shifts from other programs. That seemed appropriate, as the lands with Wilderness designations made up about 20 percent of the

National Forest System while receiving only a bit more than 1 percent of the overall budget for management. It didn't seem to me that a shift of 1 or 2 percent, thereby doubling funding for Wilderness management—should raise red flags.

Those actions were an opening gambit in my effort to bring the management of Wilderness Areas to a more equitable position relative to other USFS activities. What I proposed seemed to be a collection of good first "baby steps" to focus attention on and improve resources for the management of Wilderness Areas. And, strategically, what better time for such action than the thirtieth anniversary of the Wilderness Act?

In retrospect, it seems likely that I dramatically overrated both my power and political acumen to alter the status quo. In addition, I had too much faith in the logic of my proposal. Alterations in the status quo in federal land require careful construction of a foundation and a carefully planned and executed campaign for change. But I still believe that the time for enhanced attention to the management of Wilderness Areas will come. One of my great regrets of my tenure as chief of the USFS was to have failed in that regard.

THE SIXTH NATIONAL
WILDERNESS CONFERENCE

NOVEMBER 18, 1994

I am on my way from Albuquerque, New Mexico, back home to Washington, D.C., after attending the Sixth National Wilderness Conference, which I considered a roaring success. There were some 600 wilderness aficionados and managers in attendance. Many more had been turned away due to lack of space. Political personalities from both Republican and Democratic parties had been invited in equal numbers. Only those of the Democratic persuasion chose to accept. Maybe there was a message in that. I wondered about the reason for the absence of the Republican faction. First, I suspected that the Republicans did not view those interested in the establishment and protection of Wilderness Areas as a significant constituency. Second, they viewed being associated with anything or anyone labeled as "environmentalist" or "preservationist" as an outright political liability among their "base."

I had come to expect that in nearly every conflict regarding natural resources management there would be a three-way split: "them that's for it," "them that's against it," and "them that don't give a rat's ass." Many of the speakers during the first two days of the conference made a point—most unfortunately, in my view—of bashing congressional Republicans. Several old war horses of the wilderness movement—including David Brower and Mo Udall—railed against the results of the last national election, in which Republicans took control of both the House of Representatives and the Senate. That was apt to make my life more than a bit difficult, as I was not only President Clinton's selection as chief of the USFS but also head of the teams that dealt with constructing plans for the northern spotted owl and old-growth forests in the Pacific Northwest.

Speakers pointed out that the voting records of the new Senate majority leader (Robert "Bob" Dole) and Speaker of the House (Newt Gingrich) were equally abysmal in terms of addressing environmental concerns. They believed the election results were a harbinger of a determined effort to dismantle the gains made by environmentalists over the past thirty years relative to additions to the National Wilderness Preservation System. That mood was reflected by speaker after speaker in both their presentations and their responses to questions from the press. Clearly the speakers felt themselves on the defensive. Yet the overall mood of the conference, which celebrated the thirtieth anniversary of the signing of the Wilderness Act of 1964, was upbeat, celebratory, and focused toward the future. Assistant Secretary of the Interior Robert "Bob" Armstrong (who was responsible for the Bureau of Land Management), Assistant Secretary of the Interior George Frampton (who was responsible for the National Park Service and the U.S. Fish and Wildlife Service), and I (the USFS chief) were the banquet speakers.

During the banquet that preceded the speeches, John Twiss (the USFS's lead staffer in the Washington office on Wilderness matters) whispered in my ear and encouraged me to "work on" George Frampton and encourage him to assign one appropriate representative each from the BLM, National Park Service, and the U.S. Fish and Wildlife Service to the Interagency Arthur Carhart Wilderness Training Center, recently established at the University of Montana in Missoula. And, while I was at it, would I please encourage the appointment of a scientist from the Fish and Wildlife Service's National Biological Survey to the Aldo Leopold Wilderness Research Center, also at the University of Montana?

That was a no-brainer. Buoyed by the spirit of the moment, I turned to Frampton and made the pitch. I pointed out the potential benefits and the apropos moment presented by this gathering. He could use his after-dinner speech to make the announcement. He listened, thought for a minute, and nodded. "That's a cheap date. I'll do it!" My jaw dropped. Now, there was a decisive leader!

I motioned for Twiss and the USFS directors of the Carhart and Leopold centers to join us on the podium so that Frampton could give them the news. This was the achievement of a goal that they had worked toward for several years. Suddenly it seemed to be done deal. It was an example of carrying through on the ancient dictum *Carpe diem*! The stage was set, the time was right, and then suddenly the deed was done. Sometimes, I thought, the old magic really did work.

George Frampton, a former director of the Wilderness Society, is an extremely bright Ivy Leaguer with a pronounced competitive streak. And as wilderness was his bag, this audience was his audience. Earlier in the day I had given him a copy of my speech in which I had listed some of the potential policy actions of the USFS that would be significant to this audience of dedicated wilderness buffs and advocates. What he had planned to say in his speech did not go beyond expressing strong support for the nation's Wilderness System and its appropriate management.

Now, being on the spot, he sensed the power of the moment when he committed to the "cheap date." It was the right thing to do, the smart thing to do; the stars were in alignment at this most opportune moment. What a rare thing in governmental affairs it is to see power exercised so decisively and so expeditiously. I was proud of George Frampton. I leaned over and whispered in his ear, "You done real good, partner!" I meant it, and he knew I meant it. Now we would have to see if we could make it stick.

In my remarks, which closed out the program, I traced the USFS's role in the evolution of the concept of Wilderness (with a capital *W*). I announced several actions being taken by the USFS that should enhance the agency's management of wild lands. I said that we intended to be leaders in the management of Wilderness Areas and invited all federal land management agencies to join the USFS in fully funding, staffing, and operating the Arthur Carhart National Wilderness Training Center and the Aldo Leopold National Wilderness Institute. Frampton and Armstrong nodded their assent.

Then I announced the creation of the Frank Church–River of No Return Wilderness Management Unit. It was the crown jewel of the USFS's Wilderness System and would be managed by a single wilderness supervisor (the equal of a forest supervisor) of senior grade who would report to the regional forester. That was a first step—an experiment—in elevating attention and support for the Wilderness System. In addition, performance standards were to be developed and instituted for regional foresters and forest supervisors to assure high-quality management of USFS Wilderness Areas. I was betting that increased funding for wilderness management and research would follow, reflecting increased emphasis on ecosystem monitoring, assessment, and management. The position of director of Wilderness Management, to join the directors of the Timber, Fish and Wildlife, Recreation, Range, Watershed, and Lands divisions, was announced.

In closing, I said, "I hope what I say here tonight captures the essence and theme of this historic conference. The spirit lives! That same spirit lived in Henry David Thoreau and in Chief Seattle. That same spirit was manifest in John Muir and Arthur Carhart. It shone through in Aldo Leopold, Bob Marshall, and Howard Zahniser. And it shines through today in such stalwarts as Bill Worf and Tom Kovalicky and many others, some present in this room. That spirit lives in each of you. It lives in me. I ask of those dedicated to the stewardship of our lands and waters, 'What more could we ask than to be who we are, to be at this place at this point in history, with a chance to make a difference?' So let us, individually and collectively, resolve to do all that we can to assure that the spirit lives ever more vibrantly and becomes manifest in others. We can do that by a constant striving to enhance our knowledge and maintain the ecological function, integrity, values, status, and spirit of the Wilderness System. I pledge myself to those ends! Will you join me?"

The audience was on its feet, applauding, whistling, making wolf calls, and whooping. I had given many speeches in my professional career—including a couple of barn burners—and had never received a reception like that. I interpreted the response to be a resounding yes. Alas, that was but a dream.

The reality was that what I had proposed was a very long shot, especially the establishment of new areas or the expansion of existing areas. Resistance from the newly elected Republican-dominated Congress, flexing its muscles and responding to constituencies more interested in enhanced exploitation for timber, grazing, mining, and recreation than in conservation, was to be expected. And such was not long in coming.

But, I thought, those who chose to take on the spirit manifested in the room might best bring a lunch, as the fight would be prolonged. As I left the podium, an old Chinese blessing—or was it a curse?—came to mind: "May you live in interesting times!" Indeed, the Wilderness issue was headed for interesting times. I wondered how many in this crowd understood just how "interesting" the times emanating from the power shift of the last election would be for the management of the public lands, especially for the Wilderness System.

I thought it would be a fierce struggle to just hold on to the gains of the past three decades, much less to improve on the situation. But that has always been the name of the game in the conservation arena—two steps forward and one or two steps back. Veterans of the struggles for conservation understand, no matter how galling the waits and the defeats, the importance of being patient, preparing carefully, making what gains are possible when the time and circumstances are right, and hanging tough for the backlash. Conservationists could count on backlash and pushback from those who would profit from enhanced exploitation—no matter how inappropriate—of the public's lands.

At the moment, those entities may well have overplayed their hand. Both their rhetoric and actions will serve to vitalize their opposition. I had learned at least one lesson in four decades in the conservation game: make all the gains possible when circumstances permit and make those gains in yards. When the tide turns, and it always seems to turn, hang tough and give ground in inches and feet. A long-term view is essential, and setbacks can be converted into a stimulus for renewed efforts. All defeats and all victories are temporary—it is the long-term trends that count. Earth abides.

The initiative that I proposed relative to Wilderness issues met immediate and intense resistance, both internally and from the newly elected Republican majorities in the House and the Senate. The Clinton administration, having bigger fish to fry, chose not to spend any political chips on wilderness management issues. There was a lesson for me in the experience: I had overrun my headlights and seriously overestimated my abilities to "get 'er done." I had feared, likely correctly, that this was a last best chance for improvement in wilderness management, and though it seemed a good approach, it worked poorly when I tried it. I took a private oath to learn from the experience and do better next time. Down deep, I was glad we made the good effort. Such chances come along but rarely. In spite of my embarrassing failure, I was not sorry to have tried—after all, it might have worked and I deemed it the right thing to do. Maybe next time?

PUBLISHER'S NOTE

The Boone and Crockett Club would like to recognize several individuals whose hard work, diligence, and support—both financially and professionally—made this book project possible. As with most publishing projects, this was indeed a group effort.

First and foremost we must thank the author, Jack Ward Thomas. He is a true conservationist, biologist, and hunter beyond reproach. His contributions to our natural world will be felt for generations to come. Jack's choice of the Boone and Crockett Club as the recipient of his journals and manuscripts is an honor for which our publishing program is deeply indebted. This generosity was facilitated by two Boone and Crockett Club Honorary Life Members, John P. Poston, and Daniel H. Pletscher. These two gentlemen initially met with Jack and through several conversations approached the Club's publications program with the idea that we should publish this trilogy of Jack's journals and memoirs. Who better to publish this great conservationist's work than Boone and Crockett—founded in 1887 by Theodore Roosevelt and George Bird Grinnell, with over 120 years of publishing experience. We are indebted to John and Dan for their foresight and their tenacity.

A special acknowledgment and debt of gratitude needs to be extended to John Poston for his financial support that made this project happen. It would not have been possible otherwise to move this project from an idea in the fall of 2014 to three finished books by the summer of 2015. John's support, reflecting his friendship and respect

Fresh snow in the Eagle Cap Wilderness,
a welcome sight during elk season.

for Jack Ward Thomas, allowed us to get the ball rolling on a much faster schedule than anyone could have hoped for. We can only hope to have a faithful friend like John Poston in our lifetime!

The Boone and Crockett Club has a long history with publishing books about outdoor adventure, conservation, and hunting. The Club's publishing program is overseen by myself and Jeffrey A. Watkins (Cartersville, Georgia). Jeff's enthusiasm, suggestions, and oversight were instrumental in developing the publishing concept. Most importantly we are fortunate to have the assistance of Julie Tripp, B&C's director of publication. Julie is the foundation helping Jeff and me develop a working plan to get the project underway and see it through to completion. Julie especially enjoyed her trips down the Bitterroot Valley from B&C headquarters in Missoula to visit with Jack and his wife Kathy throughout the publishing process. Time was spent pulling photographs, going through edits, selecting authors to write the forewords, but more importantly, just "shooting the breeze" with Jack. If only we had had a stand-around fire to set the stage for those conversations!

There are a few others whose hard work made these books happen, and we'd be remiss not to mention them here. Fellow Texican Alison Tartt did an exemplary job editing and arranging the three manuscripts into their final form. B&C Lifetime Associate Hanspeter Giger (Charlotte, North Carolina) volunteered countless hours of his time providing a final read-through of the books before they went to the printer.

Thank you to everyone who helped us in the creation of this worthwhile project. It is our hope that these books will entertain, inform, teach, and induce reflection in the readers about the natural world we all have the privilege to enjoy.

Howard P. Monsour Jr., M.D.
CHAIRMAN, B&C PUBLICATIONS COMMITTEE
HOUSTON, TEXAS

AUTHOR'S ACKNOWLEDGMENTS

This book project has been decades in the making. Along the way, I was blessed with two strong women in my life who need to be acknowledged for their part in this great process.

Farrar Margaret ("Meg") Thomas and I were married in June of 1957, the week after I graduated from Texas A&M. We were full partners for the next thirty-six years—including, in the beginning, some very lean years when she taught piano lessons and I worked on weekends and holidays at part-time jobs to make ends meet. She never, not even once, complained. She also taught music in the public schools, and privately, to enhance our meager income.

Though she was no hunter, she seemed to relish going hunting with me. She seemed, especially, to enjoy my hunting bob-white and blue quail. I think she was partial to the bird dogs. When, in 1977, I asked her what she thought about leaving Texas so I could take a job with the U.S. Forest Service in West Virginia, she said she would go anywhere if she didn't have to cook and eat venison "nearly every damn day." We were off to West Virginia—and she still cooked and ate a lot of venison. But for the first time in our married life she didn't have to. That made all the difference.

She died of cancer in 1993 in Washington, D.C. Though severely ill, she insisted that "we" accept President Clinton's offer for me to be the thirteenth chief of the U.S. Forest Service. The president referred to Meg as the "First Lady of American Conservation."

In 1996, I was married to Kathleen Hurley Connelly, who worked with me in the Washington office of the U.S. Forest Service as the Deputy Chief for Administration. She was not a "country girl" and even referred to herself as "Subway Girl." Though no hunter herself, she relished accompanying me on hunting trips in the United States and foreign lands. Shortly after we married, we moved to Missoula, Montana, when I accepted an offer to become the Boone and Crockett Professor of Wildlife Conservation in the College of Forestry at the University of Montana. I enjoyed teaching and dealing with graduate students. Kathy served us all as "Mom in Residence." And thoroughly relished the role.

I had a number of bosses over my forty-year professional career. Those bosses—every single one—guided me with a loose rein, which was bound to be, from time to time, a bit nerve-racking. They, in general, gave me the opportunity to "be all that I could be" in both the professional and personal sense. Over a half-century career, my supervisors—in both wildlife research and land management—guided me well and supported me, while "looking the other way" on numerous occasions. There are too many such colleagues to mention by name, but we both know who you are.

My idea of heaven would be to, simply, do it all over again.